E-COMMERCE

[For B.Tech (CSE/IT) and all Computer Science Students]

E-COMMERCE

[For B.Tech (CSE/IT) and all Computer Science Students]

Second Edition

SARIKA GUPTA
Asstt. Prof.
MCA. M.Tech, MBA, Ph.D(CSE)*
CSE/IT Deptt. Dronacharya College of Engineering
Greater Noida, Uttar Pradesh (INDIA)

ER. GAURAV GUPTA
Manager Client Services
Rightwave Info. Solution Pvt. Ltd.
Noida

KHANNA BOOK PUBLISHING CO. (P) LTD.
PUBLISHER OF ENGINEERING AND COMPUTER BOOKS
4C/4344, Ansari Road, Darya Ganj, New Delhi-110002
Phone : 011-23244447-48 Mobile: +91-99109 09320
E-mail : contact@khannabooks.com; Website : www.khannabooks.com

Dear Readers,

To prevent the piracy, this book is secured with HIGH SECURITY HOLOGRAM on the front title cover. In case you don't find the hologram on the front cover title, please write us to at contact@khannabooks.com or whatsapp us at +91-99109 09320 and avail special gift voucher for yourself.

Specimen of Hologram on front Cover title:

Moreover, there is a SPECIAL DISCOUNT COUPON for you with EVERY HOLOGRAM.

How to avail this SPECIAL DISCOUNT:

Step 1: Scratch the hologram
Step 2: Under the scratch area, your "coupon code" is available
Step 3: Logon to www.khannabooks.com
Step 4: Use your "coupon code" in the shopping cart and get your copy at a special discount
Step 5: Enjoy your reading!

Thanks,
Khanna Publishing House

Price: ₹ 550.00

E-COMMERCE

by **Sarika Gupta and Gaurav Gupta**

ISBN: 978-93-82609-54-4

Reprint: 2024, **2026**

To view complete list of books, please scan the QR Code:

Published by:
Khanna Book Publishing Co. (P) Ltd.
CIN: U22110DL1998PTC095547

Visit us at: www.khannabooks.com
Write us at: contact@khannabooks.com

Printed in Bharat.

This book is dedicated to-

OUR FAMILY

Preface

It gives us great pleasure in presenting the first edition of this book to our esteemed readers. "**E-Commerce**" is written with several goal in mind. It is designed to provide all essential information you'll need to learn **E-Commerce**. It can be used as a test-cum-reference book by students of B.Tech (CS/IT) / MCA and M.Tech.

I am sure that the text's user friendly approach will encourage the students to read the book and will make them understand the concept in easy way.

We always welcome emails with comments and suggestions from researchers, academicians, students and other to improve the quality of this book.

Sarika Gupta
Gaurav Gupta

Acknowledgements

I take this opportunity to express my deep sense of gratitude to Dr. Ajay Matto (CEO, DCE group) and Prof. R.N.Sharma (Principal, DCE group) for their constant inspiration and encouragement. I am also greatful to Prof. Aswani (Administrator, DCE group) and Prof. Kaul (Registrar, DCE group) for their kind support.

I also want to express my heartiest thanks to Prof. Anil Chopra (Head CSE/IT/MCA), S.K. Srivastava for their valuable suggestions, support, guidance and encouragement.

Last but not the least, I would like to thank Mr. Chand s Nagar of Limited Colors, who designed the book. Thanks are also due to Mr. Puneet Khanna and Mr. Mukul Seth of Khanna Publishing Co. Pvt. Ltd., for managing the publishing agreement and production process.

Sarika Gupta

Gaurav Gupta

Contents

UNIT-1

UNIT-3

UNIT-4

UNIT-5

UNIT – 1

1. Introduction of E-Commerce
2. Network Infrastructure for E-Commerce

CHAPTER

1

Introduction of E-Commerce

1.1 INTRODUCTION

In the emerging global economy, E-Commerce and E-Business have increasingly become a necessary component of business strategy and a strong catalyst for economic development. The integration of information and communications technology (ICT) in business has revolutionized relationships within organizations and those between and among organizations and individuals. Specifically, the use of ICT in business has enhanced productivity, encouraged greater customer participation, and enabled mass customization, besides reducing costs.

With developments in the Internet and Web-based technologies, distinctions between traditional markets and the global electronic marketplace-such as business capital size, among others-are gradually being narrowed down. The name of the game is strategic positioning, the ability of a company to determine emerging opportunities and utilize the necessary human capital skills (such as intellectual re- sources) to make the most of these opportunities through an E-Business strategy that is simple, workable and practicable within the context of a global information milieu and new economic environment. With its effect of leveling the playing field, E-Commerce coupled with the appropriate strategy and policy approach enables small and medium scale enterprises to compete with large and capital-rich businesses.

On another plane, developing countries are given increased access to the global marketplace, where they compete with and complement the more developed economies. Most, if not all, developing countries are already participating in E-Commerce, either as sellers or buyers. However, to facilitate E-Commerce growth in these countries, the relatively underdeveloped information infrastructure must be improved.

Among the areas for policy intervention are:

- High Internet access costs, including connection service fees, communication fees, and hosting charges for websites with sufficient bandwidth;
- Limited availability of credit cards and a nationwide credit card system;

- Underdeveloped transportation infrastructure resulting in slow and uncertain delivery of goods and services;
- Network security problems and insufficient security safeguards;
- Lack of skilled human resources and key technologies (i.e., inadequate professional IT workforce);
- Content restriction on national security and other public policy grounds, which greatly affect business in the field of information services, such as the media and entertainment sectors;
- Cross-border issues, such as the recognition of transactions under laws of other ASEAN member-countries, certification services, improvement of delivery methods and customs facilitation; and
- The relatively low cost of labor, which implies that a shift to a comparatively capital intensive solution (including investments on the improvement of the physical and network infrastructure) is not apparent.

It is recognized that in the Information Age, Internet commerce is a powerful tool in the economic growth of developing countries. While there are indications of e- commerce patronage among large firms in developing countries, there seems to be little and negligible use of the Internet for commerce among small and medium sized firms. E-Commerce promises better business for SMEs and sustainable economic development for developing countries. However, this is premised on strong political will and good governance, as well as on a responsible and supportive private sector within an effective policy framework. This primer seeks to provide policy guidelines toward this end.

1.2 CONCEPTS AND DEFINITIONS

1.2.1 E-Business Definition

eBusiness (electronic business) is, in its simplest form, the conduct of business on the Internet. It is a more generic term than E-Commerce because it refers to not only buying and selling but also servicing customers and collaborating with business partners.

Every business has both tacit and explicit knowledge. One is undocumented, and the other is documented about what is "known" in the company. This knowledge may include information about products and services or information about how the company works with a particular supplier. No matter what type of knowledge an E-Business has, the company must put into place processes for organizing that knowledge.

Knowledge management includes managing intellectual capital, such as best practices, critical business processes, and operating metrics. Establishing ongoing processes for acquiring, organizing, and distributing this knowledge about customers, products, and processes is critical to success. The business domains, CRM, SCM and core business operations, are dependent on this information and these intellectual assets.

In every successful E-Business, the business process domains (CRM, SCM and core business operations) are an integral part of the continuous optimization process. The advantage and thus, the return on investment for an E-Business integrating its business process domains is that it extends the organization's business directly to customers and suppliers.

When business process domains are integrated, they can increase productivity and improve customer and supplier satisfaction. For example, when a repeat customer views a successful E-Business's Web site, an integrated CRM system presents that individual with offers or items of interest based on previous orders. After the customer places an order, this same E-Business allows that individual to view the status of his order in real time as it moves through the supply chain.

Business process domains are aggregations of core business processes. Although there is growing popularity of business process domains as their own entities (CRM, SCM, and core business operations), they are commanding a mind-share in the marketplace (and each has attracted various vendors and products to support it). These domains must operate together as a key component to the overall E-Business strategy.

In a successful E-Business, convergence is the driving connection of all of the business process domains. When there appears to a customer or a supplier to be no barrier between departments, the business process domains are tightly integrated with the business and IT strategies.

1.2.2 Customer Relationship Management

Customer relationships are becoming a more important factor in differentiating one business from another. In order to stay competitive, E-Businesses in every industry have begun to analyze these relationships with customers using CRM solutions.

In the past, customers would place an order via the telephone and wait until the company's purchasing department processed and shipped the order. Today's customers place an order electronically and then demand to be able to check the status of their order within minutes.

CRM enables an organization to adopt a comprehensive view of the customer and maximize this relationship. These CRM systems enable a business to identify, attract, retain, and support customs centers, direct mail, and retail facilities. In an efficient E-Business, there are CRM processes in place to handle:

Analytical CRM: The analysis of data created on the operational side of the CRM equation for the purpose of business performance management; utilizing data warehousing technologies and leveraging data marts

Customer interactions: Sales, marketing, and customer service (call center, field service) via multiple, interconnected delivery channels and integration between front office and back office

Operational CRM: The automation of horizontally integrated business processes involving "front office" customer touch points

Personalization: The use of new and traditional groupware/Web technologies to facilitate customer and business partner communications

1.2.3 Supply Chain Management

Integration of the SCM functions is emerging as one of the greatest challenges facing today's E-Businesses. SCM is the integration of business processes from end user through to original supplier. The goal of SCM is to create an end-to-end system that automates all the business processes between suppliers, distribution partners, and trading partners. The new mantra for this process, according to industry analysts, is "replacing inventory with information." In an effective E-Business, the following SCM independent processes must be highly integrated

Demand management: These are shared functions, including demand planning, supply planning, manufacturing planning, and sales and operations planning.

Inbound/outbound logistics: These include transportation management, distribution management, and warehouse management.

Supply management: These include products and services for customer order fulfillment

E-Businesses also need to develop and operate complex transaction processing systems that support their core business operation. These core operations include the operational systems that support their particular business, such as claims processing, trade execution, enterprise resource planning (ERP), and enterprise resource management (ERM).

1.3 TYPES OF E-BUSINESS MODELS

A business model is a description of how a company operates. Some business models are more complicated than others. Like traditional, bricks-and-mortar businesses, E-Businesses also need to have solid models to generate revenue.

1.3.1 Brokerage Model

Brokerage sites are meant to bring buyers and sellers together. The sellers offer their goods and services, and the buyers purchase these goods and services. These sites generally charge a fee for use. Examples of such sites include eBay, Etsy and Amazon.

1.3.2 Advertising Model

Like traditional advertisers, businesses that follow the advertising E-Business model provide a combination of content and ads. This model is most effective when there is a high level of traffic. One example of such a model is on-line newspapers, which feature news content as well as advertisements.

1.3.3 Merchant Model

Merchants have been selling wares since time immemorial. E-Commerce is simply the latest manifestation of this trend. Merchant websites sell their goods and services to buyers. Barnes and Noble's and Land's End's websites are examples of this model.

1.3.4 Community Model

This type of business capitalizes on the trend of online communities. Members of online communities make new friends, write content or post photos. The business can earn money through advertising revenue, selling products or voluntary donations by members. Flickr and Wikipedia operate under this model.

1.3.5 Subscription Model

E-Businesses that operate under the subscription model charge users a fee to use their services. Netflix and AOL are two examples.

1.4 ADVANTAGE AND DISADVANTAGES OF E-BUSINESS

E-Business is a vast term encompassing the various business processes that aim to integrate the vendors or traders with the consumers and suppliers using the Internet. The entire process of setting up a website, helping the prospective customers navigate through the website, showing them the available products, offering discounts and vouchers and doing everything possible to what the prospective clients and converting them into customers, comes under the purview of E-Business. E-Commerce, on the other hand, is a subset of E-Business and refers to online transactions that can be accounted for in monetary terms. For instance, accepting credit card payment for products sold to consumers or making payments for shopping online are examples of E-Commerce. In other words, E-Commerce refers to the last stage of E-Business which involves collecting payments for the goods sold by the business firm.

1.4.1 Advantages of E-Business

Worldwide Presence: This is the biggest advantage of conducting business online. A firm engaging in E-Business can have a nationwide or a worldwide presence. IBM was one of the first companies to use the term E-Business to refer to servicing customers and collaborating with business partners from all over the world. Dell Inc. too had a flourishing business selling PCs throughout the US, only via telephone and the Internet till the year 2007. Amazon.com is another success story that helps people buy internationally from third parties. Hence, worldwide presence is ensured if companies rethink their business in terms of the Internet.

Cost Effective Marketing and Promotions: Using the web to market products guarantees worldwide reach at a nominal price. Advertising techniques like pay per click advertising ensure that the advertiser only pays for the advertisements that are actually viewed. Affiliate marketing, where customers are directed to a business portal because of the efforts of the affiliate who in turn receive a compensation for their efforts meeting with success, has emerged on account of E-Business. Affiliate marketing has helped both the business and the affiliates. Firms engaging in E-Business have managed to use cost effective online advertising strategies to their advantage.

Developing a Competitive Strategy: Firms need to have a competitive strategy in order to ensure a competitive advantage. Without an effective strategy, they will find it impossible to maintain the advantage and earn profits. The strategy, that the firms can pursue, can be a be a cost strategy or a differentiation strategy. For instance, till the year 2007, Dell Inc. was selling computers only via the Internet and the phone. It adopted a differentiation strategy by selling its computers online and customizing its laptops to suit the requirements of the clients. Thus, E-Business resulted in Dell Inc. managing to capture a vast segment of the market using the differentiation strategy.

Better Customer Service

E-Business has resulted in improved customer service. Many a times, on visiting a website, the customer is greeted by a pop-up chat window. Readily available customer service may help in encouraging the customer to know more about the product or service. Moreover, payments can be made online, products can be shipped to the customer without the customer having to leave the house.

1.4.2 Disadvantages of E-Business

Sectoral Limitations

The main disadvantage of E-Business is the lack of growth in some sectors on account of product or sector limitations. The food sector has not benefited in terms of growth of sales and consequent revenue generation because of a number of practical reasons like food products being perishable items. Consumers do not look for food products on the Internet since they prefer going to the supermarket to buy the necessary items as and when the need arises.

Costly E-Business Solutions for Optimization: Substantial resources are required for redefining product lines in order to sell online. Upgrading computer systems, training personnel, and updating websites requires substantial resources. Moreover, Electronic Data Management (EDM) and Enterprise Resource Planning (ERP) necessary for ensuring optimal internal business processes may be looked upon, by some firms, as one of the disadvantages of E-Business.

It's evident that the advantages clearly outweigh the disadvantages of E-Business. Every business has to eventually change its modus operandi and adopt E-Business practices in order to ensure survival and success.

1.5 COMMERCE

The trading of goods, has been a major drive of human survival since the beginning of recorded history and beyond. The mass adoption of Internet has created a paradigm shift in the way businesses are conducted today. The past decade has seen an emergence of a new kind of commerce, the buying and selling of goods, through human-computer interaction over the Internet. Today, the line between E-Commerce and traditional commerce is becoming more blurred as more businesses start and continue to integrate the Internet and E-Commerce technologies into their business processes.

1.5.1 What is E-Commerce

Electronic commerce or E-Commerce refers to a wide range of online business activities for products and services. It also pertains to "any form of business transaction in which the parties interact electronically rather than by physical exchanges or direct physical contact."

E-Commerce is usually associated with buying and selling over the Internet, or conducting any transaction involving the transfer of ownership or rights to use goods or services through a computer-mediated network. Though popular, this definition is not comprehensive enough to capture recent developments in this new and revolutionary business phenomenon. A more complete definition is: E-Commerce is the use of electronic communications and digital information processing technology in business transactions to create, transform, and redefine relationships for value creation between or among organizations, and between organizations and individuals.

1.6 E-COMMERCE THE SAME AS E-BUSINESS

While some use E-Commerce and E-Business interchangeably, they are distinct concepts. In E-Commerce, information and communications technology (ICT) is used in inter-business or inter-organizational transactions (transactions between and among firms/organizations) and in business-to-consumer transactions (transactions between firms/organizations and individuals).

In E-Business, on the other hand, ICT is used to enhance one's business. It includes any process that a business organization (either a for-profit, governmental or non-profit entity) conducts over a computer-mediated network. A more comprehensive definition of E-Business is: "The transformation of an organization's processes to deliver additional customer value through the application of technologies, philosophies and computing paradigm of the new economy."

Three primary processes are enhanced in E-Business:

1. **Production processes**, which include procurement, ordering and replenishment of stocks; processing of payments; electronic links with suppliers; and production control processes, among others;
2. **Customer-focused processes,** which include promotional and marketing efforts, selling over the Internet, processing of customers' purchase orders and payments, and customer support, among others.
3. **Internal management processes**, which include employee services, training, internal information-sharing, video-conferencing, and recruiting. Electronic applications enhance information flow between production and sales forces to improve sales force productivity. Workgroup communications and elec- tronic publishing of internal business information are likewise made more efficient.

1.6.1 Internet Economy Synonymous with E-Commerce and E-Business

The Internet economy is a broader concept than E-Commerce and E-Business. It includes E-Commerce and E-Business.

The Internet economy pertains to all economic activities using electronic networks as a medium for commerce or those activities involved in both building the net- works linked to the Internet and the purchase of application services such as the provision of enabling hardware and software and network equipment for Web-based/ online retail and shopping malls (or "e-malls"). It is made up of three major segments:

- physical (ICT) infrastructure, business infrastructure, and commerce. It is made up of three major segments:
- physical (ICT) infrastructure, business infrastructure, and commerce.

The CREC (Center for Research and Electronic Commerce) at the University of Texas has developed a conceptual framework for how the Internet economy works. The framework shows four layers of the Internet economy-the three mentioned above and a fourth called intermediaries (see Table 1).

If the purpose of your small business Web site is to sell a product or service, E-marketing can lead to E-Commerce. E-Commerce is the act of doing business electronically over the Internet. No matter the size, age or type of your business, E-Commerce offers benefits that cannot be attained with a brick and mortar store.

Table 1.1: Internet Economy Conceptual Frame

Internet Economy Layer	Layer 1 - Internet Infrastructure: Companies that provide the enabling hardware, software, and networking equipment for Internet and for the World Wide Web	Layer 2 - Internet Applications Infrastructure: Companies that make software products that facilitate Web transactions; companies that provide Web development design and consulting services	Layer 3 - Internet Intermediaries Companies that link E-Commerce buyers and sellers; companies that provide Web content; companies that provide market places in which E-Commerce transactions can occur	Layer 4 - Internet Commerce Companies that sell products or services directly to conusmers or businesses
Types of Companeis	Networking Hardware/Software Companies Line Acceleration Hardware Manufacturers Internet Backbone Providers Internet Services Providers (ISPs)	Internet Commerce Applications Web Development Software Internet Consultants Online Training Search Engine Software Web-Enabled Databases Multimedia Applications	Market Makers in Vertical Industries Online travel Agents Online Brokerages Content Aggregators Online Advertisers Internet Ad Brokers Portals/contents Providers	E-Tailers Online entertainment and Professional Services Manufactures Selling Online Airlines Selling Online Tickets Free/Subscription-Based Companies
Examples	Cisco AOL AT&T Qwest	Adobe *Microsoft *IBM Oracle	e-Steel Travelocity e-Trade Yahoo! ZDNet	Amazon.com Dell

E-Commerce, a prime driver of the global economy, has changed business processes worldwide, increasing logistical efficiencies and facilitating the buying, selling, and marketing of goods. Similarly, E-Commerce has benefited millions of consumers through decreased prices, increased competition, and faster order and delivery times.

Large and small companies across multiple industries depend on E-Commerce applications to survive and compete in local, national, and global economies. These companies use e-mail to communicate with customers and suppliers and the Internet to handle marketing and electronic transaction processing and settlement. They rely on myriad hardware and software solutions to manage large databases and carry out sophisticated analysis of complex business operations, support back office automation, assist document sharing, and facilitate communication with clients, customers and colleagues.

While E-Commerce has advanced most rapidly in developed countries, companies in developing countries increasingly use E-Commerce to strengthen their core business practices and spin off new businesses.

Electronic commerce (or E-Commerce) encompasses all business conducted by means of computer networks. Advances in telecommunications and computer technologies in recent years have made computer networks an integral part of the economic infrastructure. More and more companies are facilitating transactions over web. There has been tremendous competition to target each and every computer owner who is connected to the Web. Although business-to-business transactions play an important part in E-Commerce market, a share of E-Commerce revenues in developed countries is generated from business to consumer transactions. E-Commerce provides multiple benefits to the consumers in form of availability of goods at lower cost, wider choice and saves time. People can buy goods with a click of mouse button without moving out of their house or office. Similarly online services such as banking, ticketing (including airlines, bus, railways), bill payments, hotel booking etc. have been of tremendous benefit for the customers. Most experts believe that overall E-Commerce will increase exponentially in coming years. Business to business transactions will represent the largest revenue but online retailing will also enjoy a drastic growth. Online businesses like financial services, travel, entertainment, and groceries are all likely to grow.

E-Commerce (electronic commerce or EC) is the buying and selling of goods and services on the Internet, especially the World Wide Web. In practice, this term and a newer term, E-Business, are often used interchangeably. For online retail selling, the term e-tailing is sometimes used.

1.7 E-Commerce in India

Electronic commerce (or E-Commerce) encompasses all business conducted by means of computer networks. Advances in telecommunications and computer technologies in recent years have made computer networks an integral part of the economic infrastructure. More and more companies are facilitating transactions over web. There has been tremendous competition to target each and every computer owner who is connected to the Web. Although business-to-business transactions play an important part in E-Commerce market, a share of E-Commerce revenues in developed countries is generated from business to consumer transactions. E-Commerce provides multiple benefits to the consumers in form of availability of goods at lower cost, wider choice and saves time. People can buy goods with a click of mouse button without moving out of their house or office. Similarly online services such as banking, ticketing (including airlines, bus, railways), bill payments, hotel booking etc. have been of tremendous benefit for the customers. Most experts believe that overall E-Commerce will increase exponentially in coming years. Business to business transactions will represent the largest revenue but online retailing will also enjoy a drastic growth. Online businesses like financial services, travel, entertainment, and groceries are all likely to grow.

E-Commerce (electronic commerce or EC) is the buying and selling of goods and services on the Internet, especially the World Wide Web. In practice, this term and a newer term, E-Business, are often used interchangeably. For online retail selling, the term e-tailing is sometimes used.

E-Commerce can be divided into

- E-tailing or "virtual storefronts" on Web sites with online catalogs, sometimes gathered into a "virtual mall"
- The gathering and use of demographic data through Web contacts
- Electronic Data Interchange (EDI), the business-to-business exchange of data
- E-mail and fax and their use as media for reaching prospects and established customers (for example, with newsletters)
- Business-to-business buying and selling
- The security of business transactions

1.8 HISTORY OF E-COMMERCE

The meaning of the term electronic commerce has changed over time. Originally, "electronic commerce" meant the facilitation of commercial transactions electronically, usually using technology like Electronic Data Interchange (EDI) to send commercial documents like purchase order s or invoice s electronically.

Today it includes activities more precisely termed "Web commerce" the purchase of goods and services over the World Wide Web via secure servers (note HTTPS , a special server protocol which encrypts confidential ordering data for customer protection) with e- shopping cart s and with electronic pay services, like credit card pay authorizations.

1.8.1 Several Factors Have Critical Importance in the Success of any E-Commerce Venture

They include:

- Providing value to customers. Vendors can achieve this by offering a product or product line that attracts potential customers at a competitive price.
- Providing service and performance. This can be done by offering a fast, user-friendly purchasing experience.

- Providing an attractive site. This can be done by the tasteful use of colour, graphics, animation, photographs, fonts, and white space percentage.
- Providing an incentive to buy and to return. This can be done with sales promotions like coupons, special offers, and discounts. Cross-linked web sites, and advertising affiliate programs can also be used.
- Providing personal attention. This can be done by personalized web sites, purchase suggestions, and personalized special offers.
- Providing a sense of community. This can be done with chat-rooms, message boards, soliciting customer input, and affinity programs.
- Providing reliability and security. Parallel servers, fail-safe technology, information encryption, and firewalls can enhance this requirement.
- Providing a 360-degree view of the customer relationship, defined as ensuring that all employees, suppliers, and partners have a complete view, and the same view, of the customer.
- Owning the customer's total experience. This can be done by treating any contacts with a customer as part of a total experience, an experience that becomes synonymous with the brand.
- Streamlining business processes. This can be done through re-engineering and information technologies.
- Letting customers help themselves. Provision of a self-serve site, easy to use without assistance, can help in this respect.
- Helping customers do their job. E-tailer s can provide such help through ample comparative information and good search facilities.
- Constructing a sound business model. If this key success factor had appeared in textbooks in 2000, many of the dot.coms might not have gone bust.
- Engineering an electronic value chain in which one focuses on a "limited" number of core competencies .
- Operating on or near the cutting edge of technology and staying there as technology changes. Creating an organization of sufficient alertness and agility to respond quickly to any changes in the environment.

1.9 TYPE OF E-COMMERCE/ E-COMMERCE MODEL

E-Commerce is the use of Internet and the web to transact business but when we focus on digitally enabled commercial transactions between and among organizations and individuals involving information systems under the control of the firm it takes the form of E-Business. Nowadays, 'e' is gaining momentum and most of the things if not everything is getting digitally enabled. Thus, it becomes very important to clearly draw the line between different types of commerce or business integrated with the 'e' factor.

There are mainly five types of E-Commerce models:

1. Business to Consumer (B2C)

As the name suggests, it is the model involving businesses and consumers. This is the most common E-Commerce segment. In this model, online businesses sell to individual consumers. When B2C started, it had a small share in the market but after 1995 its growth was exponential. The basic concept behind this type is that the online retailers and marketers can sell their products to the online consumer by using crystal clear data which is made available via various online marketing tools. E.g. An online pharmacy giving free medical consultation and selling medicines to patients is following B2C model. Business to Customer or B2C refers to E-Commerce activities that are focused on consumers rather than on businesses. For instance, a book retailer would be a B2C company such as Amazon.com and other companies that follow a merchant model or brokerage business models. Other examples could also be purchasing services from an insurance company, conducting online banking and employing travel services.

Example: In this case transactions take place between consumers and business houses. Here individuals are also involved in the online business transactions.

2. Business to Business (B2B)

It is the largest form of E-Commerce involving business of trillions of dollars. In this form, the buyers and sellers are both business entities and do not involve an individual consumer. It is like the manufacturer supplying goods to the retailer or wholesaler. E.g. Dell sells computers and other related accessories online but it is does not manufacture all those products. So, in order to sell those products, it first purchases them from different businesses i.e. the manufacturers of those products.

Business to Business or B2B refers to E-Commerce activities between businesses. An E-Commerce company can be dealing with suppliers or distributors or agents. These transactions are usually carried out through Electronic Data Interchange or EDI. EDI is an automated format of exchanging information between businesses over private networks.

This allows more transparency among business involved; therefore business can run more efficiently, for instance, a supplier can respond faster to diminishing stock of a particular product. EDI is composed of standards that enable businesses' computers to conduct transactions with each other without human intervention. In general, B2Bs require higher security needs than B2Cs. For example, manufacturers and wholesalers are B2B companies.

With the help of B2B E-Commerce, companies are able to improve the efficiency of several common business functions, including supplier management, inventory management and payment management.

Using E-Commerce enabled business applications, companies are able to better control their supplier costs by reducing PO (purchase order) processing costs and cycle times. This has the added benefit of being able to process more POs at a lesser cost in the same amount of time. E-Commerce technology can also serve to shorten the order-ship-bill cycle of inventory management by linking business partners together with the company to provide faster data access. Businesses can improve their inventory auditing capabilities by tracking order shipments electronically, which results in reduced inventory levels and improves upon the ability of the company to provide "just-in-time" service.

This E-Commerce technology is also being used to improve the efficiency of managing payments between a business and its partners and distributors. By processing payments electronically, companies are able to lower the number of clerical errors and increase the speed of processing invoices, which results in lowered transaction fees.

Example : Here the seller and the buyer participate as business entities. Here the business is carried out the same way a manufacturer supplies goods to a wholesaler.

3. Consumer to Consumer (C2C)

It facilitates the online transaction of goods or services between two people. Though there is no visible intermediary involved but the parties cannot carry out the transactions without the platform which is provided by the online market maker such as eBay. Customer to Customer or C2C refers to E-Commerce activities, which use an auction style model. This model consists of a person-to-person transaction that completely excludes businesses from the equation. Customers are also a par of the business and C2C enables customers to directly deal with each other.

Example: Consumer-to-Consumer (C2C) model is applicable when the business transaction is carried between two individuals. But for this type of E-Commerce, the individuals require a platform or an intermediary for business transactions

4. Peer to Peer (P2P)

Though it is an E-Commerce model but it is more than that. It is a technology in itself which helps people to directly share computer files and computer resources without having to go through a central web server. To use this, both sides need to install the required software so that they can communicate on the common platform. This type of E-Commerce has quite low revenue generation as from the beginning it has been inclined to the free usage due to which it sometimes got entangled in cyber laws.

Example: Peer-to-Peer (P2P) is another model of E-Commerce. This model is technologically more sound than the other E-Commerce models. During this type of transactions, people can share computer resources. Here it is not required to use a common server; instead a common platform can be used for the transactions.

With technological advancements, the business transactions can be done through mobile devices. The latest model for E-Commerce is the M-Commerce. The E-Commerce sites can be specially optimized and programmed so that they can be viewed and used through mobiles. Here two mobile users can contact each other to carry out the business transactions.

5. M-Commerce

It refers to the use of mobile devices for conducting the transactions. The mobile device holders can contact each other and can conduct the business. Even the web design and development companies optimize the websites to be viewed correctly on mobile devices.

6. *Customer to Business (C2B)*

Customer to Business or C2B refers to E-Commerce activities, which use reverse pricing models where the customer determines the prices of the product or services. In this case, the focus shifts from selling to buying. There is an increased emphasis on customer empowerment.

In this type of E-Commerce, consumers get a choice of a wide variety of commodities and services, along with the opportunity to specify the range of prices they can afford or are willing to pay for a particular item, service or commodity. As a result, it reduces the bargaining time, increases the flexibility and creates ease at the point of sale for both the merchant and the consumer.

There are other types of E-Commerce business models too like Business to Employee (B2E), Government to Business (G2B) and Government to Citizen (G2C) but in essence they are similar to the above mentioned types. Moreover, it is not necessary that these models are dedicatedly followed in all the online business types. It may be the case that a business is using all the models or only one of them or some of them as per its needs.

1.10 HOW E-COMMERCE WORKS?

E-Commerce allows people to create completely new business models. Unless you have been living under a rock for the last few years, you have probably heard about E-Commerce. And you have heard about it from several different angles. You may have: heard about all of the companies that offer E-Commerce.

Our secure shopping cart allows your customers to purchase their products online without worry. The orders placed by your customers online will appear in your Control Panel as invoices, where you can print and process them the way you do all your regular orders. Also, and email copy of the invoice is automatically sent to the customer and to an email address you have chosen for your own information.

There is no need for you to have a Merchant Account (an account which allows you to actually capture credit card dollars online in real-time)...but if you decide you want one, a special area within your Control Panel will show you step by step how to set one up with just a few clicks.

Unless you have been living under a rock for the last few years, you have probably heard about **E-Commerce**. And you have heard about it from several different angles. You may have:

- heard about all of the companies that offer E-Commerce because you have been bombarded by their TV and radio ads
- read all of the news stories about the shift to E-Commerce and the hype that has developed around E-Commerce companies
- seen the huge valuations that Web companies get in the stock market, even when they don't make a profit
- purchased something on the Web, so you have direct personal experience with E-Commerce
- Still, you may feel like you don't understand E-Commerce at all. What is all the hype about? Why the huge valuations? And most importantly, is there a way for you to participate? If you

have an E-Commerce idea, how might you get started implementing it? If you have had questions like these, then this article will help out by exposing you to the entire E-Commerce space.

Fig. 1.1: E-Commerce allows people to create completely new

1.11 BENEFITS OF E-COMMERCE

E-Commerce is one of the most important facets of the Internet to have emerged in the recent times. E-Commerce or electronic commerce involves carrying out business over the Internet with the assistance of computers, which are linked to each other forming a network. To be specific ecommerce would be buying and selling of goods and services and transfer of funds through digital communications.

- Enhance sales with less investment.

  Potentially unlimited customer base.

  Build profitable and professional online carts.

  Reach your targeted customers with effective marketing tools & new strategies.

  Empowers consumers by letting them handle their own transaction.

  Allows businesses to focus on selling a product or service while easily developing effective business relationships.
- E-Commerce allows people to carry out businesses without the barriers of time or distance. One can log on to the Internet at any point of time, be it day or night and purchase or sell anything one desires at a single click of the mouse.
- The direct cost-of-sale for an order taken from a web site is lower than through traditional means (retail, paper based), as there is no human interaction during the on-line electronic purchase order process. Also, electronic selling virtually eliminates processing errors, as well as being faster and more convenient for the visitor.
- E-Commerce is ideal for niche products. Customers for such products are usually few. But in the vast market place i.e. the Internet, even niche products could generate viable volumes.

- Another important benefit of E-Commerce is that it is the cheapest means of doing business.
- The day-to-day pressures of the marketplace have played their part in reducing the opportunities for companies to invest in improving their competitive position. A mature market, increased competitions have all reduced the amount of money available to invest. If the selling price cannot be increased and the manufactured cost cannot be decreased then the difference can be in the way the business is carried out. E-Commerce has provided the solution by decimating the costs, which are incurred.
- From the buyer's perspective also ecommerce offers a lot of tangible advantages.
  - Reduction in buyer's sorting out time.
  - Better buyer decisions
  - Less time is spent in resolving invoice and order discrepancies.
  - Increased opportunities for buying alternative products.
- The strategic benefit of making a business 'ecommerce enabled', is that it helps reduce the delivery time, labor cost and the cost incurred in the following areas:
  - Document preparation
  - Error detection and correction
  - Reconciliation
  - Mail preparation
  - Telephone calling
  - Data entry
  - Overtime
  - Supervision expenses

Operational benefits of E-Commerce include reducing both the time and personnel required to complete business processes, and reducing strain on other resources. It's because of all these advantages that one can harness the power of ecommerce and convert a business to ebusiness by using powerful turnkey ecommerce solutions made available by ebusiness solution providers.

1.12 E-COMMERCE TECHNOLOGY AND PROSPECTS

With the preceding in mind, the dynamic nature of the new economy, and particularly the Internet, calls for decision makers to develop policies that stimulate growth and advance consumer interests. But, in order to create the foundation for the rapid growth of E-Commerce, enterprises must adopt the effective E-Commerce technology policies that embrace the following four crucial principles:

Strong intellectual property protection: Innovation drives E-Commerce technology, and rewarding creativity fosters innovation. Thus, strong copyright, patent, and other forms of intellectual property protection are key to invigorating the information economy.

Online trust: security and privacy: Without consumer confidence in the safety, security, and privacy of information in cyberspace, there will be no E-Commerce and no growth. Protecting information and communications on the Internet is an absolute prerequisite to the continued success of the Internet and the information economy.

Free and open international trade: Closed markets and discriminatory treatment will stifle E-Business. The Internet is a global medium, and the rules of the information economy must reflect that fact. Only in an open, free market will the Internet's potential be realized.

Investing in an E-Commerce technology infrastructure: Supporting the physical infrastructure necessary to deliver digital content (primarily through telecommunications deregulation and government efforts to reduce the digital divide) is vital to spurring technological growth.

For hundreds of years, protection of creative material has given authors and other innovators powerful incentives to develop and distribute exciting new products. Throughout, respect for private property (whether in its tangible or intellectual form) has been a core value of market-driven economies.

In the information economy, such protection is even more vital, because the core currency of the Internet is nearly exclusively intellectual property. Today, software developers and other authors of creative works depend on the rights granted by copyright laws to develop new, more functional, and more powerful products. Overall, U.S. copyright-based industries (particularly the software, film, music, and publishing industries) are among the fastest growing segments of the American economy. Of those industries dependent on copyright for their business models, the high-tech industries comprise an ever-growing share, particularly those creating software and hardware products.

Industry leaders estimate that, within five years, an astonishing two thirds of software sales will be conducted over the Internet. Furthermore, one third of all software exports from the United States will be distributed electronically. Failure to properly protect this vital intellectual currency means its value will evaporate and the global economy will suffer greatly.

1.12.1 Copyright in the Internet Age

Digital piracy (the online theft of creative property) poses one of the single greatest threats to the success of the information economy. It undermines the confidence that creators and consumers place in their commercial interactions over networks.

The very nature of the online world that makes it so attractive in the marketplace also renders the work of copyright violators easier. Now that unlimited, flawless copies of creative works in digital form can be made and distributed globally in a matter of seconds, intellectual property on the Internet can be at great risk. Internet piracy is real, accurate and growing, demanding strong protections in the digital arena.

1.12.2 Software Piracy Is the Industry's Most Serious Problem

Piracy is the most significant problem facing the software industry globally. Every day, pirates steal millions of copies of copyrighted computer programs. Some of these are stolen by users making illegal copies personally, others by professional counterfeiting, and still others **Governments Must Combat**

1.12.3 Copyright Theft

Stemming these massive losses requires a concerted, multifaceted effort to combat the theft of copyrighted material. Although technological measures to fight piracy and increased public education about copyright are essential, the key to copyright protection lies in governments worldwide adopting and vigorously enforcing strong laws prohibiting this theft.

1.12.4 Copyright Laws Must Be Enforced

Strong words in a statute are not enough. These laws must be backed by vigorous enforcement by governments and must allow private parties to pursue fast and inexpensive remedies when their rights have been infringed. Strong copyright protection includes:

- Deterrent civil and criminal penalties
- Sustained criminal enforcement
- Copyright-related law enforcement efforts must be funded sufficiently
- Court-ordered and court-appointed piracy inspections must be available

1.12.5 Deterrent Civil and Criminal Penalties

Effective copyright laws must provide strong civil remedies, including permanent injunctions against further infringement, the seizure of illegal software (and articles used to defeat copyright protection), compensation, and fines. They must also provide for minimum criminal penalties when piracy is committed knowingly and for commercial purposes or to satisfy the internal demands of a business or other entity. In the United States, both criminal penalties and civil remedies are available and, increasingly, other countries are adopting similar legal models.

1.12.6 Sustained Criminal Enforcement

Sustained criminal enforcement is absolutely necessary in order to deter piracy and send the message that piracy is a serious crime with serious consequences. In the United States, the No Electronic Theft (NET) Act enables law enforcement officials to prosecute individuals who steal software by distributing it over the Internet, even if they do not profit economically from their activities. The NET Act has proven to be an effective antipiracy tool and has resulted in numerous convictions. In countries where such laws do not exist, however, customs and other governmental agencies must vigorously investigate and enforce traditional copyright laws as a first step toward addressing Internet-based piracy.

1.12.7 Copyright-Related Law Enforcement Efforts Must Be Funded Sufficiently

Despite the very real economic damage caused by software piracy, copyright enforcement actions too often are forced to take a back seat to other criminal prosecutions. For authorities to make a real dent in copyright crimes, governments must provide adequate funding and explicit direction to those agencies responsible for copyright enforcement.

1.12.8 Court-Ordered and Court-Appointed Piracy Inspections Must Be Available

Given even minimal warning, a pirate can swiftly and easily eliminate evidence of software theft with the touch of a button. As a result, the prosecution of software piracy, whether in civil or criminal contexts, requires court-ordered inspections without advance notice to the suspected software pirate (as required under the Trade-Related Intellectual Property Rights [TRIPs] Agreement). To ensure fairness, such searches should be court-supervised, with court-appointed experts being permitted to search and inspect for the suspected piracy.via illicit sales or auctions on the Internet.

1.12.9 What technologies are necessary for E-Commerce

The short answer is that most information technologies and Internet technologies that we discuss throughout the book are involved in E-Commerce systems, viz.–

- The Internet, intranets, and extranets are the network infrastructure or foundation of E-Commerce.
- Customers must be provided with a range of secure information, marketing, transaction, processing, and payment services.
- Trading and business partners rely on Internet and extranets to exchange information and accomplish secure transactions; including electronic data interchange (EDI) and other supply chain and financial systems and databases.
- Company employees depend on a variety of Internet and intranet resources to communicate and collaborate in support of their EC work activities.
- Information system professionals and end users can use a variety of software tools to develop and manage the content and operations of the websites and other EC resources of a company.

1.13 WHAT FORCES ARE FUELLING E-COMMERCE

There are at least three major forces fuelling E-Commerce: economic forces, marketing and customer interaction forces, and technology, particularly multimedia convergence.

1.13.1 Economic Forces

One of the most evident benefits of E-Commerce is economic efficiency resulting from the reduction in communications costs, low-cost techno- logical infrastructure, speedier and more economic electronic transactions with sup-pliers, lower global information sharing and advertising costs, and cheaper customer service alternatives.

Economic integration is either external or internal. External integration refers to the electronic networking of corporations, suppliers, customers/clients, and independent contractors into one community communicating in a virtual environment (with the Internet as medium). Internal integration, on the other hand, is the networking of the various departments within a corporation, and of business operations and processes. This allows critical business information to be stored in a digital form that can be retrieved instantly and transmitted electronically. Internal integration is best exemplified by corporate intranets. Among the companies with efficient corporate intranets are Procter and Gamble, IBM, Nestle and Intel.

1.13.2 Market Forces

Corporations are encouraged to use E-Commerce in marketing and promotion to capture international markets, both big and small. The Internet is like-wise used as a medium for enhanced customer service and support. It is a lot easier for companies to provide their target consumers with more detailed product and service information using the Internet.

1.13.3 Technology Forces

The development of ICT is a key factor in the growth of e- commerce. For instance, technological advances in digitizing content, compression and the promotion of open systems technology have paved the way for the convergence of communication services into one single platform. This in turn has made communication more efficient, faster, easier, and more economical as the need to set up separate networks for telephone services, television broadcast, cable television, and Internet access is eliminated. From the standpoint of firms/businesses and consumers, having only one information provider means lower communications costs.

Moreover, the principle of universal access can be made more achievable with convergence. At present the high costs of installing landlines in sparsely populated rural areas is a disincentive to telecommunications companies to install telephones in these areas. Installing landlines in rural areas can become more attractive to the private sector if revenues from these landlines are not limited to local and long distance telephone charges, but also include cable TV and Internet charges. This development will ensure affordable access to information even by those in rural areas and will spare the government the trouble and cost of installing expensive landlines.

1.14 NEED OF E-COMMERCE

There are some points which elaborate the need of E-Commerce

1. E-Commerce Hosting Plan with Online Shopping Cart

Online Shopping Cart software is another example of a vehicle to move credit card and ordering information. Your customers can efficiently order 24 hours a day. A shopping cart also eliminates some potential for error as there is only one human involved in the process rather than two. With our E-Commerce plans, we offer the Miva Merchant shopping cart.

The Shopping Cart is a vehicle that enables you to:

- Display your products on your website
- Get the ordering information from your customer
- Verify via email to the customer that his order has been placed
- Deliver the notification and ordering information to the seller

2. Choose your Payment Options

- **Off-line Credit Card Processing:** This is a good option if you currently have a Merchant Account with a local bank. Your customer's credit card information is captured and stored on our server for later authorization and transaction processing through a traditional card swipe terminal or through a computer. However, if you are clearing more than 100 transactions a month, you may want to consider the real-time payment processing option.
- **Real-time payment processing enabled by Merchant Accounts:** To process credit cards transactions in real time through your website you need to either (1) Open a Merchant Account with a financial institution; OR (2)Sign up with a payment gateway, for example, Authorize Net Merchant Accounts give you the ability to take credit card information from your prospective customers over the Internet. Miva Merchant (E-Commerce shopping cart) offer seamless integration with the CardService online payment gateway, providing you with a completely integrated E-Commerce solution.

3. Secure your E-Commerce website

When you are accepting credit card and other sensitive information online, you will need to make sure that all information are routed through a Secure Socket Layer (SSL) encrypted connection. We have a SSL installed on each server that is available for you to use for free. We offer 128-bit encrypted SSLs through GeoTrust that can be purchased for an additional fee if you prefer not to use the shared SSL.

Your business must also have a merchant number; a number you can get from a bank or credit union that will allow you to accept credit cards both online or in the real world. Some of these institutions are uncomfortable dealing with online transactions and set high premiums and costs as a result.

There are also banks and other companies that put together "store front" or "shopping cart" packages for you, handling much of the headaches. These vary in price, but plan on spending over a thousand dollars to set it up and $500-1000 and up per month in costs. If you plan on doing a lot of business, these options can be a good choice. However, they may not be your first choice.

As always, there are a few companies out there who will do some of this for free. iCat allows you 10 products to sell over the Internet for no fee, at least for now. More products than 10 and you have to get an account with them. Also, there is still a certain amount of work involved and you should be comfortable with HTML and general Internet knowledge if you don't have someone doing it for you.

1.15 INCENTIVES FOR ENGAGING IN E-COMMERCE

A basic fact of Internet retailing is that all retail websites are created equal as far as the "location, location, location" imperative of success in retailing is concerned. No site is any closer to its web customers and competitors offering similar goods and services may be only a mouse click away. This makes it vital that businesses find ways to build customer satisfaction, loyalty, and relationships, so customers keep coming back to their web stores. Thus, the key to E-Commerce success is to optimize several key factors such as selection and value, performance and service efficiency, the look and feel of the site, advertising and incentives to purchase, personal attention, community relationships, and security and reliability. The incentives for engaging in E-Commerce are listed as follows:

1. **Selection and Value.** Attractive product selections, competitive prices, satisfaction guarantees, and customer support after the sale.
2. **Performance and Service.** Fast, easy navigation, shopping, and purchasing, and prompt shipping and delivery.
3. **Look and Feel.** Attractive web storefront, website shopping areas, multimedia product catalog pages, and shopping features.
4. **Advertising and Incentives.** Targeted web-page advertising and e-mail promotions, discounts and special offers, including advertising at affiliate sites.
5. **Personal Attention.** Personal web pages, personalized product recommendations, web advertising, and e-mail notices, and interactive support for all customers.
6. **Community Relationships.** Virtual communities of customers, suppliers, company representatives, and others via newsgroups, chat rooms, and links to related sites.
7. **Security and Reliability.** Security of customer information and website transactions, trustworthy product information, and reliable order fulfillment.

1.15.1 Transaction Management

Electronic networking minimizes impacts of time & distance. The promise of E-Commerce is that transaction costs can be constrained to minimum that is appropriate to each type of transaction. Institutional adjustments and new approaches to organizational and inter-organizational management is required to allow new kinds of market relationships to involve in an electronic market-places.

At another level, there is the need to cope with escalation in the generation of transaction-associated data. Distributing information electronically not only facilitates more efficient storage and retrieval, but also helps ensure that operators of these systems always access the most up-to-date manuals, not only is the amount of transaction-related data increasing, but the awareness of the potential value of this data is increasing also.

1.15.2 Business Efficiency

E-Commerce support advanced design and manufacturing concepts like Just-in-Time, Quick Response, and Concurrent Engineering, all oriented to co-ordination and often integrating various aspects of the production and distribution processes. It facilitates new kind of on-demand marketing concepts throughout a wide range of products.

E-Commerce generates transaction information immediately in the form that permits sophisticated processing and quick distribution and can be used to plan and support changes designed to increase the responsiveness, flexibility, efficiency and accountability of business process. As in E-Commerce use of customer database increases, new security, privacy and legal issues arises. For this purpose business & government co-operation and support is essential.

1.15.3 New Market Development

E-Commerce is used by many firms not only to mere automation, but for creating business opportunities. E-Commerce is now a standard business tool, moving beyond cost saving and strategic objectives altogether. Many highly visible new markets for intangible products are being created around changing patterns of work & leisure-allowing consumers to access such services as banking, insurance and travel reservations directly from their homes and businesses, both in and out of normal business hours. In media, entertainment and communication sector, E-Commerce is the interactive tool widely used to develop world wide customers. Education and Training is an important area where E-Commerce can build up the infrastructure of skills upon which new generations of Electronic services markets will develop.

The view of major firms across the world is that the changes in access media would have to be customer driven. Customers will gravitate to the medium that is easiest, quickest and most convenient to use, and prefer to stay with that medium until it is obvious to them that a different medium is superior. The fast and speedy growth and development of E-Commerce requires government support and encouragement. Development of other networking-based activities-the convergence of different access technologies, ranging from telephone to television is must.

In this global scenario, Internet Commerce stands at a critical juncture. After an exhilarating start-up, further development hinges on bridging the chasm between early adopter and a true mass market. We envision Eco System ad the foundation of that bridge.

1.16 APPLICATION OF E-COMMERCE

There are lot of E-Commerce applications some of which are as given below-

An example – supply chain management

Before looking at the wide variety of E-Commerce application areas that have flourished over the last decade in more detail, it is worth looking at one which may not be familiar to a reader, but which saves companies huge amounts of resources. The application involves a **supply chain.** A supply chain is a set of relationships between a number of companies who have a symbiotic relationship with each other in that one company supplies commodities or services to other companies which, in turn, supply commodities or services to other companies, and so on.

Figure 1.2 shows the information flows in this supply chain. This is an example of a **supply chain**. It represents a typical E-Business application. There are a number of commercial imperatives for Warner Lambert: first, it should not overstock bottles of Listerine and incur costs because its resources are tied up in unsold goods; on the other hand, it should always stock enough bottles to satisfy demand in the time that the reordering and replenishing processes can take place. Second it should be able to get as quick a response to an order for raw materials as possible. This requires every company in the supply chain to move quickly to process an order from a company which follows it in the chain. An empty warehouse would be a disaster for Warner Lambert.

A third commercial imperative is for the elimination of waste bureaucracy and indirect connections between companies from the supply chain. This is again connected with responsiveness:

the more paper that is used and the more companies have to communicate using devices such as email the slower the process of reorder and replenishment will be. The ideal here is for a company higher up in the supply chain to share its data with companies further down the chain. For example, Warner Lambert should ideally be able to look at the stocks of the wholesalers and initiate a replenishment of those stocks when it discerns that they are becoming low – provided, of course, that some pre-agreement has been made about the quantities involved. An important point about an application such as this one is that information should be kept confidential as it flows across the internet.

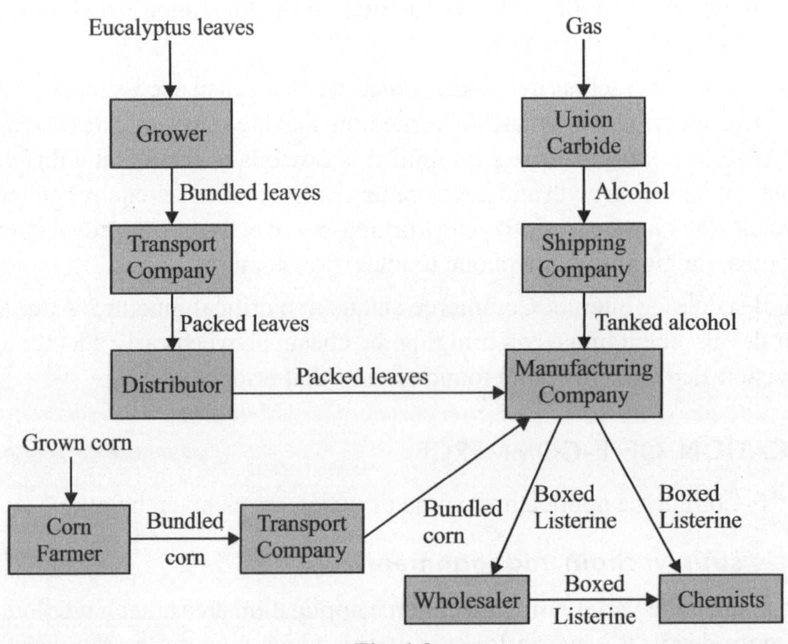

Fig. 1.2

1.16.1 E-tailing

The next example is probably the one that you expected me to introduce first: that of selling goods over the internet. However, I deliberately introduced supply chain management first since it is an area where companies are making huge savings in their investment in internet technology. The investments in retailing using the internet **(e-tailing)** are only gradually being realised.

The archetypal e-tailing application is that of a bookseller such as Amazon. This company is renowned for the fact that it only sells books over the internet and doesn't even take telephone orders. It has one of the best organised websites and is continually referred to by journalists as an E-Commerce success story.

1.16.2 Procurement

The term **procurement** is used to describe the purchase of goods and services which are not directly used in the main business of a company. For example, a car manufacturer will procure stationery for its employees or procure training courses for them to attend in order to improve their skills.

A typical conventional procurement process consists of a number of steps:

- the person making the procurement expresses their need by typing in details of a requisition using either a computer-based or paper-based form;
- the form is then dispatched to a member of staff who checks that it has been filled in correctly, that the amount is no larger than the amount that they are able to authorise and that there are sufficient funds available for purchase;
- If the form is authorised then it is sent on to a member of staff who is concerned with the purchasing of the good or service that is required; they then fill in a purchase requisition and send it off to the company who supplies the item that is to be purchased. If the item is over the limit for authorisation, then it is sent to someone who can authorise greater amounts.

This is in contrast to an e-procurement system which would automatically take the form produced by the person making the procurement, check that it satisfies all the company rules for procuring the item that is required, carry out authorisation if it is below a certain limit or send the form to someone who can carry out authorisation and then log the purchaser into the site of the supplier. He or she is then able to use this site to make the purchase, quoting an automatically generated procurement requisition number.

1.16.3 Auction Sites

These are sites on the web which run conventional auctions. There are two types of auction: those that are carried out in real time, where participants log in to an auction site using a browser at a specified time and bid for an article until the highest price is reached and no other bids are forthcoming. The other type of site and the most common is where an item is offered for sale and a date advertised after which no more bids are accepted. Such sites make a profit from two sources: first they usually charge a commission on the items that are sold and, second, they display adverts which are viewed by visitors to the site. The auction site will then receive some fee for displaying the advert, a further fee if a visitor clicks on an advert and it takes them to the advertiser's website and another fee if they purchase something from this site. Again, this is just an online analogue of a conventional business.

1.16.4 Other Commercial Websites

So far I have detailed E-Commerce applications which are connected with very large organisations; to conclude this section it is worth looking at a number of smaller applications, many of which are distinguished by the fact that they are novel. They are in contrast to the applications discussed in previous subsections which mainly consist of standard functions such as order processing

1.16.5 Search engines

The web contains a huge amount of material. Finding specific information is a huge problem; even in the early days of the internet this was a problem which threatened to slow the growth of the net. Fortunately a partial solution to this problem emerged: the **search engine**. This is a program which accesses a huge database of information about the World Wide Web; it contains individual words in web documents and the location of the documents containing the words. When the user of a search engine wants to find any document they type a **query**: a series of keywords joined by Boolean connectives such as 'and' and 'or' or, in some cases, a natural language sentence. For example, the query Java & compiler would return with the addresses of all those web documents which contain the words 'Java' and 'compiler'.

1.17 E-COMMERCE APPLICATIONS: ISSUES AND PROSPECTS

Various applications of E-Commerce are continually affecting trends and prospects for business over the Internet, including e-banking, e-tailing and online publishing/online retailing.

A more developed and mature e-banking environment plays an important role in E-Commerce by encouraging a shift from traditional modes of payment (i.e., cash, checks or any form of paper-based legal tender) to electronic alternatives (such as e- payment systems), thereby closing the E-Commerce loop.

What are the existing practices in developing countries with respect to buying and paying online

In most developing countries, the payment schemes available for online transactions are the following:

A. *Traditional Payment Methods*

- **Cash-on-delivery.** Many online transactions only involve submitting purchase orders online. Payment is by cash upon the delivery of the physical goods.
- **Bank payments.** After ordering goods online, payment is made by depositing cash into the bank account of the company from which the goods were ordered. Delivery is likewise done the conventional way.

B. *Electronic Payment Methods*

- **Innovations affecting consumers**, include credit and debit cards, automated teller machines (ATMs), stored value cards, and e-banking.
- **Innovations enabling onlinE-Commerce** are e-cash, e-checks, smart cards, and encrypted credit cards. These payment methods are not too popular in developing countries. They are employed by a few large companies in specific secured channels on a transaction basis.
- **Innovations affecting companies** pertain to payment mechanisms that banks provide their clients, including inter-bank transfers through automated clearing houses allowing payment by direct deposit.

1.18 ECONOMIC POTENTIAL OF ELECTRONIC COMMERCE

Electronic Commerce is a marriage between a rapidly evolving technical environment and an increasingly pervasive set of ideas as to how markets should function. However, markets involve complex interaction between specific business/organizational factors, and general economic, social and political factors. The full economic potential of Electronic Commerce can only be evaluated against a backdrop of rapid change on all of these fronts. There are strong current indications that massive changes have already begun to occur across the entire business spectrum.

There are difficulties in assessing the commercial potential of the Internet. The Internet is the first multifunctional digital information environment that is available to a wide spectrum of users, ranging from large organizations to individuals, and it will likely become a focal point for the convergence of access media and the development of interactive services.

Although growth in the Internet is not the same phenomenon as growth in E-Commerce, ne vistas for Electronic Commerce are continually opening up on the Internet. In particular, the spectacular rates of increase in the numbers of households with Internet access has drawn special attention to prospects for direct sales to individual consumers. Companies are learning to identify the many new consumer communities that are emerging in the Internet environment, and to evaluate their product and service needs. Relatively mature communities have developed already around electronic services in the areas of travel and tourism, road navigation and health.

Consumers are pushing retailers to the wall, demanding lower process, better quality, a large selection of in-season goods. Retailers are scrambling to fill the order. They are slashing back-office costs, reducing profit margins, reducing cycle times, buying more wisely, and making huge investments in technology. They are revamping distribution channels to make sure that warehouse costs are down by reducing their average inventory levels and coordinating the consumer demand and supply patterns. In the push to reduce prices, more and more retailers are turning to overseas suppliers, in part because of cheaper labor costs. The effect of E-Commerce can also be seen over the retail industry and marketing.

1.18.1 E-Commerce and Retail Industry

Retailers are in the immediate line of fire and are first to bear the brunt of cost cutting. They are putting that pressure on the manufacturing and supplier end of the pipeline. At the same time, the quest for efficiencies has led to turmoil and consolidation within the retail industry. The pressure experienced by retailers and suppliers can be seen in the disappearance of jobs, in mergers, and in the increase in business failures in the manufacturing sector.

The problems are indeed serious. Electronic markets could provide a partial solution by promising customers more convenience and merchants greater efficiency and interactivity with suppliers to revitalize the troubled retailing sector.

1.18.2 E-Commerce and Marketing

Electronic commerce is forcing companies to rethink the existing ways of doing target marketing (isolating and focusing on a segment of the population), relationship marketing (building and sustaining a long-term relationship with existing and potential customers), and even event marketing (setting up a virtual booth where interested people come and visit). Consider the case of conventional direct marketers, who devote some 25 percent of their revenues to such costs as printing and postages for catalogs. Interactive marketing could help cut such expenses and may even deliver better results.

Interactive marketing is accomplished in electronic markets via interactive multimedia catalogs that give the same look and feel as a shopping channel. Users find moving images more appealing than still images and listening more appealing than reading text on screen. Those are two powerful reasons why every text-based and still-picture-based interactive experimental-based service has ever generated anywhere near the volume of retail merchandise orders that televised shopping channels have achieved. Maximum public acceptance will require that interactive catalog services have a more entertaining visual appearance than traditional text-intensive catalogs have had. Ideally, an interactive shopping program should produce full-motion demonstrations of selected products, but such a practical and economical technology has yet to be developed.

At this stage in the development of E-Commerce, a many of the aspects of inter-corporate and consumer E-Commerce applications must be evaluated separately in terms of their economic potential. However, developments like the Internet already bringing the consumer and corporate E-Commerce environments steadily together. The workplace (including schools & universities) is the most common source of computer awareness and skills that become transferred to the household.

The significance and growth potential of E-Commerce is linked interactively to the broader socialization of the electronic networking environment, a phenomenon that looks certain to proliferate with each generation. Indeed, evidence for this is already accumulating.tands at a critical juncture. After an exhilarating start-up, further development hinges on bridging the chasm between early adopter and a true mass market. We envision Eco System ad the foundation of that bridge.

1.19 ADVANTAGES OF E-COMMERCE

With the astonishing growth of the Internet, many companies are finding new and exciting ways to expand upon their business opportunities. There are very few successful companies that do not use computers in their everyday business activities, which also mean there are few companies that do not use E-Commerce. These are the advantages of Internet and E-Commerce in general:

1. **Speed.** The Internet and World Wide Web give businesses opportunities to exchange messages or complete transactions almost instantaneously. Even with the slowest connections, doing business electronically is much faster than traditional modes. With increased speeds of communication, the delivery time is expedited and that makes the whole transaction from start to finish more efficient. Even more significant is the fact that information appearing on the Internet can be changed extremely rapidly. This gives business owners the ability to inform

customers of any changes to the service that you are offering. This also allows for you to update marketing and promotional materials as often and as frequently as you would like.

2. **Cost Saving.** By using the Internet, marketing, distribution, personnel, phone, postage and printing costs, among many others, can be reduced. You can start doing business in cyberspace for as little as thousand of rupees. Most businesses will spend more than this but compared to the cost of opening a physical store, the savings are tremendous. These funds can then be diverted to marketing and advertising of your product or service.
3. **No Boundaries.** Cyberspace does not know any national boundary. That means you can do business all over the world as easily as you can in your own neighborhood. Since the Internet connects everyone in cyberspace, information is transmitted at the speed of sound or the speed of light, depending on your connection. Either way, distance becomes meaningless, which makes you able to link to anyone on the globe and anyone on the globe can link to you. The ability to provide links makes doing business on the Internet attractive to customers in any part of the world.
4. **Ease of Networking.** One advantage of the Internet is that is allows people to easily meet, gather data/information and stay in touch with others at a very low cost. Now almost everyone can automatically expose his/her business to the international market. The web will enable firms to build on the assets that they already possess, like brand name recognition, operational infrastructure, information, and customer relationships in order to develop new markets and distribution channels. Meeting with new network locally and from other countries can be done anytime and anywhere now.

1.19.1 Advantages to Customers

1. **Reduced Prices**—Costs of products are reduced since stages along the value chain are decreased. For instance, intermediaries can be eliminated by the company directly selling to the consumer instead of distributing through a retail store.
2. **Global Marketplace**—Consumers can shop anywhere in the world. Currently, according to the World Trade Organization (WTO) there are no custom duties put on products bought and traded globally electronically. This also provides wide selection of products and services to consumers.
3. **24-Hour Access**—Online businesses never sleep as opposed to brick and mortar businesses. E-Commerce allows people to carry out businesses without the barriers of time or distance. One can log on to the Internet at any point of time, be it day or night and purchase or sell anything one desires at a single click of the mouse.
4. **More Choices**—Provides consumers with more choices. For example, before making any purchase, customer can study about all the major brands and features of any item. It also provides consumers with less expensive products and services by allowing them to shop in many places and conduct quick comparisons.
5. **Quicker Delivery**—Allows quick delivery of products and services (in some cases) especially with digitized products.

6. Consumers can receive relevant and detailed information in seconds, rather than in days or weeks.
7. Makes it possible to participate in virtual auctions.
8. Allows consumers to interact with other consumers and electronic communities and exchange ideas as well as compare experiences.

1.19.2 Advantages to Businesses

1. **Increased Potential Market Share**—The Internet enables businesses to have access to international markets thereby increasing their market share. Companies can also achieve greater economies of scale.
2. **Low-cost Advertising**—Advertising on the Internet costs less than advertising on print or television depending on the intricacies and extent of the advertisement. A company can still spend a lot on advertising on the Internet if the company hires an external party to create their advertisements but advertising on the Internet itself is less costly since there is less cost associated with it in terms of printing and limited television spots.
3. **Low Barriers to Entries**—Anyone can start up a company on the Internet. Start-up costs are a lot lower for companies since there is less need for money for capital.
4. **Strategic Benefit**—The strategic benefit of making a business 'E-Commerce enabled' is that it helps reduce the delivery time, labour cost and the cost incur red in the following areas:
    - Document preparation
    - Error detection and correction
    - Reconciliation
    - Mail preparation
    - Telephone calling
    - Data entry
    - Overtime
    - Supervision expenses

1.19.3 Advantages to Society

1. Enables people in Third world countries and rural areas to enjoy products and services which otherwise are not available to them.
2. Facilitates delivery of public services at a reduced cost, increases effectiveness, and/or improves quality.
3. Enables more individuals to work at home, and to do less traveling for shopping, resulting in less traffic on the roads, and lower air pollution.
4. Allows some merchandise to be sold at lower prices since organization may not need a physical place and full inventory.

1.19.4 Advantages to Women

People in general think that women unlike men are reluctant to purchase online.

On the contrary, NPD research found that women tend to shop online more than men in most product categories. The study asserts that women were more likely to shop toys, clothing, games and make up online more than men.

In short all the major advantages of E-Commerce can be summarized as follows:

1. Cost reduction due to competitiveness in the procurement of products. Many suppliers of the product compete for customer patronage in open electronic markets. This competition brings down the product price.
2. Cost reduction due to reducing the paper work. The cost effective electronic documents will be delivered almost instantly and safely. This enables both parties to take quick decisions.
3. Information dissemination at a wider level is possible. Information about the product, cost, size, specification etc. may be made available to the customer located at widely distant geographical boundaries.
4. Improved customer relationship may be achieved by fast dissipation of the information to the potential customers.
5. Because all orders and inquiries are processed online, the product is directly supplied to the customer. This eliminates the need for wholesalers and retailers and brings down the product prices.
6. Total time reduction in the order processing, as E-Commerce minimizes the time taken from order to delivery.
7. Provides better, fast and effective linkage with the clients. Since all information has to be processed in the electronic medium, that is online, it is possible to identify the customers' requirements that lead to quick product design.
8. Opens new vistas for the organization and generates better business avenues because of easy and cheap reach to the potential customer base.
9. Enhances the organization's product and market analysis as the organization gets faster feedback from the customer. These feedbacks may be processed online.

1.20 E-COMMERCE DISADVANTAGES

Although the list of E-Commerce advantages is long, yet the E-Commerce environment is far from perfection. In fact, some of the E-Commerce disadvantages cause both consumers and businesses to suffer considerable misfortune. Although cost savings are usually mentioned, there are hidden costs that can quickly turn a credit into a debit. In addition, the technology is not perfect, for example, the network unreliability is a continuing concern.

Moreover, some other concerns involve security, the loss of privacy, low and remote service levels, and complex legal issues. Let us discuss these disadvantages one by one.

1.20.1 Hidden Costs

Although buying on-line is convenient, the cost of this convenience is not always clear at the front end. For example, on-line purchases are often accompanied by high shipping and re-stocking fees, a lack of warranty coverage, and unacceptable delivery times. The online purchases must be shipped and the shipping charges may be considerable.

In fact, too many E-Commerce companies have developed a reputation of overcharging for shipping and handling.

1.20.2 Network Unreliability

With a user population of well over 100 million in North America alone, the Internet is a very busy information highway. Although the Internet is designed to overcome the single point of failure problem, there have been several well- network failures during the past few years. An E-Commerce website that cannot serve its customers loses sales, credibility, and even customers. In effect, a network failure can be compared to having a location at an exclusive mall that is in middle of nowhere and has no access roads that lead to it. Network reliability problems may be generated by such factors as:

- Equipment failure in the network connection provider or ISP.
- Long response time due to increased network traffic or inadequate bandwidth.
- Accidental problems caused by nature such as lightning, floods, earthquakes that affect communication lines or by human error such as a road construction worker severing a network line by accident.

1.20.3 Cost of Staying in Business

We included operational cost savings and lower barriers of entry in the list of ecommerce advantages. That is, getting into business is relatively easier in an E-Commerce environment. Unfortunately, the flip side of the coin is that staying in business may be more difficult. Remember that the easy access means increased competition, thus causing businesses to operate with very thin profit margins. To be profitable, E-Businesses must maintain high sales volumes, which in turn means developing and maintaining a big and loyal customer base. Attracting customers and transforming them into repeat buyers is the key to profitability. To survive and remain competitive, businesses must invest heavily in often-costly technology. The introduction of computer technology within a business not only automates the business process but it also changes the way the company does business internally and externally. Such synergy between technology and business operations makes the company more dependent on technology, therefore making it more vulnerable to the pace and network failures.

1.20.4 Lack of Security

One of the main roadblocks to the wide acceptance of E-Commerce by businesses and consumers alike is the perceived lack of adequate security for on-line transactions. For example, consumers are growing increasingly weary about providing credit card information over the Internet. During the past few years, the press has been filled with reports about hackers breaking into E-Business websites and stealing credit card information. In many cases, the break-ins passed inadvertently for several months before either the seller or the buyer discovered the problem.

Securing on-line transaction data during its generation and then safeguarding it after it has been stored in the database are critical issues to be faced. For example, in June of 2001, a small computer retailer exposed credit card information through its website. The problem, caused by a coding error in a web page, allowed unauthorized access to stored order and credit card information for thousand of customers, dating as far back as one year.

1.20.5 Lack of Privacy

Ensuring the security of the data is of paramount importance to customers and to the credibility of the business. Customers also worry about the privacy implications of publicized incidents of data gathered by organizations of all types and sizes. The incredible data collection process is a mixed blessing to customers. Even at the simplest data level, sales information is stored in databases connected to web servers, thus exposing the information to cyber criminals. Because data gathering on the web is so easy, databases routinely contain information about customer purchasing habits, demographic data, credit information, and so on. In many cases, companies sell customer database information to marketing companies.

In turn, the marketing companies engage in massive e-mail campaigns to attract new customers. It doesn't take long for the customer's e-mail box to be filled with unwanted and unsolicited e-mail (also known as "spam"). The growing sales of personal firewalls and the large number of "hits" on websites that deal with privacy issues are testimony to the fact that customers are growing increasingly worried about their online privacy, and that they are seeking ways to protect themselves from cyber attackers.

1.20.6 Low Service Levels

Another common complaint about doing business online is the low level of customer service that online companies tend to provide. Although technology has automated business transactions to a large extent, there remains a real need for the human touch. Therefore, customer service has become a major differentiating factor. Because the web buying experience is much more impersonal than the traditional one, providing good customer service is critical to the survival of any E-Business. Therefore, E-Commerce websites must provide

- a pleasant and problem-free pre-ordering and ordering experience. The website design is an important interface.
- readily available easily used feedback options. Major customer complaints include the lack

of contact information on websites and the difficulty of contacting a customer service representative.

- quick and courteous complaint resolution.
- timely and low-cost shipping and prompt delivery of merchandise to customers.

1.20.7 Legal Issues

Legal problems encountered in the E-Commerce environment include

- Software and copyright infringements. The amount of illegal content flowing freely on the Internet is illustrated by the so-called Napster case. Napster, a popular music website website, was sued by the Recording Industry Association because it hosted millions of illegal digital copies of copyrighted songs that were freely downloaded by millions of users worldwide. After court action, Napster was forced to change its business model and to eliminate all illegal material from its website.
- Credit card fraud and stolen identities. The lack of security we mentioned earlier has put credit card fraud on the proverbial front burner. In addition, lack of security makes it relatively easy to assume another person's identity in order to make fraudulent transactions. Loss of confidence in the security of online transactions is a brake on the E-Business train.

1.21 EVOLUTION OF ECOMMERCE

The evolution of E-Commerce can be attributed to a combination regulatory reform and technological innovation. Through Internet (which played an important role in the evolution) appeared in the late 1960s, E-Commerce now took off with the arrival of the World Wide Web and browsers in the 1990s.

E-Commerce were first developed in the early 1970s with innovations like:

- **Electronic funds transfer (EFT)** – funds can be routed electronically from one organization to another.
- **Electronic data interchange (EDI)** – used to electronically transfer routine documents, that expanded electronic transfers from financial transactions to other types of transaction processing.
- **Interorganizational system (IOS)** – a system which allows the flow of information to be automated between organizations in order to reach a desired supply-chain management system, which enables the development of competitive organizations.

The Internet has changed the way consumers and businesses conduct transactions. Because the web is such a dynamic medium, first generation web sites have quickly given way to dynamic and interactive E-Commerce sites that incorporate the 7 C's of next generation web sites. This article looks at the evolution of E-Commerce technology, strategy, and marketing issues that have undergone drastic changes in the past few years.

Less than five years ago, companies started to view the Internet as a medium over which business could be conducted. Standardization, security, privacy issues were being considered by companies who were testing the waters of E-Commerce by putting up electronic storefronts that displayed products and services. Soon order entry was being enabled on E-Commerce sites and a new era had dawned that allowed customers to experience a different experience while conducting business using the Internet. Amazon was a pioneer and reaped the benefits of being first-to-market. Internet time is now measured in days rather than months or years which companies of "old-economy" were used to when deciding to implement or shift business strategy decisions.

From the Internet to Intranets to Extranets has been a speedy journey in the past 5 years. The 3 C's of first generation E-Commerce: Content, Community, and Commerce have now evolved into 7 C's of second generation E-Commerce: Content (e.g. Yahoo), Community (Ivillage), Commerce (e.g. Amazon), Communication (e.g. Doubleclick), Connectivity (e.g. Cisco), Collaboration (Mercata - now defunct), and Customization (e.g. Netperceptions). Each of these C's reflect an evolution of features that has its roots in first enabling automated processes (such as procurement) to extending these processes externally with other consumers as well as business partners.

1.21.1 Business Models

B2C (Business to Consumer) models have been tried and tested during the first generation of E-Commerce boom, but the newer trends are toward B2B (Business to Business) and Click-and-Mortar models. B2B provides advantages of close integration and communication with partners and suppliers, Click-and-Mortar provide takes advantage of offline and online channels being established in physical store locations but at the same time offering onlinE-Commerce convenience.

Companies have quickly realized that E-Commerce sites are more than digital storefronts that display products and allow customers to place an order. Business processes should extend to the back-end with systems in place to optimize the company's supply chain and distribution system. A holistic approach will offer the company insights on creating maximum efficiencies to support all business processes. E-Commerce business models are more than technology solutions. The right strategy focuses on a company's core services and products, and one that encompasses the entire E-Business value chain. Although technology plays an important part in the business goals, technology by itself is a means to an end rather than the end itself. If used properly, technology can be used to leverage the e-marketplace for competitive advantage in today's fast paced economy.

The traditional model of Manufacturer -> Wholesaler/Distributor -> Retailer -> User is being disinter mediated by providing a direct link between Manufacturer and End User (e.g. Dell). Companies are extending E-Commerce capabilities of electronic storefronts to back-end processes using Supply Chain Management and Enterprise Resource Planning software.

Supply Chain Management is the process of tracking the availability, delivery, and pricing of supplies and materials required to meet customer demands for goods. Part of supply-chain management process includes forecasting which helps managers determine how quickly they can get necessary supplies and at what cost. Results are arrived at by looking at orders, inventories, production capacity, transportation availability, and other factors that affect cost of material.

Enterprise Resource Planning is more complex and integrates order entry, monitoring inventory, and balancing financial records. Companies deploying ERP software that include functions of supply chain management, planning, warehousing, and transportation can make more knowledgeable decisions. Web based Supply Chain Management and Enterprise Resource Planning (ERP) applications are being deployed by corporations for significant cost savings. For companies that had operational centers all over the world, sharing data between facilities was a very complex task. The ubiquitous nature of Internet has provided an opportunity to share supply chain data by consolidating information and providing access to it in real-time for planning decisions.

1.21.2 Strategy

Online and offline business strategies differ significantly. Companies planning to enter the E-Commerce arena must have proper strategies to ensure their profitability, growth, and survival in the electronic marketplace. The business plan must traverse all parts of the organization and systems must be in place to react quickly to changing market conditions. Stovepipe processes must be replaced by integrated and collaborative environment that generate more value. Outsourcing technology to Application Service Providers may be an option for companies whose core competencies lie in business and not in technology. Technology must be a support mechanism for business and optimize information flow internally and externally to leverage efficiencies and strategic advantage in every aspect of business.

1.21.3 Marketing

With new business models emerging (e.g. Priceline), companies should balance experimentation with risk-taking to achieve optimum efficiencies. A new way of presenting information to customers over a digital medium has also required companies to re-think ways of keeping customers loyal ("stickiness" of web sites) since competitors are only one click away.

Consumers are more responsive now to new business models and what was sure to fail in the 'old economy' has a chance of success in the digital world if marketed correctly. E-Commerce strategy should include Customer Relationship Management (CRM) to help retain customers on a long-term basis. The digital arena provides new challenges as compared to traditional brick-and-mortar business models. Knowledge management techniques are being used for effective CRM. Tracking customer orders, responding to customer queries when the order is shipped results in satisfied customers who believe the vendor is involved beyond the point when a order has been placed, products shipped, and funds transferred. Another strategy for companies that have electronic storefronts and physical location has been the merging of two models (click-and-mortar), in which a customer may be able to place an order on a web site and pickup the product at the store, or return a product to the store that had been received as a shipment from placing the web order. With satisfied customers, acquisition and retention costs are lowered.

1.21.4 Security

As electronic commerce becomes acceptable by businesses and consumers, transactions are now routinely carried over computer networks. This necessitates the need for network resources to be not only available, but also reliable to provide data integrity in transit. The Internet today is the leading source of fraud. Last year credit card company Visa reported that although only 2% of its total transactions were done on the internet, 50% of all disputes were as a result of orders placed on the Internet. Security of E-Commerce site remains a big concern for big and small corporations and policies must be implemented to protect business strategy that relies heavily on technology. Denial of service attacks on web sites and e-mail viruses have a direct impact on productivity and reduced confidence in the e-marketplace. Ignoring security issues can endanger entire system integrity as well as expose a company's most critical data to theft or damage. Policies for use of network resources by employees and business partners, privacy issues, etc. must be carefully considered and implemented to reduce liability, theft, and wasted computing resources. This problem has been exasperated by lack of qualified personnel needed to design and maintain secure E-Commerce sites. As a result of today's digital economy, one of the most lucrative career paths is in the field of Information Security.

1.22 ARCHITECTURAL FRAMEWORK FOR E-COMMERCE

Architectural framework of E-Commerce means the synthesizing of various existing resources like DBMS, data repository, computer languages, software agent-based transactions, monitors or communication protocols to facilitate the integration of data and software for better applications.

The architectural framework for E-Commerce consists of six layers of functionality or services as follows:

1. Application services.
2. Brokerage services, data or transaction management.
3. Interface and support layers.
4. Secure messaging, security and electronic document interchange.
5. Middleware and structured document interchange, and
6. Network infrastructure and the basic communication services.

1. **Applications:** In the application layer services of E-Commerce, it is decided that what type of E-Commerce application is going to be implemented. There are three types of distinguished E-Commerce applications i.e., consumer to business application, business-to-business application and intra-organizational application.
2. **Information Brokerage and Management Layer:** This layer is rapidly becoming necessary in dealing with the voluminous amounts of information on the networks.

   This layer works as an intermediary who provides service integration between customers and information providers, given some constraint such as low price, fast services or profit maximization for a client. For example, a person wants to go to USA from India. The person checks the sites of various airlines for the low-price ticket with the best available service.

For this he must know the URLs of all the sites. Secondly, to search the services and the best prices, he also has to feed the details of the journey again and again on different sites. If there is a site that can work as information broker and can arrange the ticket as per the need of the person, it will save the lot of time and efforts of the person. This is just one example of how information brokerages can add value.

Another aspect of the brokerage function is the support for data management and traditional transaction services. Brokerages may provide tools to accomplish more sophisticated, time-delayed updates or future-compensating transactions.

3. **Interface and Support Services:** The third layer of the architectural framework is interface layer. This layer provides interface for E-Commerce applications. Interactive catalogs and directory support services are the examples of this layer.

   Interactive catalogs are the customized interface to customer applications such as home shopping. Interactive catalogs are very similar to the paper-based catalog. The only difference between the interactive catalog and paper-based catalog is that the first one has the additional features such as use of graphics and video to make the advertising more attractive.

   Directory services have the functions necessary for information search and access. The directories attempt to organize the enormous amount of information and transactions generated to facilitate E-Commerce.

   The main difference between the interactive catalogs and directory services is that the interactive catalogs deal with people while directory support services interact directly with software applications.

4. **Secure Messaging Layer:** In any business, electronic messaging is an important issue. The commonly used messaging systems like phone, fax and courier services have certain problems like in the case of phone if the phone line is dead or somehow the number is wrong, you are not able to deliver the urgent messages.

   In the case of courier service, if you want to deliver the messages instantly, it is not possible as it will take some time depending on the distance between the source and destination places. The solution for such type of problems is electronic messaging services like e-mail, enhanced fax and EDI.

   The electronic messaging has changed the way the business operates. The major advantage of the electronic messaging is the ability to access the right information at the right time across diverse work groups.

   The main constraints of the electronic messaging are security, privacy, and confidentiality through data encryption and authentication techniques.

5. **Middleware services:** The enormous growth of networks, client server technology and all other forms of communicating between/among unlike platforms is the reason for the invention of middleware services. The middleware services are used to integrate the diversified software programs and make them talk to one another.

6. **Network Infrastructure:** We know that the effective and efficient linkage between the customer and the supplier is a precondition for E-Commerce. For this a network infrastructure

is required. The early models for networked computers were the local and long distance telephone companies. The telephone company lines were used for the connection among the computers. As soon as the computer connection was established, the data traveled along that single path. Telephone company switching equipment (both mechanical and computerized) selected specific telephone lines, or circuits, that were connected to create the single path between the caller and the receiver. This centrally-controlled, single connection model is known as **circuit switching.**

However, circuit switching does not act well for sending data across a large network. In order to implement circuit switching, point-to-point connections for each pair of senders/ receivers has to be established which is both expensive and difficult to manage. There is one more technique that is used by the Internet. It is called a packet switching network. In a packet switching network, files and messages are broken down into packets that are labeled electronically with codes that indicate both their origin and destination.

Packets travel from computer to computer along the network until they reach their destination. The destination computer collects the packets and reassembles the original data from the pieces in each packet. In packet switching, as the packet passes through various computers on its line the computers determine the best way to move the packet forward to its destination.

1.23 IMPACTS OF E-COMMERCE ON BUSINESS

E-Commerce has made a profound impact on society. People can now shop online in the privacy of their own homes without ever having to leave. This can force larger brick and mortar retailers to open an online division. In some cases, it can also force smaller businesses to shut their doors, or change to being completely online. It also changes the way people look at making purchases and spending money. E-Commerce has changed the face of retail, services, and other things that make our economy work. Undoubtedly, it will continue to influence how companies sell and market their products, as well as how people choose to make purchases for many years to come. The following are the impact of E-Commerce on the global economy.

1.23.1 Impacts on Direct Marketing

Product promotion E-Commerce enhances promotion of products and services through direct, information-rich, and interactive contact with customers.

New sales channel E-Commerce creates a new distribution channel for existing products. It facilitates direct reach of customers and the bi-directional nature of communication.

Direct savings The cost of delivering information to customers over the Internet results in substantial savings to senders when compared with non -electronic delivery. Major savings are also realized in delivering digitized products versus physical delivery.

Reduced cycle time The delivery of digitized products and services can be reduced to seconds. Also, the administrative work related to physical delivery, especially across international borders, can be reduced significantly, cutting the cycle time by more than 90 percent.

Customer service Customer service can be greatly enhanced by enabling customers to find detailed information online. Also, intelligent agents can answer standard e-mail questions in seconds and human experts' services can be expedited using help-desk software.

Corporate image On the Web, newcomers can establish corporate images very quickly. Corporate image means trust, which is necessary for direct sales. Traditional companies such as Intel, Disney, Dell, and Cisco use their Web activities to affirm their corporate identity and brand image.

1.23.2 Other Marketing Impacts

Customization

E-Commerce provides for customization of products and services, in contrast to buying in a store or ordering from a television, which is usually limited to standard products. Dell Computers Inc. is a success story of customization. Today, we can configure not only computers but also cars, jewelry, gifts, and hundreds of other products and services. If properly done, one can achieve mass customization. It provides a competitive advantage as well as increases the overall demand for certain products and services.

Advertisement

With direct marketing and customization comes as one-to-one or direct advertisement, which is much more effective than mass advertisement. This creates a fundamental change in the manner in which advertisement is conducted not only for online trades but also for products and services that are ordered in traditional ways.

Ordering System

Taking orders from customers can drastically be improved if it is done online. When taken electronically, orders can be quickly routed to the appropriate order-processing site. This saves time and reduces expenses. So sales -people have more time to sell. Also, customers can compute the cost of their orders, saving time for all parties involved.

Markets

The physical market disappears as does the need to deliver the goods to the marketplace. In a market space, which is an electronic market, goods are delivered directly to buyers when purchasing is completed making markets much more efficient. For those products that are digitally based-software, music and information-the changes will be dramatic. Already, small but powerful software packages are delivered over the Internet. This fundamentally affects packaging and greatly reduces the need for historical distribution.

New selling models such as shareware, freeware are emerging to maximize the potential of the Internet. New forms of marketing will also emerge, such as Web-based advertising, linked advertising, direct e-mail, and an increased emphasis on relationship marketing. Customer's convenience is greatly enhanced, availability of products and services is much greater, and cheaper products are offered. All these provide EC with a competitive advantage over the traditional direct sales methods. Some people predict the "fall of the shopping malls," and many retail stores and brokers of services are labeled by some as "soon to be endangered species."

1.24 IMP ACTS ON ORGANIZATIONS

1.24.1 Technology and Organizational Learning

Rapid progress in E-Commerce will force companies to adapt quickly to the new technology and offer them an opportunity to experiment with new products, services, and processes. New technologies require new organizational approaches. For instance, the structure of the organizational unit dealing with E-Commerce might have to be different from the conventional sales and marketing departments. To be more flexible and responsive to the market, new processes must be put in place. This type of corporate change must be planned and managed.

1.24.2 Changing Nature of Work

The nature of work and employment will be transformed in the Digital Age; it is already happening before our eyes. Driven by increased competition in the global marketplace, firms are reducing the number of employees down to a core of essential staff and outsourcing whatever work they can to countries where wages are significantly less expensive. The upheaval brought on by these changes is creating new opportunities and new risks and forcing us into new ways of thinking about jobs, careers, and salaries.

The Digital Age workers will have to become very flexible. Few of them will have truly secure jobs in the traditional sense, and all of them will have to be willing and able to constantly learn, adapt, make decisions, and stand by them.

1.24.3 New Product Capabilities

E-Commerce allows for new products to be created and existing products to be customized in innovative ways. Such changes may redefine organizations' missions and the manner in which they operate. E-Commerce also allows suppliers to gather personalized data on customers. Building customer profiles as well as collecting data on certain groups of customers, can be used as a source of information for improving products or designing new ones.

Mass customization, as described earlier, enables manufacturers to create specific products for each customer, based on his or her exact needs. For example, Motorola gathers customer needs for a pager or a cellular phone, transmits them electronically to the manufacturing plant where they are manufactured, along with the customer's specifications and then sends the product to the customer within a day.

1.24.4 Impacts on Manufacturing

E-Commerce is changing manufacturing systems from mass production to demand-driven and possibly customized, just-in-time manufacturing. Furthermore, the production systems are integrated with finance, marketing, and other functional systems, as well as with business partners and customers. Using Web-based ERP systems, orders that are taken from customers can be directed to designers and to the production floor, within seconds. Production cycle time is cut by 50 percent or more in many cases, especially when production is done in a different country from where the designers and engineers are located.

Companies like IBM, General Motors, are assembling products for which the components are manufactured in many locations. Sub-assemblers gather materials and parts from their vendors, and they may use one or more tiers of manufacturers. Communication, collaboration, and coordination become critical in such multitier systems. Using electronic bidding, assemblers get sub-assemblies 15 percent to 20 percent cheaper than before and 80 percent faster.

1.24.5 Impacts on Finance

E-Commerce requires special finance and accounting systems. Traditional payment systems are ineffective or inefficient for electronic trade. The use of the new payment systems such as electronic cash is complicated because it involves legal issues and agreements on international standards. Nevertheless, electronic cash is certain to come soon and it will change the manner in which payments are being made. In many ways, electronic cash, which can be backed by currency or other assets, represents the biggest revolution in currency since gold replaced cowry shells. Its diversity and pluralism is perfectly suited to the Internet. It could change consumers' financial lives and shake the foundations of financial systems and even governments.

E-Commerce will change the way the businesses are being carried on. It will lead to the emergence of new businesses as well as business practices and also a new role for intermediaries. Indeed, all the functional areas of business will undergo change as follows:

- The new technology will transform business processes, the way products and services are created and marketed, dynamics of competitions, the organization structure of the enterprise and the nature of the enterprise itself. This will include marketing, supply management, customer and sales management, product development etc.
- Local proximity may no longer be a significant factor in retaining customer. Local markets will be replaced by global markets. Indeed it may bring to reality the goal of making the whole world as one family.
- Transparency and openness continue and will continue, to be effective business strategy. Already many businesses have started recognizing key customers, employees and suppliers more like a partner in the business. E-Commerce will lead to better customer service, more personalized products, reduced costs, supply chain efficiency and faster time to market. The most significant aspect of E-Commerce is new market development. The E-Commerce links and the infrastructure, initially set up, can be successfully used in other sectors.
- The change in the business functions will lead to new business models and create new set of facts and circumstances that can materially change the incidence of taxation.

The Internet will emerge as a new platform for marketing of products and services that will displace and rebuild existing economy. It will affect organizational structure; require different skills for negotiation, new regulatory and legal framework, electronic money, taxation and many other things. The evolution of E-Commerce will have profound impact on competition, mobility of enterprises, effect on consumer behavior, changes in the way the work is defined and managed. The net will enable businesses to save time on product design, design according to the individual customer specification, order and delivery of components, tracking sales and getting feedback from customers.

- The businesses can have virtual project team, virtual learning space so that the employees who are dispersed over various countries can work together as if they are together in one physical room. Business can be connected to the retail points in order to ascertain market trends, demand of the products and with the suppliers upstream to order the desired requirements. Better demand forecasting and stock replenishment can lead to significant reduction in the cost.

1.25 SUCCESS OF E-COMMERCE

The difference between a successful E-Commerce venture and a "dot bomb" is a mixture of many elements.

These critical areas are primarily:

1.25.1 Customer Service

Outstanding customer service is a major failing of many enterprises. Online customers have a choice, they are not restricted by geographical boundaries. If you don't offer excellence, they will go somewhere that does. There is much more about critical customer service that is beyond the scope of this website. However, we plan to bring you an in-depth study in the near future.

1.25.2 Marketing

The final primary blunder was the poor marketing. Money was poured into allsorts of irrelevant areas for advertising. Even down to paid listings in Search engines. Many of which did not even serve the population of that country to any relevant degree.

If we can get the "big four" above right, we have a grounding for success. Add to this the possibility of selling advertising space, affiliate programs etc. We can top up our income. To add to the formula for success, we need to realise the importance of the following secondary criteria;

1.25.3 Customer Power

Much more information is available to the customer to make informed decisions before committing to a purchase. Knowing this, they should always be treated with the respect of an industry expert. The likelihood is you really don't know the level of their understanding.

SUMMARY

Electronic commerce or E-Commerce refers to a wide range of online business activities for products and services. It also pertains to “any form of business transaction in which the parties interact electronically rather than by physical exchanges or direct physical contact.”

E-Commerce is usually associated with buying and selling over the Internet, or conducting any transaction involving the transfer of ownership or rights to use goods or services through a computer-mediated network.

Though popular, this definition is not comprehensive enough to capture recent developments in this new and revolutionary business phenomenon. A more complete definition is: E-Commerce is the use of electronic communications and digital information processing technology in business transactions to create, transform, and redefine relationships for value creation between or among organizations, and between organizations and individuals.

First generation E-Commerce sites running HTML have paved the way for more complex and dynamic web sites that tie together processes from order-entry to inventory control to financial record keeping. Wireless devices are now being web enabled and for conducting business to consumer E-Commerce transactions. Success in the e-marketplace will depend on companies being able to respond to needs of the ever-changing marketplace and forming partnerships, alliances, and collaborations with others to deliver value that may not have been possible with individual efforts. The ability to innovate, change, recover from setbacks will be hallmarks of success in this competitive arena. Generic models of B2C commerce are outdated and newer efforts are needed to leverage the untapped potential offered in the digital medium.

There is an acute shortage of personnel with the right mix of technology and managerial competencies. With continuing education and real-world experience that reflects trends in current marketplace, today’s IT professionals should seize opportunities that are available in the dynamic E-Commerce field and position themselves to be leaders of the next generation E-Commerce that is constantly creating rapid transformation in Internet time.

EXERCISE

1. What do you mean by Electronic Commerce.
2. What are the Technology and Prospects Electronic Commerce.
3. Definition of E-Business and E-Commerce.
4. What is Economic potential of electronic commerce
5. Describe the Incentives for engaging in electronic commerce.
6. What are the Forces behind E-Commerce.
7. Write down the Advantages and Disadvantages of Electronic Commerce
8. Describe Architectural framework of Electronic Commerce.
9. Write down the impact of E-Commerce on business.

CHAPTER

2

Network Infrastructure for E-Commerce

2.1 NETWORK INFRASTRUCTURE

In information technology and on the Internet, infrastructure is the physical hardware used to interconnect computers and users. Infrastructure includes the transmission media, including telephone lines, cable television lines, and satellites and antennas, and also the routers, aggregators, repeaters, and other devices that control transmission paths. Infrastructure also includes the software used to send, receive, and manage the signals that are transmitted.

In some usages, infrastructure refers to interconnecting hardware and software and not to computers and other devices that are interconnected. However, to some information technology users, infrastructure is viewed as everything that supports the flow and processing of information.

Infrastructure play a significant part in evolving the Internet, both in terms of where the interconnections are placed and made accessible and in terms of how much information can be carried how quickly.

Network architecture is the design of a communications network. It is a framework for the specification of a network's physical components and their functional organization and configuration, its operational principles and procedures, as well as data formats used in its operation.

In telecommunication, the specification of a network architecture may also include a detailed description of products and services delivered via a communications network, as well as detailed rate and billing structures under which services are compensated.

The network architecture of the Internet is predominantly expressed by its use of the Internet Protocol Suite, rather than a specific model for interconnecting networks or nodes in the network, or the usage of specific types of hardware links.

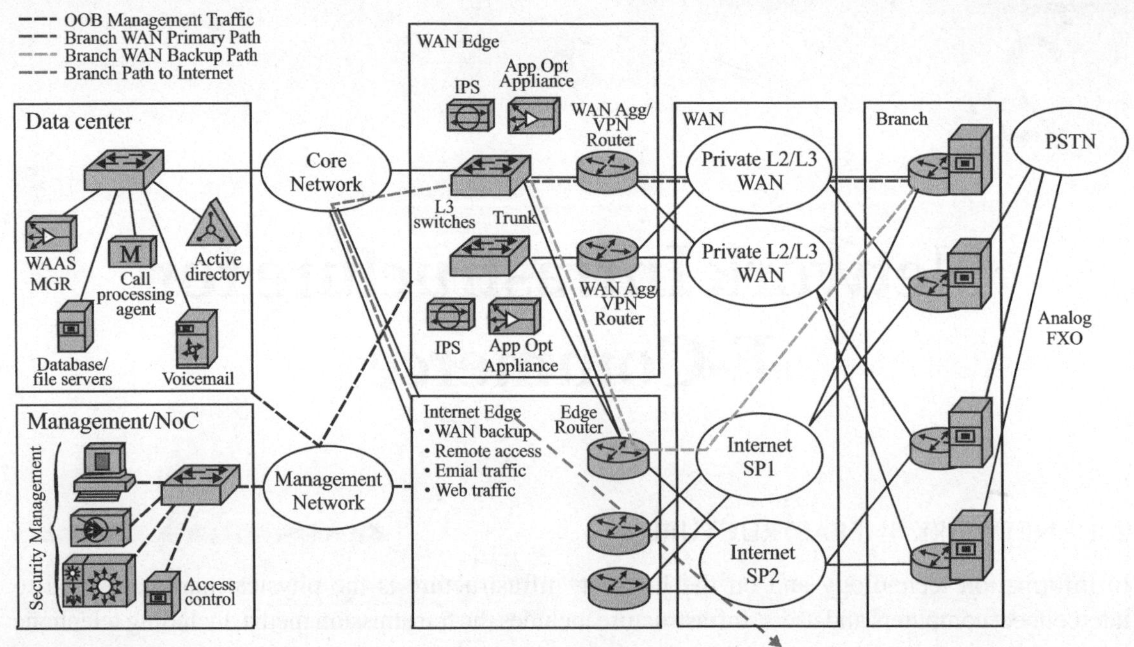

Fig. 2.1

By Definition

A Network's Infrastructure includes the physical hardware used to transmit data electronically such as routers, switches, gateways, bridges, and hubs.

Backbone: The backbone is the main line of wire that connects networks to one another.

Routers: A router is located at the gateway where it directs the flow and determines the route of packets as they travel from one network to another network(s). A router can be either a hardware device or a software application.

Switches: A switch directs the flow and determines the route of packets as they travel from one segment of a Local Area Network (LAN) to another on that samc LAN.

Bridge: A bridge connects one Local Area Network (LAN) to another. While it can determine to which LAN a packet should be sent, it does not examine or analyze the packet.

Gateway: A gateway is the point at which the network connects to another network. A gateway can be composed of software, hardware or a mixture of the two.

Hub: A hub connects segments of a Local Area Network (LAN) and directs packets to their correct location.

Cabling: Several types of cable are used to connect computers on a network. Coaxial cables and twisted pair cables are both composed of copper; the cable television industry primarily uses coaxial cables while the telephone industry relies upon twisted pair. Fiber optic cables can carry more information than copper wires can, and transmit data as pulses of light.

Modem: A modem is a hardware peripheral used to connect a computer to a network through a telephone, DSL or a cable connection.

A network infrastructure is an interconnected group of computer systems linked by the various parts of a telecommunications architecture. Specifically, this infrastructure refers to the organization of its various parts and their configuration from individual networked computers to routers, cables, wireless access points, switches, backbones, network protocols, and network access methodologies. Infrastructures can be either open or closed, such as the open architecture of the Internet or the closed architecture of a private intranet. They can operate over wired or wireless network connections, or a combination of both.

The simplest form of network infrastructure typically consists of one or more computers, a network or Internet connection, and a hub to both link the computers to the network connection and tie the various systems to each other. The hub merely links the computers, but does not limit data flow to or from any one system. To control or limit access between systems and regulate information flow, a switch replaces the hub to create network protocols that define how the systems communicate with each other. To allow the network created by these systems to communicate to others, via the network connection, requires a router, which bridges the networks and basically provides a common language for data exchange, according to the rules of each network.

When multiple computers in a single household share the same Internet connection, it is considered a basic form of network infrastructure, whether or not the computers also share information with each other. The Internet itself is a more advanced network infrastructure, in which individual systems access a global network that houses information on various systems, and allows access using web standards and protocols, most commonly framed as web addresses, also known as URLs.

Office intranets are similar to the global Internet, but operate on a closed network infrastructure accessible only by those within it. This generally consists of a central data store one or more computers known as servers as well as ethernet cabling, wireless access points, routers, switches, and the individual computers with access to the central data store. The individual computers connect to the network via either cabling or wireless access. The routers and switches then determine what level of access they are allowed to have, and act as traffic directors to point them to the central data store on the servers. As the individual computers send or receive data, the routers ensure it reaches the appropriate place.

Today's networks are becoming increasingly complex. Support for critical enterprise applications and converged communication systems have created unparalleled expectations for network availability and performance.

Insight Networking's core competency is architecting and deploying real time infrastructure.

We understand what it takes to successfully plan, design and implement complex and secure networks.

2.1.1 Network Infrastructure Benefits

Most internal network teams face a steep learning curve as they begin to deploy advanced network technologies. Insight's network consultants are 100% focused on designing and implementing client centric networks.

- We have worked on hundreds of networks and bring extensive infrastructure experience.
- We lead the industry with deployment expertise for advanced network technologies.
- We employ strong project management and service delivery methodologies to ensure a successful outcome.

2.2 NETWORK INFRASTRUCTURE OF E-COMMERCE

Network infrastructure is required for E-Commerce to transport content. I-way is a high-capacity, interactive electronic pipeline used to transfer content in case of E-Commerce. I-way can transfer any type of context like, text, graphics, audio, video. In other words, multimedia contents are easily transported through I-way.

Components of I-way: - Consumer access equipment. - Local on-ramps, and - Global information distribution networks.

Consumer access equipment are devices used by consumers to access the multimedia interactive contents of E-Commerce. In this segment, hardware and software vendors are also included. Local or access road, or on-ramps: This segment of I-way simplify linkages between businesses, universities, and homes to the communications backbone. There are four different types of provider of access ramps: - telecom-based - cable TV-based - wireless-based and - computer-based online information services. These providers link users and E-Commerce application providers. Global information distribution networks are the infrastructure that are connecting countries and continents.

There are seven major issues to be discussed about I-way: cost, subsidies, allocation of scarce resources, regulation, universal access, privacy and social issues. Cost: Who will pay for constructing the I-way? Subsidies: Who are to be given subsidies, Allocation of scarce resources: Investment of the allocation of different scarce resources would be wasted or not. Regulation: Who will fund for the highway and who will write and enforce the rules to use the highway, Universal access: who can access and at what cost? Privacy: Is using online activities secure, Social and religious barriers: In cyberspace, everybody has right to write anything or publish.

2.3 BUSINESS MODELS FOR INTERNET BASED E-COMMERCE

The success of Internet based businesses in the Business to Customer segment in recent years is an indication of the events to unfold at the dawn of the new millennium. It is widely projected that the Business to Business segment is poised for a spectacular growth. However, a consistent definition and a framework for a business model for the Internet based business is still non-existent.

We propose a three dimensional framework for defining a business model and apply it to the emerging market structure. Furthermore, we also identify certain factors that would guide organizations in their choice of an appropriate business model. We also identify possibilities for further theory building in this area. The growth of Internet based businesses, popularly known as dotcoms is anything but meteoric. It has dwarfed the historical growth patterns of other sectors of the industry.

Over years, several organizations doing business through the Internet have come out with their own set of unique propositions to succeed in the business. For instance Amazon.com demonstrated how it is possible to "dis-intermediate" the supply chain and create new value out of it. Companies such as Hotmail, and Netscape made business sense out of providing free products and services.

On the other hand companies such as AOL and Yahoo identified new revenue streams for their businesses. It is increasingly becoming clearer that the propositions that these organizations employed in their business could collectively form the building blocks of a business model for an Internet based business. Several variations of these early initiatives as well as some new ones being innovated by recent Internet ventures have underscored the need for some theory building in this area.

A good theory is a statement of relations among concepts with in a set of assumptions and constraints. Wallace outlined a systematic approach to theory building, which broadly consists of observation, induction and deduction. Theory building in a new area often begins with individual observations that are highly specific and essentially unique items of information. By careful measurement, sample summarization and parameter estimation, it is possible to synthesize empirical generalizations. The next stage in theory building involves concept formation, proposition formation and proposition arrangement. Using sampling the hypothesis that occasioned the construction of the proposition could be tested. Eventually, the results of hypothesis testing enables confirmation, modification or rejection of the theory.

Another key aspect of theory building is the use of alternative classification schemes often employing typologies and taxonomies. Typological classification has a twofold function: codification and prediction. A typology creates order out of the potential chaos of discrete and heterogeneous observations. But in so codifying the phenomena, it also permits the observer to seek and predict relationship between phenomena that do not seem to be connected in any obvious way. This is because a good typology is not a collection of undifferentiated entities but is composed of a cluster of traits, which in reality hang together. Indeed systematic classification and the explication of rationale for classification are tantamount to the codification of the existing state of knowledge in a discipline.

This is an effort on the theory building process that incorporates several of the above features such as observation, induction and classification. We particularly identify and focus on two broad issues concerning organization engaging in Internet based business: Is there a basis on which one can classify these new propositions and are there any factors that could potentially influence an organization in identifying an appropriate sub-set of these propositions for its business? We propose to address these issues in this topic.

It proposed a four-layer framework for measuring the size of the Internet economy as a whole. The Internet infrastructure layer addresses the issue of backbone infrastructure required for conducting business via the net. Expectedly, it is largely made up of telecommunication companies and other hardware manufacturers such as computer and networking equipment. The Internet applications layer provides support systems for the Internet economy through a variety of software applications that enable organizations to commercially exploit the backbone infrastructure. Over years, several applications addressing a range of issues from web page design to providing security and trust in conducting various business transactions over the net have been developed. The Internet intermediary layer includes a host of companies that participate in the market making process in several ways. Finally, the Internet commerce layer covers companies that conduct business in an over all ambience provided by the other three layers.

The Internet infrastructure layer and the applications layer play a crucial role in moderating and trend setting the growth of Internet economy.

2.4 INTRANET BASED E-COMMERCE—ISSUES, PROBLEMS AND PROSPECTS

2.4.1 What is Intranet

Intranet is a network based on the Internet that is accessed by the employees of an organization. An Intranet provides easy access to internal files and documents to the various employees of the organization, from their individual workstations. Sharing of data, made possible through the Intranet, not only helps in saving time of employees, but also allows employees from various levels to access data. It also contributes to a paperless office.

2.4.2 Benefits of Intranet

Most of today's modern businesses are adopting intranet technology due its competitive advantages in dealing with the corporate information essential for any business. The various benefits of intranet to business can be broadly classified as under:

Communication

Intranet is extremely useful for communication and collaboration between the employees for successful functioning of any business organization. Intranet provides this to businesses in the form of tools like discussion groups, Intranet forms, and bulletin boards. Using intranet tools help in conveying and distributing necessary information or documents among the employees of an organization. This results in easy communication and sound relationship between the employees and top level management. Today, many business houses working on projects use intranet tools, discussion forms, chats, emails, electronic bulletin boards, etc. that help in communicating between different departments of an organization.

Time Saving

All businesses know the importance of time. Using Intranet technology allows to distribute valuable information among the employees in a fast and efficient manner. Intranet saves time by interactivity, i.e employees can access information at a relevant times that suit them, rather than sending and waiting for email and email replies.

Productivity

Intranet technology provides fast information to employees and helps to perform their various tasks with responsibility. A employee can access any data from any database of the organization without wastage of time. Employees working on projects can collaborate easily, ensuring better and faster results.

Reduce Costs

An important benefit of Intranet is that it is cost effective. This can be attributed to the fact that it is paperless. As Intranet supports online publishing, it definitely cuts down the printing and distribution costs as well. All the documents of the company can be published through the Intranet using web pages, as compared to spending money on printing documents. The information can be accessed from the respective workstations of the employees. Intranet results in reduced costs for corporate training, administrative and operational purposes.

Incorporated and Distributed Computing Environment

Intranet supports an active distribution of stored information through different types of operating systems and computer types, from which the employees can access information. Intranet results in distributing information at a lower cost due to the web architecture feature of intranet.

Increases Collaboration

As intranet allows all employees to access data, this helps build team work within the organization. Also certain contents of intranet like declaration section, help desk, FAQ, handbook of employee, etc., aids in collaboration among the employees.

Rich in Format

Intranet allows employees to view documents in various rich format applications as well as video and audio. Multimedia programs can be used with intranet as well, allowing for better communication and information being shared very fast.

Apart from these benefits, Intranet also promotes equal corporate culture in information viewing. Intranet helps in maintaining good communication between different departments and also facilitates an immediate updation of operations. It provides teleconferencing software for interactive communication within the organization.

Implementing Intranet in a business organization helps save significant time and money in the long run. Truly a boon to all business organizations, the benefits of intranet to business has made it a necessity rather than a luxury, for most organizations.

2.5 INTERNET, INTRANET AND EXTRANET

There's one major distinction between an intranet and the Internet: The Internet is an open, public space, while an intranet is designed to be a private space. An intranet may be accessible from the Internet, but as a rule it's protected by a password and accessible only to employees or other authorized users.

From within a company, an intranet server may respond much more quickly than a typical Web site. This is because the public Internet is at the mercy of traffic spikes, server breakdowns and other problems that may slow the network. Within a company, however, users have much more bandwidth and network hardware may be more reliable. This makes it easier to serve high bandwidth content, such as audio and video, over an intranet.

(unless you work for the United States Marine Corps. Then you don't get to watch video's. And they Block 80% of any kind of "fun" or entertaining website available on the Internet)

The Extranet is a portion of an organization's Intranet that is made accessible to authorized outside users without full access to an entire organization's intranet.

2.6 DIFFERENCE BETWEEN INTRANET AND VPN

2.6.1 Intranet vs VPN

Intranets and VPN are two technologies that are commonly used in business environments. It is important to note though that while Intranet is just a term that is used to describe an internal network that simulates the Internet while VPN, which stands for Virtual Private Network, is one methodology used to remotely connect to a network as if you are connected locally.

An Intranet is just a local network that utilizes the same technologies that the Internet does (i.e. HTTP, SMTP, FTP) in order to simplify things and make it a lot easier for members of the organization to access resources and share data. Using the said technologies make it easier for administrators to provide different levels of access in a manner that is already familiar with most people. On the other hand, VPN was created to address the need of inexpensive and secure connections between distant offices. Prior to VPN, leased lines provided a secure but very expensive means of achieving this.

A VPN utilizes a much bigger public network like the Internet to pass the data along since the origin and destination are probably not in the same locale. To prevent snoopers from getting the data, encryptions are utilized to make it "unreadable". With Intranets, the computers are usually located in the same vicinity so there is little or no need to utilize the Internet and employ complicated encryption systems.

Although it is not necessary to use the Internet to have a fully functional Intranet, doing so can extend the usability of the Intranet. This is often achieved by tunneling the Intranet through a VPN so that remote users can still access the resources of the Intranet as if they are connected locally. There is no need to add security measures to the Intranet as the data would be automatically encrypted once it goes through the VPN and decrypted after it reaches the destination. Accessing the Intranet via a VPN is no different than accessing it locally once you've successfully established a connection.

2.7 INTERNET AND INTRANET BASED PROBLEM IN E-COMMERCE

An Internet business is similar to a brick mortar business in that it is not all sunshine and roses. While the Internet does make starting a business and earning money a reality for many, you will still face roadblocks along the way. The good news is that there are solutions to these common Internet business problems. Read on to find out two common problems and how you can fix them.

What are two of the biggest problems that people have on the Internet in the small business market

Problem 1: Many people are delusional as far as how much money can be made on the Internet quickly. It is very different when you are a newbie versus an Internet business that has established a track record, credibility, and experience. In the beginning making money online can be a slow process. You have to build your business day by day.

Too many Internet business newbie give up after they don't achieve big money right away. They don't realize that it takes time. Remember, Rome wasn't built in a day. Have the mindset that your Internet business success will take time. If you are in it for the long haul then you will have a much better chance of obtaining this level of achievement.

Problem 2: People new to the Internet tend to be cheap. They don't invest in products, learning, and tools that they need. They don't take the risk that will reap rewards in the long term instead of the short term. Successful Internet businesses, on the other hand, recognize that you have to take risks. They know that not everything has a guarantee. They are willing to accept this risk in order to receive a greater reward.

Don't play defense. If you do then you decrease the odds of being successful. If you are proactive and play from an offensive perspective then the probability of successful will be stacked in your favor. You have to be positive and realize that you are in it for the long haul. You know you will face obstacles, but you will view them as opportunities, learn from them, and grow from them.

2.8 NETWORK ACCESS EQUIPMENTS

Networking equipment typically refers to equipment facilitating the use of a computer network. Typically, this includes routers, switches, hubs, gateways, access points, network interface cards, Networking cables, network bridges, modems, ISDN adapters, firewalls and other related hardware.

The most common kind of networking hardware today is copper-based Ethernet adapters, helped largely by its standard inclusion on most modern computer systems. Wireless networking has become increasingly popular, however, especially for portable and handheld devices.

Other hardware prevalent within computer networking is datacenter equipment (such as file servers, database servers and storage areas), network services (such as DNS, DHCP, email etc) as well as other specific network devices such as content delivery.

As technology grows and IP-based networks are integrated into building infrastructure and household utilities, network hardware becomes an ambiguous statement owing to the increasing number of 'network capable' endpoints.

2.9 BROADBAND COMMUNICATION

Broadband communication is a type of telecommunication that supplies multiple channels of data in single communications platform using some form of wave or frequency division multiplexing. In other words, broadband refers to the telecommunication in which a wide band of frequencies are available to transmit data. To receive broadband services you must have broadband access, and broadband access is the major issue for allowing new applications to be utilized. Broadband offers a new brand of services where data, voice, and video commonly known as multimedia can be delivered together as one packet.

Some of the networks that are available for providing these types of services are Asynchronous Transfer Mode (ATM), frame relay, and leased lines. These networks are instrumental in supplying customers with broadband services and potentially overtaking the traditional dial-up Internet. Broadband communication systems distribute broadband services on the transmit end and also allow access to the services transmitted by the broadband provider on the receive end.

2.9.1 ATM (Asynchronous Transfer Mode)

ATM (asynchronous transfer mode) is a dedicated-connection switching technology that organizes digital data into 53-byte cell units and transmits them over a physical medium using digital signal technology. Individually, a cell is processed asynchronously relative to other related cells and is queued before being multiplexed over the transmission path.

Because ATM is designed to be easily implemented by hardware (rather than software), faster processing and switch speeds are possible. The prespecified bit rates are either 155.520 Mbps or 622.080 Mbps. Speeds on ATM networks can reach 10 Gbps. Along with Synchronous Optical Network (SONET) and several other technologies, ATM is a key component of broadband ISDN (BISDN).

2.9.2 ISDN (Integrated Services Digital Network)

ISDN (Integrated Services Digital Network) is an all digital communications line that allows for the transmission of voice, data, video and graphics, at very high speeds, over standard communication lines. ISDN provides a single, common interface with which to access digital communications services that are required by varying devices, while remaining transparent to the user. Due to the large amounts of information that ISDN lines can carry, ISDN applications are revolutionizing the way businesses communicate. ISDN is not restricted to public telephone networks alone; it may be transmitted via packet switched networks, telex, CATV networks, etc.

There are two levels of service: the Basic Rate Interface (BRI), intended for the home and small enterprise, and the Primary Rate Interface (PRI), for larger users. Both rates include a number of B-channels and a D-channels. Each B-channel carries data, voice, and other services. Each D-channel carries control and signaling information.

2.9.3 Frame Relay

Frame Relay is a protocol standard for LAN internetworking which provides a fast and efficient method of transmitting information from a user device to LAN bridges and routers.

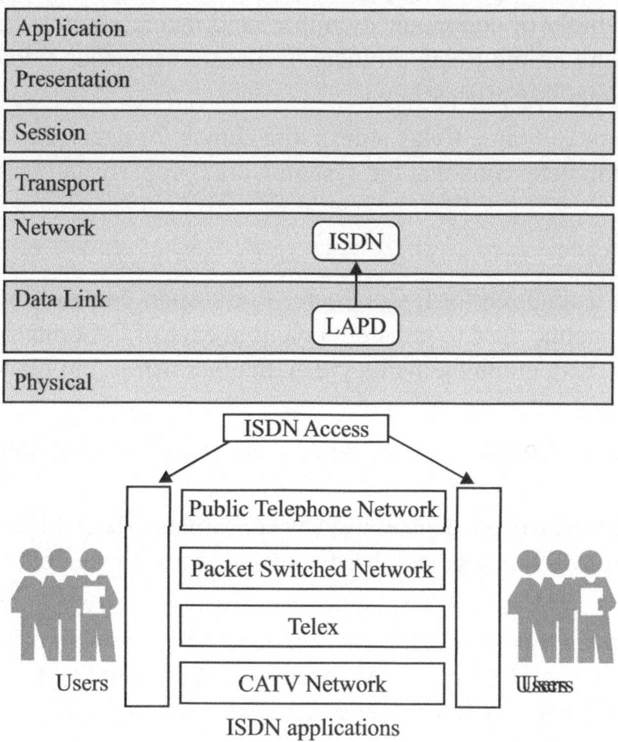

Fig. 2.2

The Frame Relay protocol uses a frame structured similar to that of LAPD, except that the frame header is replaced by a 2-byte Frame Relay header field. The Frame Relay header contains the user-specified DLCI field, which is the destination address of the frame. It also contains congestion and status signals which the network sends to the user.

2.9.4 Virtual Circuits

The Frame Relay frame is transmitted to its destination by way of virtual circuits (logical paths from an originating point in the network) to a destination point. Virtual circuits may be permanent (PVCs) or switched (SVCs). PVCs are set up administratively by the network manager for a dedicated point-to-point connection; SVCs are set up on a call-by-call basis.

2.9.5 Advantages of Frame Relay

Frame Relay offers an attractive alternative to both dedicated lines and X.25 networks for connecting LANs to bridges and routers. The success of the Frame Relay protocol is based on the following two underlying factors:

Because virtual circuits consume bandwidth only when they transport data, many virtual circuits can exist simultaneously across a given transmission line. In addition, each device can use more of the bandwidth as necessary, and thus operate at higher speeds.

The improved reliability of communication lines and increased error-handling sophistication at end stations allows the Frame Relay protocol to discard erroneous frames and thus eliminate time-consuming error-handling processing.

These two factors make Frame Relay a desirable choice for data transmission; however, they also necessitate testing to determine that the system works properly and that data is not lost.

SUMMARY

Network infrastructure is required for E-Commerce to transport content. I-way is a high-capacity, interactive electronic pipeline used to transfer content in case of E-Commerce. I-way can transfer any type of context like, text, graphics, audio, video. In other words, multimedia contents are easily transported through I-way.

Components of I-way: - Consumer access equipment. - Local on-ramps,and - Global information distribution networks.

Consumer access equipment are devices used by consumers to access the multimedia interactive contents of E-Commerce. In this segment, hardware and software vendors are also included.

Local or access road, or on-ramps: This segment of I-way simplify linkages between businesses, universities, and homes to the communications backbone. There are four different types of provider of access ramps: - telecom-based - cable TV-based - wireless-based and - computer-based online information services. These providers link users and E-Commerce application providers.

Global information distribution networks are the infrastructure that are connecting countries and continents.

There are seven major issues to be discussed about I-way: cost, subsidies, allocation of scarce resources, regulation, universal access, privacy and social issues. Cost: Who will pay for constructing the I-way? Subsidies: Who are to be given subsidies, Allocation of scarce resources: Investment of the allocation of different scarce resources would be wasted or not. Regulation: Who will fund for the highway and who will write and enforce the rules to use the highway, Universal access: who can access and at what cost? Privacy: Is using online activities secure? Social and religious barriers: In cyberspace, everybody has right to write anything or publish.

EXERCISE

1. What are Internet and Intranet based E-Commerce Issues, write down all these.
2. Describe all the problems and prospects of Internet and Intranet based E-Commerce.
3. Whai is the Network Infrastructure.
4. Write down all the Network Access Equipments used in E-Commerce.
5. Describe Broadband telecommunication (ATM, ISDN, FRAME RELAY).

UNIT – 2

3. Mobile Commerce

CHAPTER

3

Mobile Commerce

3.1 INTRODUCTION

M-commerce (mobile commerce) is the buying and selling of goods and services through wireless handheld devices such as cellular telephone and personal digital assistants (PDAs). Known as next-generation E-Commerce, m-commerce enables users to access the Internet without needing to find a place to plug in. The emerging technology behind m-commerce, which is based on the Wireless Application Protocol (WAP), has made far greater strides in Europe, where mobile devices equipped with Web-ready micro-browsers are much more common than in the United States.

Mobile Commerce, also known as **M-Commerce** or **mCommerce**, is the ability to conduct commerce using a mobile device, such as a mobile phone, a Personal digital assistant PDA, a smartphone, or other emerging mobile equipment such as dashtop mobile devices. Mobile Commerce has been defined as follows: "Mobile Commerce is any transaction, involving the transfer of ownership or rights to use goods and services, which is initiated and/or completed by using mobile access to computer-mediated networks with the help of an electronic device."

Mobile commerce (m-commerce) is defined as the buying and selling of products and services through the use of wireless mobile devices. M-commerce is considered the next generation of E-Commerce and this particular technology will allow users to shop through the Internet without a plug-in terminal.

In order to exploit the m-commerce market potential, handset manufacturers such as Nokia, Ericsson, Motorola, and Qualcomm are working with carriers such as AT&T Wireless and Sprint to develop WAP-enabled smart phones, the industry's answer to the Swiss Army Knife, and ways to reach them. Using Bluetooth technology, smart phones offer fax, e-mail, and phone capabilities all in one, paving the way for m-commerce to be accepted by an increasingly mobile workforce.

As content delivery over wireless devices becomes faster, more secure, and scalable, there is wide speculation that m-commerce will surpass wireline E-Commerce as the method of choice for digital commerce transactions. The industries affected by m-commerce include:

- Financial services, which includes mobile banking (when customers use their handheld devices to access their accounts and pay their bills) as well as brokerage services, in which stock quotes can be displayed and trading conducted from the same handheld device
- Telecommunications, in which service changes, bill payment and account reviews can all be conducted from the same handheld device
- Service/retail, as consumers are given the ability to place and pay for orders on-the-fly
- Information services, which include the delivery of financial news, sports figures and traffic updates to a single mobile device.

Over the past 10 years mobile phones have changed the way that we live and work. What is the nature of this change, On the one hand, it's a change in personal freedom. The mobile phone seems to give us more power as individuals to do what we want and be who we want to be. Many people consider mobile phones as extensions of themselves. This is shown by the wide variety of mobile phones available and the myriad ways of transforming each phone into a truly personal device.

These days it's more likely that you'll forget your keys than your mobile phone when you leave home in the morning. As technology advances, mobile phones are able to be used to extend the reach of the person and delegate many functions that would previously have been more time consuming or would have to be carried out in person. As individuals, we expect to be able to do things whenever we want to and mobile phones are core devices enabling this expectation to be fulfilled. This means that there is a fundamental shift in our perception of space and time - of what is possible where and when.

On the other hand, mobile phones are connecting people more than ever before and becoming new glue holding together social interactions and relationships. A mobile phone makes us available to others, be they businesses or individuals, 24 hours a day, 7 days a week. This is an enormous break with the past, when we needed to know where a person was in order to contact them. It gives enormous opportunities for businesses to really connect with and understand consumers and for consumers to have more meaningful relationships with businesses.

3.2 MOBILE COMMERCE BEYOND E-COMMERCE

Throughout the 1990s the introduction of the internet and E-Commerce reshaped the way that businesses do business and the way that consumers interact with businesses. Businesses took the opportunity to automate many processes that before would have been handled manually, from ordering to customer service. One clear example is the way that spending on advertising has begun to shift from traditional off-line media to online and digital media as advertisers have seen an opportunity to better connect with their target audience. IBM forecasts 22% growth in mobile, digital and interactive advertising formats between 2006 and 2010 against 4% growth in traditional advertising formats.

Mobile commerce, often referred to as mcommerce, builds on the advances made by E-Commerce (such as automated, electronic processes) but makes interaction available to a wider audience in a more personalised way. Like any emerging market, there are many propositions about how to use this technology. Some organisations adopt an aggressive policy and want to get something moving as fast as possible whilst others adopt a wait-and-see approach. As a result, proprietary solutions are developed that make integration with existing systems or by multiple partners complex and costly. At the same time, multiple solutions create a complex landscape for businesses and consumers alike - making it difficult to choose which solution to use.

The other difference between E-Commerce and m-commerce is the opportunity to connect information with objects in a more direct way than has been possible until now. This is the world predicted by the *Internet of Things*, a report published by the International Telecommunications Union (ITU) in 2005, where objects have a life and history of their own that we can use to our advantage. The mobile phone can be the tool that connects the physical and virtual world. At the base of this vision is the ability to identify objects uniquely. GS1, with over 30 years experience developing identification standards for the supply chain that have been adopted globally, clearly has a role to play here. In this context, mobile phones are enablers of an *Internet of Things*. What is special about mobile phones is the fact that they have massive adoption globally.

Many more people have access to a mobile phone that to a computers and this means that m-commerce has the opportunity to connect not just big businesses but also small business and consumers on a massive scale. In this sense, mobile phones have the potential to bridge the digital divide and allow organizations and individuals to reach out to one another more easily than ever before.

We're moving into a world where digital goods are becoming as important as physical goods. Due to the internet, value is created not just by goods themselves but by the exchanges of those goods. Organizations that can facilitate that exchange (for example by creating communities of users with similar interests) have a significant competitive advantage in this networked world. Furthermore, these communities can be leveraged to increase sales of physical goods through more engaged users. We know we can't predict the future. This document is a way to reflect on the future together and to stimulate ideas about how to shape it.

Key actors in mobile commerce

Actor	Stakeholders	Expected roles
Consumer		Interact with businesses through mobile phones
Companies	Manufactures Distribution/wholesalers Logistics/Transporters (3PL) Relailers	Relevant applications, provide content and transact with consumer
Mobile Industry	Mobile Phone Manufacturers Mobile Network Operators/Carriers Service Providers (IT companies) Marketing Agencies	Develop technology • Device • Data Source • Network
Enables and	Government Agencies Standards Organisations Consumer/user accociations	Provide regulations, standards and guidelines

3.3 SUCCESS FACTORS FOR MOBILE COMMERCE

Mobile commerce is an emerging market. As with any emerging market there are significant opportunities and significant risks. The temptation at this stage is for key players to impose their own rules based on their own business models.

Although this can be beneficial for a few in the short-term and in some markets may be the only way to start doing mobile commerce, in the long-term this will have a negative impact on business because lack of interoperability and higher operating costs will create barriers to growth and adoption. However a dynamic market needs an environment that favours innovation and a diversity of stakeholders.

It is for this reason that the GS1 Mobile Com group advocates an approach where building an interoperable standards-based eco-system for mobile commerce is central. This way, all players will be able to benefit from the system created, as they already do with the existing GS1 identification and communication standards. This section defines four success factors which the GS1 Mobile Com group believes are key to making mass mobile commerce happen across the globe:

1. *Innovative Business Models*

Companies that want to take advantage of the opportunities presented by this new technology will have to understand how this technology fits with existing business models or provokes new ones.

- Retailers and manufacturers have to consider that they have the opportunity to become providers of services as well as providers of products. Providing services requires different resources, different internal organisation and different thinking to providing products, but there are many benefits to be gained from embracing a service-based approach that will strengthen core business.
- Mobile Network Operators need to consider how mobile commerce can be integrated with existing tools for revenue generation such as SMS, Premium SMS and MMS as well as the huge potential to drive data traffic (which in most markets is still priced highly and discourages increases usage). Additionally, the fact that mobile operators have an existing billing structure is of great advantage, particularly as far as payments for low amounts are concerned.
- Mobile Phone Manufacturers need to consider how to provide mobile devices that suit the needs of the market but also drive the market in new directions, with open architecture and tools allowing new applications to develop based on their devices and platforms.
- Solution Providers need to understand how to collaborate with different players, bearing in mind that in many mobile commerce applications they will only be one part of a solution.

2. *Consumer adoption*

Mobile phones are already starting to become a basic device available to everyone: anytime, anywhere. This means that the question is not so much "Will every consumer adopt his mobile phone as a universal interface to connect to any digital service?" as "When will consumers do this, under what circumstances, how much will they use it and how quickly will this adoption take place".

For mass adoption of this technology to take place quickly, consumers must:

- be able to access services as easily as possible ("just a few clicks and no more").
- be convinced that the services are useful and make a difference to their lives.
- be confident about the costs of these services (for free, part of the monthly fee they already pay as a subscriber or a transparent one-off fee (such as SMS)).
- be confident about the source and reliability of the information delivered (for example bank, brand-owner, retailer, government organisation).
- be confident about respect of privacy and personal information.
- be confident that security measures protecting their devices (such as biometrics and pass codes) are effective.

For consumers to adopt any of these new services on their mobile phones confidently, they will need to be able to use these services whatever kind of mobile phone they buy, whatever kind of subscription contract they have signed and whatever mobile network operator they have chosen.

For service providers, this means that choices need to be made to support interoperability and openness, rather than to develop and use private or proprietary model. Business models need to be developed to make sure this is possible.

Once there is a global, interoperable platform available, service providers (bank, brand owners, retailers and many other stakeholders) will be able to focus their resources on creating and launching new services or on transferring existing services to mobile devices, all based on a system that is trusted by consumers.

3. Technology availability

Without certain technologies, mobile commerce is impossible. The full potential of the mobile phone as an ubiquitous object is only released when local interaction technologies are embedded, such as the combination of camera and image recognition software (to read whether bar codes or recognise specific images) and ways of exchanging and communicating wireless information with products, point-of-sale and other devices. The integration of a secure element, such as a tamperproof chip card, inside the mobile phone will provide security and trust for handling valuable data (such as personal and payment information).

Support for high quality display of the information to the users, supporting state of art internet technologies are required to provide a satisfying and consistent user experience. Mobile networks need to be able to deal with large amounts of traffic at high speed. Availability of technologies is vital to success of mobile commerce. As for internet and E-Commerce, increased user comfort and reactivity provided by high speed connections encourage use of networks for data transfer. High speed mobile network technologies are now in place in many locations.

4. Interoperable systems

Interoperable systems are essential to mass adoption of mobile commerce. Though proprietary systems may function well in limited situations, they are a barrier to any large-scale implementation.

- Can we imagine a world in which identification keys to access to mobile commerce applications are not unique and may cause conflicts when end consumers scan a bar code with their mobile phones.
- Can we imagine a world in which data carriers are different depending on the applications and need to download multiple bar code readers for the users? Significant additional costs are generated if applications providers are forced to adapt their bar code readers to each operating system in the mobile market.
- Can we imagine a world in which the communication layer is specific to a mobile device, a mobile operator or a local area? This means that whenever a consumer changes a geographic zone certain services will no longer be available. The access to the mobile service must be as simple as possible and the protocols used must be transparent for the users.
- Can we imagine a world in which data processing is built in a proprietary "logic" with no possibility of interoperability between the data pools used to store and exchange data with the services.

GS1's role is to help that businesses collaborate to make sure these success factors are on their side as they begin to use mobile commerce to enhance their business.

3.4 CURRENT AND POTENTIAL APPLICATIONS OF MOBILE COMMERCE

3.4.1 Business-to-Consumer Applications

These applications revolve around making life easier and richer for consumers and deepening the relationship between consumers and businesses, so that consumers feel they have more say in what they consume. One way to categorise these applications is to look at where they fit in the purchase cycle (as in the diagram below).

3.4.2 Advertising and Promotion

Key concept: advertising and promotional information is sent direct to mobile phones. A consumer is in a shop. She is interested in a new cosmetic product but hesitates to buy. She notices she can view an advertisement for the product by taking the picture of the bar code. She does this and views the advertisement.

A consumer notices a billboard advertising for a handbag while walking down the street. By moving closer and activating the Bluetooth function of its phone, she is able to download a coupon to get 30% off the product in any shop today. She does this and receives the coupon in an electronic format on her mobile phone. This bar code will be read by an reader at the cash desk if she buys the product. She then uses her phone to find the location of the nearest shop.

3.4.3 Store Location

Key concept: a map is displayed on a mobile phone showing where consumers can buy a product.

A consumer is visiting the website for a product he likes. He is intrigued by a bar code on the web page.

Information next to the bar code explains that by scanning the bar code with his mobile phone he can save a link to a web page that will show a map of where that product is available in relation to where he and his mobile phone are. Next time he's in town, he uses his phone to consult the map and is presented with different options for finding the product.

3.4.4 In-store Navigation

Key concept: consumers find products more easily when in a shop

A consumer comes into a store is scans an RFID tag to turn their phone into a shopping assistant. They can now search for any product in the store and know exactly where it is (aisle, shelf), how much it costs, and any other information necessary to make a purchasing decision.

3.4.5 Comparison Shopping

Key concept: consumers use their mobile phone to access information about product characteristics and price for related products.

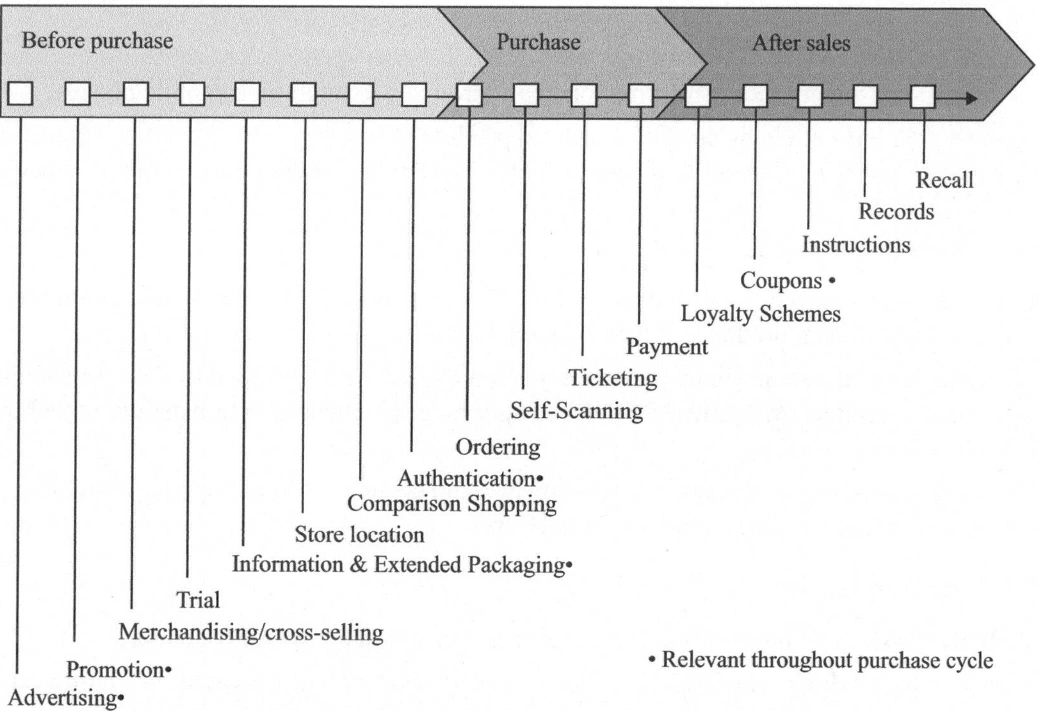

Fig. 3.1: Business-to consumer applications and the purchase cycle

A consumer is in a shop. She uses her mobile phone to access a web-based comparison shopping application. By scanning a bar code on a product, she is able to see the price of this product in different shops in her area. Having seen that the product is reasonably priced, she decided to buy it.

Using a similar set-up, consumers could also access test results from consumer organisations or customer reviews.

3.4.6 Information and Extended Packaging

Key concept: consumers access additional information about products through their mobile phone

A consumer is in a foreign country. He buys some medicine in a pharmacy, but wants to be sure he has understood the dosage instructions given by the pharmacist properly. He scans the bar code on the pack and finds is able to read the dosage instructions in his own language.

A consumer is worried about allergens in a product she has just bought. By scanning the bar code on product packaging, she is able to access a full range of product information including *information about which allergens the product contains.*

The same concepts can be used to provide consumers with nutritional information (and so diet advice) as well as instructions related to product handling, warranty or recycling. A consumer could also check whether food was GM-free or Halal/Kosher certified.

3.4.7 Data-rich Products

Key concept: consumers access information about products through their mobile phones

A consumer buys a television. Full access to product instructions and guarantee are available using a mobile phone to scan an RFID tag embedded inside the product throughout its lifecycle.

3.4.8 Self-Scanning

Key concept: consumers in supermarkets use their mobile phone (rather than a device supplied by the supermarket) to scan products as they do their shopping.

A consumer is in a shop. He uses his mobile phone to scan RFID tags placed on the shelf each time he takes a product. When he has finished shopping, payment is automatically added to his mobile phone bill.

By storing data from self-scanning, consumers could create a mobile shopping list which could then be shared with an online shopping application.

3.4.9 Authentication

Key concept: mobile phones are used to check whether or not a product is genuine.

A consumer is watching television. She sees a news report about a counterfeit pharmaceutical product. Using her mobile phone, she scans a bar code on the product packaging. She connects automatically to a anticounterfeiting application that checks the product's authenticity and tells her that the product is genuine.

3.4.10 Payment

Key concept: mobile phones are able to make payment anywhere, anytime.

A consumer walks into a small shop to buy a newspaper. By moving here mobile phone close to an RFID-enabled device on the cash desk, payment is deducted from a supply of electronic money stored on her mobile phone.

At a vending machine, a consumer can buy a canned drink by moving there phone close to an RFIDenabled phone reader. Payment is deducted from the person's mobile phone bill. A consumer pays his bills by simply scanning the barcode on the bill and using his mobile phone to process payment.

3.4.11 Ticketing

Key concept: mobile phones are used to distribute and redeem tickets.

A concert-goer buys concert tickets online. When she pays she gives her credit card number. A unique bar code is sent by SMS to her mobile phone. She gains entry to the concert by showing the bar code to a reader at the entrance.

A traveller needs to take a metro train. He has bought an electronic ticket that has automatically credited ten journeys to his mobile phone. At the ticket barrier, he moves his mobile phone close to an RFID-reader which deducts one journey from his account as the gate opens.

3.4.12 Coupons

Key concept: mobile phones used both to capture and redeem coupons and discounts.

A consumer sees an offer for a new product in a magazine. By scanning a bar code with her mobile phone, she is able to take the offer with her to the shop. At the cash-desk, she shows the bar code on mobile phone to the cashier. It is scanned at the same time as the rest of her shopping and the discount automatically calculated.

3.4.13 Loyalty Schemes

Key concept: mobile phones are used to send targeted promotional coupons.

A consumer sees an advertisement for a brand-loyalty scheme. She can accumulate points by scanning the bar codes on products that she has bought. When she has a certain number of points, she receives an SMS with discounts on further products.

3.4.14 Loyalty Cards

Key concept: mobile phones replace physical loyalty cards.

Having signed up for a supermarket loyalty scheme, a unique bar code is sent to a consumer's mobile phone. Whenever he shops at the same supermarket, he shows the bar code at the cash desk and accumulates points based on the total amount he has spent.

3.4.15 Recall

Key concept: mobile phones are used to access information about product recall easily.

A consumer is watching television. She sees a news report about a defective pharmaceutical product. Using her mobile phone, she scans the bar code on the product packaging. She connects automatically to an application that checks the products serial number and tells her that the product does not need to be recalled.

3.4.16 Interactive TV

Key concept: TV viewers can interact with what's happening on screen using their mobile phone

A consumer watches a dating programme on TV. Each of the potential dates is wearing a t-shirt with a bar code. Using her mobile phone to scan the bar code, she received extra information about the person and decides whether she is still interested.

A bar code runs under an TV advertisment for a product on TV. By scanning the bar code the consumer can purchase the product using their preferred shipping and billing information that is preconfigured.

3.4.17 Interactive Publications

Key concept: Publication readers can retrieve more information using their mobile phone

A bar code under each article and product advertisement allows readers of magazines, newspapers, and other publications tor retrieve additional information necessary to increase comprehension and to make purchasing decisions.

3.4.18 Catalogue Shopping

Key concept: mobile phones are used to place orders for products in a catalogue.

A consumer receives a catalogue by mail from a catalogue shopping company. Each product on sale is accompanied by a unique bar code. By scanning the bar codes, the consumer can buy products directly from the catalogue in a similar way to Amazon's "1-Click" buying functionality. A consumer accesses a web-based catalogue on his mobile phone which he can browse and use to order products.

3.4.19 Trial of Digital/Non-Digital Media

Key concept: mobile phones are used to trial books, magazines, music and video.

A consumer moves their mobile phone close to the shelf with an advertisement for a new magazine. Their mobile phone reads and RFID tag on the shelf and downloads a preview of an article from the magazine. Using rich media techniques, the consumer could also have the impression of turning the magazines pages on their mobile phone as well as zooming into the article to read the text.

This concept could be extended to other types of media. For example, a kiosk in a music store could allow consumers to download a song extract or an intelligent movie poster could allow consumers to download a film trailer.

3.4.20 Personal Safety

Key concept: mobile phones are used to alert current location.

A person takes a taxi at night. By moving her RFID enabled phone close to a unique RFID tag placed in the taxi, she is able to automatically send her her current location and her expected time of arrival to a friend by SMS.

3.4.21 Text to Voice

Key concept: mobile phones translate text to voice for elderly or visually-impaired consumers.

By passing their mobile phone close to an RFID tag, an elderly or visually impaired consumer can hear information about a product or promotion.

3.5 BUILDING BLOCKS FOR MOBILE COMMERCE

This section explores the individual components that can be put together to satisfy a particular business need or process. The diagram below shows how these components can be separated into:

- identification keys are numeric codes that are used to identify objects
- data carriers are physical representation that carries the numeric codes (such as a bar code or RFID tag)
- mobile devices are able to capture data from the data carrier
- network providers and technologies make it possible to exchange data across a network
- information providers provide information processing and transactional functionality

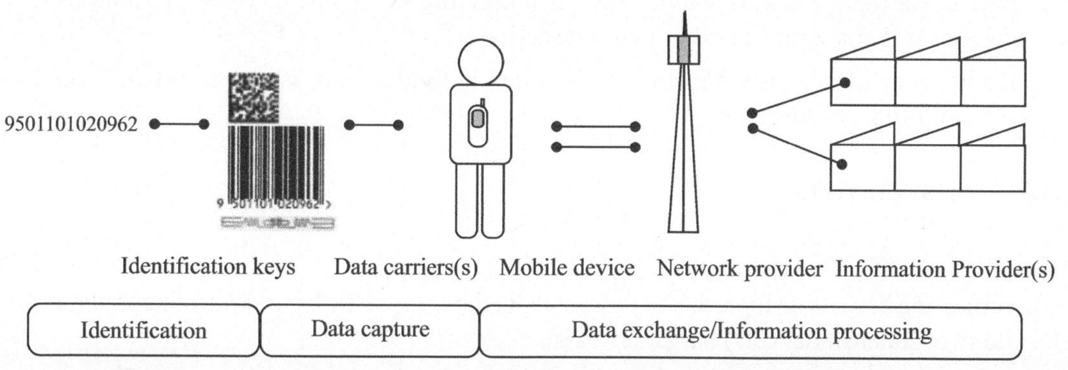

Fig. 3.2

A generic scenario could be described as follows and is represented in the Figure 3.2. Numeric identification codes are used to uniquely identify traded items, locations or services. Bar codes or RFID tags are used to represent these identifiers so that the mobile devices can capture them. An owner of a mobile device scans the bar code or tag and captures the identification code. A particular request is then issued by the mobile device and sent though a network to an information provider. Information processing takes place and the desired response is sent back to the mobile device.

The following sections explore each part of this generic scenario in more detail.

3.5.1 Identification Keys

Identification keys are needed to uniquely identify traded items, locations or consignments used in the supply chain.

Many business applications begin with using correct identification numbers to identify products. It is important to keep in mind the investment that already has been made in existing ways of identifying products as well as any interoperability considerations so that seamless integration with other applications in the supply chain is possible.

Choosing the right identification keys to use for mobile commerce can be easy if goods are already identified. This is the case for the companies already using GS1 identification, where Global Trade Item Number (GTIN) is used to identify trade items, Global Location Number (GLN) to identify business location and so on.

This task is more difficult in areas where common industry-wide identification schemes are not yet established such as identification of consumers, devices and geographical locations. Businesses should choose a method that remains open and extensible across industry or geographical boundaries.

The following areas might require further research and need for standards:

- How can a consumer or household be uniquely identified, taking in consideration privacy Aspects.
- How can a particular purchase be uniquely identified so that information can be shared between trading partners (manufacturer, retailer, marketing companies). How to identify several purchases that are processed in one transaction.
- Do items or units of use need to be identified individually or is generic identification of a class of products sufficient.

3.5.2 Data Carriers

Bar codes

An identification key can be represented physically in the form of the bar code. Both one-dimensional (1D) and two-dimensional (2D) bar codes exist.

1D bar codes (also called linear bar codes) are one of the most widespread and well-known global identification applications and can be seen anywhere in the world. Standards for 1D bar codes have been developed and adopted since the early 1970's. 1D bar codes are read by laser-based scanners (currently at point-of-sale and throughout the supply chain) and camera-based readers (by mobile phones and in specific environments).

A typical EAN-13 bar code

A typical Data Matrix bar code

Fig. 3.3

1D bar codes require that the size and printing quality match certain criteria in order to be compliant with the standards.

2D bar codes are more novel and have become commonplace in countries with faster adoption of more advanced mobile phones and networks, such as Japan and Korea. There is still rclativcly little standardisation and many divergent implementations and varieties exist. Several vendors are trying to use this situation to their advantage creating private or patented solutions.

2D bar codes are more advanced than 1D bar codes and have built-in error-correction mechanisms that accept some considerable tolerances in the quality of the printed image without any reduced performance in scanning and recognition of the symbol. 2D bar codes require camera-based scanners to be read. 2D bar codes found in Asia are standardised but proprietary (with non-claimed royalty rights) and allow a URL (web address) to be encoded.

GS1 DataMatrix is a 2D bar code developed by GS1 and based on the ECC200 ISO Standard. While providing all the advantages of other 2D bar codes GS1 DataMatrix is widely supported by important industry stakeholders and is becoming more and more popular within different sectors (such as healthcare). Mobile devices present a very good technical opportunity to act as bar code scanners to capture information stored in 1D or 2D bar codes printed on the product packaging and in other locations. More detailed requirements for mobile devices are listed further on in this section.

The following questions are intended to guide whether a business application should use 1D or 2D bar codes:

- How much information needs to be captured for the application to work, As a rule, 1D bar codes carry less information than 2D bar codes. However, emerging standards such as GS1 DataBar make it possible to have extended data set comparable with two-dimensional bar codes.
- Does the object already carry identification information If so, can that information be used to power mobile applications? People often think that mobile applications need 2D bar codes to

function. In many cases, there is no reason why 1D bar codes cannot be used. In the case of consumer products, there are good reasons for using existing 1D bar codes such as limited space on the pack or clarity for the consumer.

- Does transactional data need to be in the data carrier and human readable on the object (such as delivery dates and serial information) Take into consideration different amount of data that can be stored in different data carriers.
- Is there a need for the product to be scanned by the conventional technologies present at current POS? Again interoperability is very important here. It makes sense to use already existing data carriers if this can fulfill the business need.
- How generic should the application be As a rule 1D bar codes are generic and require more complex applications to request forwarding to related information whereas 2D bar codes can potentially encode a URL (web address) that points directly to the information provider.

  However, having a URL hardcoded in the bar code might make the application less robust and less flexible. The following cases can be observed:

  1. 1D bar code scanning requires generic framework for the URL resolution. This is also referred to as indirect or managed encoding.
  2. 2D bar code scanning with no specific URL encoded requires a generic framework for the URL resolution. This is also referred to as indirect or managed encoding.
  3. 2D bar code scanning with a specific URL encoded does not require any additional processing. This is also referred to as direct or unmanaged encoding. Each of these cases has its advantages and disadvantages. The first two cases require a more evolved infrastructure but are also more robust and can be customised to future needs more easily.
- Should a "patented" solution be chosen, There are many "proprietary" 2D bar codes currently available on the market. The GS1 Mobile Com group suggests that widely-implemented, open standards be used wherever possible.
- What happens if the mobile device is unable to capture information from the bar code,Users should have access to a fallback mechanism such as manual entry of human readable data.

3.5.3 Radio Frequency Identification (RFID) Tags

Electronic Product Codes (EPC) are assigned to physical objects, loads, locations, assets and other entities embedded in a Radio Frequency Identification (RFID) tag attached to each object. With an RFID reader, an EPC-compliant RFID tag and a distributed EPC network, a business can look up detailed information about a product or package, such as its date of manufacture or expiration.

3.5.4 EPC-compliant RFID Tags

The Electronic Product Code (EPC) is a family of coding schemes to be used with RFID tags. The EPC was created as a low-cost method of tracking goods in the supply chain using RFID technology. It is designed to meet the needs of various industries, while guaranteeing uniqueness for all EPC-compliant tags. EPC tags have been designed to identify individual items as opposed to just the manufacturer and class of products, as most bar codes do today. The EPC accommodates existing coding schemes and defines new schemes where necessary. If mobile devices should read RFID tags, they should work according to the specifications of EPC global. Several standards are available such as the tag data standard, ISO standards and other technical requirements and specifications. EPCglobal developments in the future will show which kind of technology will be standard in retail environments. Currently pallets and cases are identified and tagged with ultra high frequency (UHF) transponders using the EPC tag data standard. On consumer items high frequency (HF) technology is expected, but this difference in technology does not change the content of the tags. Information on a tag always has to follow the tag data standard.

3.5.5 Near Field Communication (NFC) Tags

Near Field Communication (NFC), is a short-range high frequency (HF) wireless communication technology, which enables the exchange of data between devices over distances of about 10cm. NFC is based on open standards by the NFC Forum (www.nfcforum.com), an organisation with over 100 members from handset, IT and other device manufacturers, plus payment organisations and application developers. The technology is an extension of the ISO 14443 proximity-card standard (contactless card, RFID) that combines the interface of a smartcard and a reader into a single device. NFC is primarily aimed to be used in conjunction with mobile phones.

3.6 MOBILE DEVICES

Hundreds of different mobile devices are available to the end consumers and the range of devices available changes freque ntly. In 2006, Nokia alone released 39 new mobile phone models. It would be a very complicated task to effectively list all of all the mobile devices that could be used for the mobile commerce purposes.

More and more devices available on the market today bring new and exciting functions that can be used by different business applications. Two examples are location-based functionality (based on Global Positioning System (GPS) or other technologies) and payment functionality. Both extend the reach of mobile devices and increase their integration with relevant business applications and processes.

To enable mobile commerce to happen widely, what defines a mobile device

- Ubiquitous (present in the mass market and available to the consumers on the day-to-day basis)
- Reasonably-priced
- Provides internet connectivity
- Able to display rich content such as images
- Portable
- Customisable
- Able to save data
- Autonomous

- Has a good quality camera with autofocus
- Screen can display barcodes
- Ability to read RFID tags

In addition mobile devices should be able to read barcodes and RFID tags to be able to interact with physical objects as described below. As mobile phones begin to be to emulate credit cards security is an important issue. Measures such as PIN (Personal Identification Number) codes and biometrics are necessary to make sure the device can only be used by its owner.

3.6.1 Bar Code Scanning

Mobile devices should be capable of reading both 1D and 2D bar codes. Ideally bar code reading should be assured by the underlying operating system of the device thus enabling robust and speedy reading and decoding of the bar codes. A camera with auto-focus is needed to effectively read the bar code. A simpler variant would be a macro lens, but this limits usability by making it more difficult to take normal (nonmacro) pictures. Latest developments in the software should also be taken into account to ensure quick and effective decoding or barcodes read by the mobile device.

3.6.2 Bar Code Display

In several business applications it might be desirable that a bar code is displayed on the screen of the mobile device so that the conventional methods of Automatic Identification and Data Capture (AIDC) could be deployed such as laser scanning at point-of-sale. Experience with the scanning of the mobile phone screens is however mixed.

3.6.3 Point-of-sale (POS) Interaction with Mobile Devices

Point-of-sale (POS) usually means a checkout counter in a shop or supermarket. More specifically, the point-of-sale often refers to the hardware and software used for checkouts - the equivalent of an electronic cash register. Point-of-sale systems are used in almost every type of retail store. Integration of the mobile technologies with point-of-sale systems brings numerous benefits such as:

- automated identification of the customer and access to his or her customer profile if such interaction is desired.
- payment at POS using a mobile device as a digital wallet.
- transmission of pre-scanned data if a mobile device is used for the self-scanning purposes.

Challenges are obviously related to robustness and effectiveness of the communication between the mobile device and POS interfaces. Several trials have shown that existing point-of-sale equipment has difficulty reading bar codes displayed on mobile phone screens. Either more specialised equipment is needed (that corrects errors caused by distortion and scratching) or RFID protocols (such as NFC) could be used to exchange data between the mobile phone and the point-of-sale. Additionally, consumer tests have shown that consumers may be reluctant to give their phones to a cashier for scanning.

3.7 MOBILE PHONES – REVOLUTIONARY DEVICES

Mobile phones are central to the lives of most people in developed countries and are growing in importance in less developed countries. Since their mainstream adoption in the 1990s, they have remained primarily communication devices. We use mobile phones to talk to other people and we carry mobile phones with us so that other people can talk to us.

However, the situation is changing. Mobile phone manufacturers have developed mobile devices that can serve many functions beyond voice communication such as taking photos and listening to music.

Mobile network operators are offering services that give greater value to subscribers, such as portable email for business users. Mobile phones are now equipped with cameras with the potential to turn them into portable bar code scanners. Handset manufacturers are developing RFID chips that can turn mobile phones into mobile wallets able to carry and exchange electronic money securely and engage in other transactions with RFID readers in the physical world.

The combination of more powerful mobile devices, more innovative mobile operators and change in the mobile network infrastructure (such as 3G networks able to carry large amounts of data at high speed as broadband connections do for computers) is setting the stage for an enormous change in a already fast-moving sector. Mobile devices are fast becoming the place where numerous technologies meet and create applications that are useful for both consumers and businesses across the globe.

The mobile phone of the future is a device that enables users to communicate, connect, transact and innovate. In most markets, phones with the characteristics below are already becoming available:

3.7.1 A Communicative Device

The mobile phone will continue to be a device that is used to communicate with others. Although this may be extended beyond voice to instant messaging and email, it is important not to forget communication is a central strength of mobile devices. As it becomes easier and cheaper to transfer larger amounts of data, sharing photos and videos with others will further extend this role.

3.7.2 A Connective Device

Mobile phones enable people to connect to other sources of data anytime, anywhere. This is what is happening with mobile email. As data on the web becomes more structured, mobile devices will become more and more powerful as entry points to tasks that have moved from offline to online but are currently still only available through fixed computers.

3.7.3 A Transactional Device

Mobile phones are ideal devices to be used for payments and transactions. There are a wide range of applications that aim to transform the mobile phone into an electronic wallet that can be used as a payment device.

3.7.4 An Intelligent Device

Mobile phones are a place where multiple applications can meet and fuse. Mobile devices that integrate a phone, a camera, a location finder (GPS) and a connection to the internet make it possible for a user to request context-dependent information such as finding out where a store selling a product they want to buy is located. As usage increases, mobile phones can become agents of change, tools that facilitate connecting things in the physical world to information about them in the digital world.

3.8 NETWORK PROVIDERS AND TECHNOLOGIES

There are several standards that govern communication between mobile device and the supporting network. The following is a non-exhaustive listing of the most influential standards and technologies:

3.8.1 GSM

Global System for Mobile communications is the most popular standard for mobile phones in the world. Its promoter, the GSM Association, estimates that 82% of the global mobile market uses the standard. Over 2 billion people use GSM phones across more than 200 countries and territories. Its ubiquity makes international roaming very common between mobile phone operators, enabling subscribers to use their phones in many parts of the world. GSM differs from its predecessors in that both signalling and speech channels are digital quality, and so is considered a second generation (2G) mobile phone system. Data communication has been built on top of the 2G system thanks to the work of the 3rd Generation Partnership Project (3GPP).

The key advantages of GSM systems to consumers have been better voice quality and low-cost alternatives to making calls, such as the Short Message Service (SMS, also called "text messaging"). The advantage for network operators has been the ease of deploying equipment from any vendor that implements the standard.

3.8.2 General Packet Data Service (GPRS)

GPRS (General Packet Data Service) is a mobile data service available to GSM users. It is important because it allows end users without access to 3G networks to have access to a mobile internet and related data services." If there are space issues here, you can add at end of final paragraph (without creating new paragraph) and you could reduce the space after the bulleted list further up the page.

3.8.3 3G

3G is the third generation of mobile phone standards and technology, after 2G. It is based on the International Telecommunication Union (ITU) family of standards under the International Mobile Telecommunications IMT-2000 programme. 3G technologies enable network operators to offer users a wider range of advanced services while achieving greater network capacity through improved spectral efficiency. Services include wide-area wireless voice telephony and broadband wireless data transmission. Typically, they provide a 5-10 Mb per second service.

3.8.4 EDGE

Enhanced Data rates for GSM Evolution (EDGE) or Enhanced GPRS (EGPRS), is a digital mobile phone technology that allows increased data transmission rates and improved data transmission reliability. Although technically a 3G-network technology, it is generally classified as the unofficial standard 2.75G, due to its slower network speed. EDGE has been introduced into GSM networks around the world since 2003, initially in North America.

EDGE can be used for any packet switched application, such as an internet connection. High-speed data applications such as video services and other multimedia benefit from increased data capacity of EGPRS.

3.8.5 Universal Mobile Telecommunications (UMTS)

Universal Mobile Telecommunications System (UMTS) is one of the third-generation (3G) mobile phone technologies. Currently, the most common form uses W-CDMA as the underlying air interface, is standardized by the 3GPP, and is the European answer to the ITU IMT-2000 requirements for 3G cellular radio systems.

3.8.6 HSPA

High-Speed Packet Access (HSPA) is a collection of mobile telephony protocols that extend and improve the performance of existing UMTS protocols. Two standards (HSDPA and HSUPA) have been established and a further standard HSOPA is being proposed.

3.8.7 Wireless Networks (Bluetooth / Wi-Fi)

More and more mobile phones support several technologies at once, not only in the respect to the communication between the handset and the carrier network but also wireless networking such as Bluetooth (short-range) or Wi-Fi (medium-range). Several pilots have been established in the retail area where consumer's handset can receive promotional info or download music files via Bluetooth connection (in-store promotions, etc.). In France, Loréal and Carrefour have collaborated on one such Bluetooth pilot.

3.8.8 SMS

SMS (Short Message Service) is the most commonly used protocol for text messaging between mobile phones. Already a multi-billion dollar industry, SMS is available on a wide range of networks and performs very well. It would be relatively easy to establish SMS as an additional data carrier for GS1 Identification Keys. All that would be needed would be guidelines on how to structure GS1-compliant SMS messages.

3.8.9 MMS

MMS (Multimedia Message Service) is a standard for sending messages with multimedia content (such as images, audio and video). Markeing messages sent via MMS are general more effective (leading for example to higher brand recall) than SMS text messages. However, not all phones and networks support MMS consistency, leading to patching adoption.

3.9 WIRELESS APPLICATION PROTOCOL (WAP)

The Wireless Application Protocol - defines a network architecture for content delivery over wireless networks. Central to the design of WAP is a network stack based on the OSI model. WAP implements several new networking protocols that perform functions similar to the well-known Web protocols HTTP, TCP, and SSL.

WAP includes the concepts of browsers, servers, URLs, and gateways. WAP browsers are intended to be implemented on small mobile devices such as cell phones, pagers, and PDAs. Instead of developing content in HTML and JavaScript, WAP developers use WML and WMLScript.

WAP is a global standard developed by the WAP Forum for wireless devices to access the Internet and telephony services. WAP can also be used to access data from corporate intranets through public or private IP networks. Figure A shows the WAP services that are currently offered.

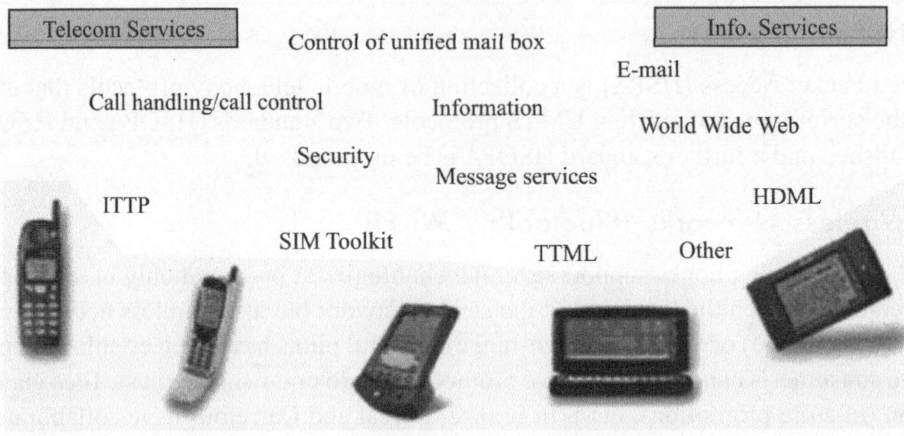

Fig. 3.4

3.10 WAP TECHNOLOGY SPECIFICATIONS

WAP is an open specification that defines a set of protocols in application, session, transaction, security, and transport layers. To leverage existing programming and development skills, it is based on existing standards and protocols such as XML, HTTP, UDP, HTML, and JavaScript.

WAP (Wireless Application Protocol) is a specification for a set of communication protocols to standardize the way that wireless devices, such as cellular telephones and radio transceivers, can be used for Internet access, including e-mail, the World Wide Web, newsgroups, and instant messaging. While Internet access has been possible in the past, different manufacturers have used different technologies. In the future, devices and service systems that use WAP will be able to interoperate.

The WAP layers are:

- Wireless Application Environment (WAE)
- Wireless Session Layer (WSL)
- Wireless Transport Layer Security (WTLS)
- Wireless Transport Layer (WTP)

The WAP was conceived by four companies: Ericsson, Motorola, Nokia, and Unwired Planet (now Phone.com). The Wireless Markup Language (WML) is used to create pages that can be delivered using WAP.

The key elements of the WAP specification include:

- A well-known applications development framework. The WAP transport model is analogous to the Internet model, except for the gateway that is inserted between the Web server and the client. This familiar model leverages the existing development skills of WWW programming.
- WML (Wireless Markup Language) as the standard markup language.
- A browser inside WAP devices that parses WML and WMLScript.
- A framework to support advanced telephony services, like WWW to mobile messaging, call forwarding, mobile to telefax access, and address book access.

Figure B compares a protocol stack based on the Internet model to WAP. As you can see, numerous networks are included in WAP, with the ultimate goal of targeting multiple networks.

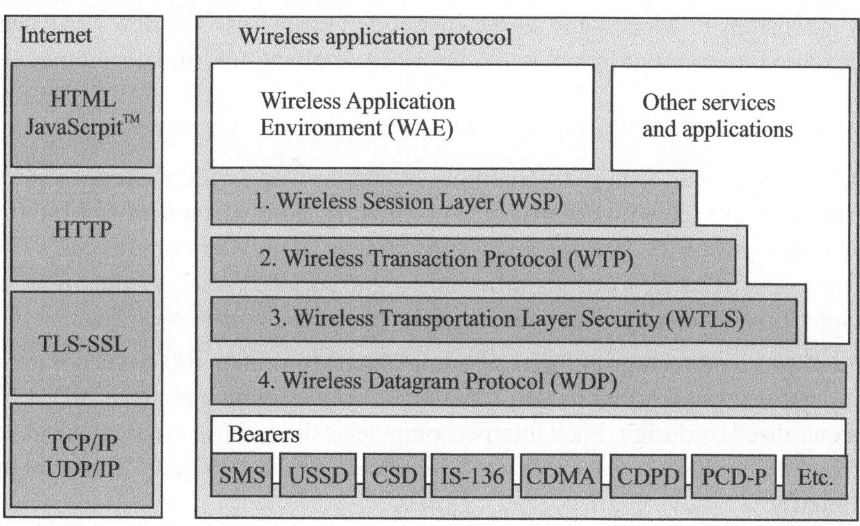

Fig. 3.5

3.10.1 How WAP Works

A typical WAP network consists of the following components:

- User with WAP-enabled device

- Gateway
- Application server

The application server can be located in either a public or private IP network. The gateway normally is located in telecom networks, but it can be set up by a company using its own computer systems. To get an idea of how these components work together, let's look at a typical scenario using WAP technology:

1. A user with a WAP device requests content from the application server.
2. The request reaches the gateway first, which does the protocol translation from WAP to HTTP and routes the HTTP request to the destination server.
3. The server returns WML output and adds HTTP headers to the gateway, depending upon whether dynamic or static pages are requested.
4. The gateway converts WML and HTTP to binary form to conserve bandwidth and returns a WAP response to the user.
5. The browser inside the WAP device interprets the WML and shows the contents.

3.10.2 WAP Limitations

Compared to PCs, wireless devices are limited in terms of processing power, memory, battery life, and display size. Other issues of low bandwidth, latency, and connection stability motivated the forum to come up with a new set of WAP standards. They have reused many of the existing standards while creating new extensions to address the above-mentioned problems. The new WAP specifications leverage the existing investment in hardware, software, applications, and development skills.

3.10.3 Internet

The Internet, or simply the Net, is the publicly available worldwide system of interconnected computer networks that transmit data by packet switching using a standardised Internet Protocol (IP) and many other protocols. It is made up of thousands of smaller commercial, academic, and government networks. It carries various information and services, such as electronic mail, online chat and the interlinked web pages and other documents of the World Wide Web.

A global network connecting millions of computers. More than 100 countries are linked into exchanges of data, news and opinions. Unlike online services, which are centrally controlled, the Internet is decentralized by design. Each Internet computer, called a host, is independent. Its operators can choose which Internet services to use and which local services to make available to the global Internet community.

Today, the Internet is a public, cooperative, and self-sustaining facility accessible to hundreds of millions of people worldwide. Physically, the Internet uses a portion of the total resources of the currently existing public telecommunication networks. Technically, what distinguishes the Internet is its use of a set of protocols called TCP/IP (for Transmission Control Protocol/Internet Protocol). Two recent adaptations of Internet technology, the intranet and the extranet, also make use of the TCP/IP protocol.

For many Internet users, electronic mail (e-mail) has practically replaced the Postal Service for short written transactions. Electronic mail is the most widely used application on the Net. You can also carry on live "conversations" with other computer users, using Internet Relay Chat (IRC). More recently, Internet telephony hardware and software allows real-time voice conversations.

The most widely used part of the Internet is the World Wide Web (often abbreviated "WWW" or called "the Web"). Its outstanding feature is hypertext, a method of instant cross-referencing. In most Web sites, certain words or phrases appear in text of a different color than the rest; often this text is also underlined. When you select one of these words or phrases, you will be transferred to the site or page that is relevant to this word or phrase. Sometimes there are buttons, images, or portions of images that are "clickable." If you move the pointer over a spot on a Web site and the pointer changes into a hand, this indicates that you can click and be transferred to another site.

Using the Web, you have access to millions of pages of information. Web browsing is done with a Web browser, the most popular of which are Microsoft Internet Explorer and Netscape Navigator. The appearance of a particular Web site may vary slightly depending on the browser you use. Also, later versions of a particular browser are able to render more "bells and whistles" such as animation, virtual reality, sound, and music files, than earlier versions.

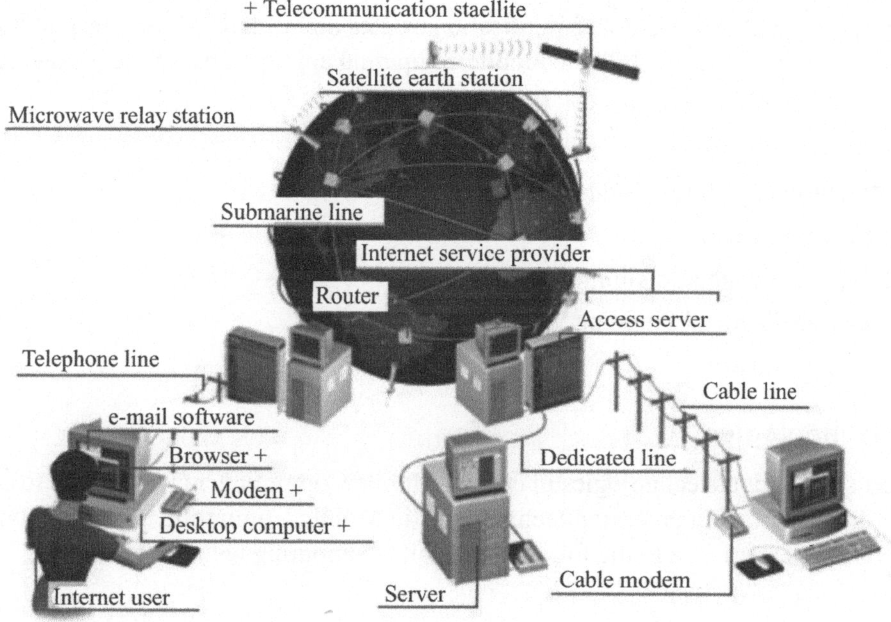

Fig. 3.6

3.11 MOBILE ACCESS INFORMATION DEVICE (MAID)

MAID stands for Mobile access Information Device Profile. MAID, combined with the Connected Limited Device Configuration (CLDC), is the Java runtime environment for today's mobile information devices (MIDs) such as phones and entry level PDAs. What MAID provides is the core application functionality required by mobile applications - including the user interface, network connectivity, local data storage, and application lifecycle management - packaged as a standardized Java runtime environment and set of Java technology APIs.The MIDP 2.0 reference implementation (RI) is available on Windows 2000, with compliant implementations available on Linux/x86 and Solaris/SPARC.

Games (stand alone, networked, multi player), messaging (e-mail, instant messaging, chat), remote directory access, location-based services (maps, driving directions, yellow pages), financial applications (stock quotes, banking), field automation (customer relationship management, supply chain management, field force automation, telemetry), consumer applications (online auctions, news services with alerts, online reservation systems), etc.

3.12 MOBILE COMPUTING APPLICATIONS

There are many applications which are used in mobile computing they are as given below:

3.12.1 Market Segments

Mobile computing applications reduce duplication of data inputs and provides instant information just-in-time. It offers secure and reliable mobile computing applications for the following verticals

- Airline and Railway Industries
- Transportation Industry
- Manufacturing & Mining Industries
- Distribution Industry
- Banking and Financial Institutions
- Insurance & Financial Planning
- Hospitality Industry

3.12.2 Technologies

It has expertise in various technologies in current Mobile Computing and continued to acquire the knowledge and expertise in emerging technologies in Mobile Computing and Communication. It has good working experience in the following Mobile Computing technologies.

- WAP
- Massaging
- SMS
- MMS
- DRM
- Bluetooth

3.12.3 Platforms

It develops Mobile solutions on various kind of devices like Palm, Nokia, Compaq iPAQ etc and built the complete expertise in the following Operating system platforms.

- Palm OS
- Linux Mobile
- Java (J2ME)
- Microsoft Windows CE
- Symbian OS

3.12.4 Databases

It develops database driven mobile applications both on client server or stand-alone application architecture. It can develop applications which can use the following mobile databases

- Oracle Lite
- Sybase SQL Anywhere
- Microsoft SQL Server CE
- DB2 EveryPlace

3.12.5 Expertise in Detail

Following are the range of mobile computing solution for various industry verticals.

3.12.6 Airline and Railway Industries

- Replace existing FCOM Manuals in the cockpit with PDAs or tablet PCs (Paperless cockpit)
- Take Load & Trim sheet to the tarmac on PDAs or Tablet PCs
- Use PDAs or tablet PCs for Grading in a Simulator Training environment
- Access reservation, flight schedule and ticketing information by busy travelers using handheld devices
- Virtual check-in for regular customers
- Airline Baggage and Cargo Control
- Flight arrival and departure information while traveling to the airport
- By airline maintenance staff – fueling and deicing information and baggage handling information
- Easier, faster and quicker checking in of baggage by scanning bar-coded information from baggage tickets directly into a database
- Pen-based work order application using a wireless local area data network
- Airport Security and Monitoring

3.12.7 Transportation Industry

- Consignment tracking application
- Computer-Aided Dispatch (CAD) about real- time drop shipments or pickups
- Exact delivery time tracking for superior customer service
- Fleet management/maintenance information
- Traffic Control and Monitoring
- Mobile networks to provide two-way communication between fleet drivers and their dispatch centers or home offices
- Real-time Traffic Reporting
- Parking Management: Automatic Fee debiting/ Space Availability
- Real-time Passenger Information Dissemination (at Kiosks, Bus Stops, Road Signs, etc.)
- Command and Control of Vehicle Fleets: City Buses, School Buses, Cabs Services Vehicles, Airport Limo Service Vehicles

3.12.8 Manufacturing and Mining Industries

- Broad-spectrum networks to resolve LAN extension problems
- Portable computers in vehicles and in mines or on shop floors
- In-process Monitoring
- Real-time Asset Management: Tools, Materials, Parts
- Instant Purchase Verification, delivery Confirmation and Order Tracking
- Industrial Controls

3.12.9 Distribution Industry

- Warehouse Inventory Applications
- Route, accounting and distribution warehousing applications

3.12.10 Banking and Financial Institutions

- Wireless banking transactions - account balance, funds transfer, bill payment from a smart phone or handheld PDA
- ATMs wirelessly connected to handheld devices through Bluetooth
- Stock Trading
- Sales professional automation in the financial industry - enabling these professionals to respond to customer queries on the spot
- Credit card authorization on mobile POS terminals equipped with wireless adapters
- Wireless e-mail, instant messaging

3.12.11 Insurance & Financial Planning

- Current client portfolio information via wireless- connected devices
- Sales illustrations, created, printed and presented to customers on the spot
- Corporate data retrieval from the clients office or home
- Wireless E-mail Access for busy professionals

3.12.12 Hospitality Industry

- Hotel Reservation software
- Guest Check-in using handheld devices - PDAs, Blackberry and cellular phones
- Sales force automation
- Mobile POS

3.13 MOBILE COMPUTING APPLICATION ISSUES

The programs used in mobile devices like mobile phones, laptops, palm computers, etc. for internet connectivity and other computer related activities are called mobile computing applications. The various issues and designs of mobile computing application are discussed under various headings below.

3.13.1 Technical Design

First comes the Technical Design Issues, which consist of network design, capacity planning, response time calculations, data compression considerations, system availability design and security issues. The technical design plays a key role in a mobile computing project and offers unique challenges to the system professionals.

3.13.2 Network Design

Issues regarding Wireless LAN design and Wide Area Radio Network Design which network design comprises are discussed below.

(a) Wireless LAN design issuess

- The number of mobile users who will use wireless LAN and the number of them active during the peak period.
- The types of LAN application accessed by them. (Keeping in mind that wireless LANs will not be acceptable for the intended users as they operate at much slower speeds than wired LANs).
- Use of notebook with a wireless NIC as a primary and user device.
- Roaming areas, location & range of needed access point.

- Impact of construction materials in single penetration.
- Preferred technology-spread spectrum or frequency hopping.
- Radio frequency interference from any other devices in office, factory or campus etc.

(b) Wide Area Radio Network Design Issues

- The need of building a private radio network.
- Most appropriate radio network technology for the suite of applications.
- Matching of user application-usage profiles to a given network capacity.
- Integration of RNA technology with a radio network infrastructure.
- Ensuring good coverage & minimum number of dead spots.
- If distributed wireless network design with several MCSSs must be used?
- Managing the way logic networks will be influenced by network design options.

3.13.3 Capacity Planning and Response Time Calculations

A mobile computing application transaction has to cover a synchronous set of hardware as well as software components before it reaches the destination server. Diverse physical links, wireless & wired line in between the end user's client application software and the information server are present in its reverse path too. So scheduling on a network requires complex rules, which makes it difficult to build a mathematical model to estimate response times. Planning reliable capacities in advance is a hard task still. The network providers give an estimate using complex queuing models or rule-of thumb calculation based on the other customer's experience.

3.13.4 Data Compression Considerations

As the bandwidth of wireless network is scarce & inexpensive it is necessary to compress data to get the maximum out of this bandwidth. This is usually done in the modem by going beyond the modem hardware in reducing the quantity of traffic on wireless networks using client application programs.

3.13.5 System Availability Design

Rather than sticking on with the general base station hardware & network controllers, redundancy & message switches are typically built on fault-tolerant platforms. Public shared network providers must be approached for details of their redundancies. MCSS is another vital component that badly needs inbuilt redundancy.

3.13.6 Security Issues

It is tough to track down securing information by unauthorized access. Common security breaches of mobile computing applications include,

- Network by criminal elements.

- Physical breach security at communication centers mainly unmanned base stations.
- Interception of credit card authorization over wireless network.
- Careful security considerations including on-the-air encryption & firewalls must be used

Other than technical design the next major issue under Mobile computing application is Ergonomics & Logistics Design where the designers evaluates the following.

- Form factor of end user device
- Battery life
- Input method-keyboard, pen, touch or voice
- Ruggedness
- Whether Portable or fixed
- Safety & Health issues.

Mobile computing application deals with the future of computer usage and is therefore of great relevance.

SUMMARY

Mobile commerce, often referred to as mcommerce, builds on the advances made by E-Commerce (such as automated, electronic processes) but makes interaction available to a wider audience in a more personalised way. Like any emerging market, there are many propositions about how to use this technology. Some organisations adopt an aggressive policy and want to get something moving as fast as possible whilst others adopt a wait-and-see approach. As a result, proprietary solutions are developed that make integration with existing systems or by multiple partners complex and costly. At the same time, multiple solutions create a complex landscape for businesses and consumers alike-making it difficult to choose which solution to use.

The other difference between E-Commerce and m-commerce is the opportunity to connect information with objects in a more direct way than has been possible until now. This is the world predicted by the *Internet of Things*, a report published by the International Telecommunications Union (ITU) in 2005, where objects have a life and history of their own that we can use to our advantage. The mobile phone can be the tool that connects the physical and virtual world. At the base of this vision is the ability to identify objects uniquely. GS1, with over 30 years experience developing identification standards for the supply chain that have been adopted globally, clearly has a role to play here. In this context, mobile phones are enablers of an *Internet of Things*. What is special about mobile phones is the fact that they have massive adoption globally.

Many more people have access to a mobile phone that to a computers and this means that m-commerce has the opportunity to connect not just big businesses but also small business and consumers on a massive scale. In this sense, mobile phones have the potential to bridge the digital divide and allow organizations and individuals to reach out to one another more easily than ever before.

EXERCISE

1. What do you mean by Mobile Commerce.
2. What is the difference between E-Commerce and Mobile Commerce.
3. What are mobile devices.
4. What is WAP explain with examples.
5. What are mobile computing applications.

UNIT – 3

4. Security
5. Firewalls

CHAPTER

4

Security

4.1 WHAT IS SECURITY

Security is a branch of computer technology known as information security as applied to computers and networks. The objective of computer security includes protection of information and property from theft, corruption, or natural disaster, while allowing the information and property to remain accessible and productive to its intended users. The term computer system security means the collective processes and mechanisms by which sensitive and valuable information and services are protected from publication, tampering or collapse by unauthorized activities or untrustworthy individuals and unplanned events respectively. The strategies and methodologies of computer security often differ from most other computer technologies because of its somewhat elusive objective of preventing unwanted computer behavior instead of enabling wanted computer behavior.

4.1.1 Security Architecture

Security Architecture can be defined as the design artifacts that describe how the security controls (security countermeasures) are positioned, and how they relate to the overall information technology architecture. These controls serve the purpose to maintain the system's quality attributes, among them confidentiality, integrity, availability, accountability and assurance."

Confidentiality is an ethical principle associated with several professions (e.g., medicine, law, religion, professional psychology, and journalism). In ethics, and (in some places) in law and alternative forms of legal dispute resolution such as mediation, some types of communication between a person and one of these professionals are "privileged" and may not be discussed or divulged to third parties. In those jurisdictions in which the law makes provision for such confidentiality, there are usually penalties for its violation. It means "ensuring that information is accessible only to those authorized to have access" and is one of the cornerstones of information security. Confidentiality is one of the design goals for many cryptosystems, made possible in practice by the techniques of modern cryptography.

Integrity is a concept of consistency of actions, values, methods, measures, principles, expectations and outcomes. In ethics, integrity is regarded as the quality of having an intuitive sense of honesty and truthfulness in regard to the motivations for one's actions. Integrity can be regarded as the opposite of hypocrisy in that it regards internal consistency as a virtue, and suggests that parties holding apparently conflicting values should account for the discrepancy or alter their beliefs.

The word "integrity" stems from the Latin adjective *integer* (whole, complete).In this context, integrity is the inner sense of "wholeness" deriving from qualities such as honesty and consistency of character. As such, one may judge that others "have integrity" to the extent that one judges whether they behave according to the values, beliefs and principles they claim to hold.

Availability. In telecommunications and reliability theory, the term **availability** has the following meanings:

- The degree to which a system, subsystem, or equipment is in a specified operable and committable state at the start of a mission, when the mission is called for at an unknown, *i.e.,* a random, time. Simply put, availability is the proportion of time a system is in a functioning condition. This is often described as a **mission capable rate**. Mathematically, this is expressed as 1 minus unavailability.
- The ratio of (a) the total time a functional unit is capable of being used during a given interval to (b) the length of the interval.

Accountability and insurance is a concept in ethics and governance with several meanings. It is often used synonymously with such concepts as responsibility, answerability, blameworthiness, liability, and other terms associated with the expectation of account-giving. As an aspect of governance, it has been central to discussions related to problems in the public sector, nonprofit and private (corporate) worlds. In leadership roles, accountability is the acknowledgment and assumption of responsibility for actions, products, decisions, and policies including the administration, governance, and implementation within the scope of the role or employment position and encompassing the obligation to report, explain and be answerable for resulting consequences.

4.2 WIRELESS SECURITY

Wireless security is the prevention of unauthorized access or damage to computers using wireless networks.

Wireless networks are very common, both for organizations and individuals. Many laptop computers have wireless cards pre-installed. The ability to enter a network while mobile has great benefits. However, wireless networking has many security issues. Hackers have found wireless networks relatively easy to break into, and even use wireless technology to crack into wired networks. As a result, it's very important that enterprises define effective wireless security policies that guard against unauthorized access to important resources. Wireless Intrusion Prevention Systems are commonly used to enforce wireless security policies.

In telecommunications, **wireless communication** is the transfer of information without the use of wires. The distances involved may be short (a few meters as in television remote control) or long (thousands or millions of kilometers for radio communications). The term is often shortened to "wireless". It encompasses various types of fixed, mobile, and portable two-way radios, cellular telephones, personal digital assistants (PDAs), and wireless networking.

The term "wireless" has become a generic and all-encompassing word used to describe communications in which electromagnetic waves or RF (rather than some form of wire) carry a signal over part or the entire communication path. Common examples of wireless equipment in use today include:

- Professional LMR (Land Mobile Radio) and SMR (Specialized Mobile Radio) typically used by business, industrial and Public Safety entities.
- Consumer Two way radio including FRS Family Radio Service, GMRS (General Mobile Radio Service) and Citizens band ("CB") radios.
- The Amateur Radio Service (Ham radio).
- Consumer and professional Marine VHF radios.
- **Cellular telephones and pagers:** provide connectivity for portable and mobile applications, both personal and business.
- **Global Positioning System (GPS):** allows drivers of cars and trucks, captains of boats and ships, and pilots of aircraft to ascertain their location anywhere on earth.
- **Cordless computer peripherals:** the cordless mouse is a common example; keyboards and printers can also be linked to a computer via wireless.
- **Cordless telephone sets:** these are limited-range devices, not to be confused with cell phones.
- **Satellite television:** allows viewers in almost any location to select from hundreds of channels.
- **Wireless gaming:** new gaming consoles allow players to interact and play in the same game regardless of whether they are playing on different consoles. Players can chat, send text messages as well as record sound and send it to their friends. Controllers also use wireless technology. They do not have any cords but they can send the information from what is being pressed on the controller to the main console which then processes this information and makes it happen in the game. All of these steps are completed in milliseconds.

4.3 SECURITY GOALS TECHNICALLY DEFINED

Confidentiality

1. Data transmitted or stored should only be revealed to an intended audience
2. Confidentiality of entities is also referred to as anonymity

Data Integrity

1. It should be possible to detect any modification of data
2. This requires to be able to identify the creator of some data

Accountability

It should be possible to identify the entity responsible for any communication event

Availability

Services should be available and function correctly

Controlled Access

Only authorized entities should be able to access certain services or information

4.4 SECURITY SERVICES – OVERVIEW

4.4.1 Authentication

The most fundamental security service which ensures, that an entity has in fact the identity it claims to have

4.4.2 Integrity

In some kind, the "small brother" of the authentication service, as it ensures, that data created by specific entities may not be modified without detection

4.4.3 Confidentiality

The most popular security service, ensuring the secrecy of protected data

4.4.4 Access Control

Controls that each identity accesses only those services and information it is entitled to.

4.4.5 Non Repudiation

Protects against that entities participating in a communication exchange can later falsely deny that the exchange occurred

4.4.6 Wireless Communication

Wireless communication is the transfer of information over a distance without the use of electrical conductors or "wires." The distances involved may be short (a few meters as in television remote control using infrared light) or long (thousands or millions of kilometers for radio communications).

Wireless networks, handheld devices and mobile applications are changing the way the government does business, making it more flexible, accessible and affordable than ever before. Our wireless capabilities include:

- 802.11a/b/g multipoint logical/physical design and implementation
- Unlicensed and licensed point-to-point backhaul design and implementation

- Interference mitigation via antenna selection, RF propagation, channel selection, polarization, and more
- In-building distribution solutions
- Traffic monitoring, reporting and analysis
- Security management and billing software
- Acquisition support
- Seamless roaming between different carrier networks and technologies (wireless ISP or public hotspots, private corporate wireless networks and cellular or PCS networks for nationwide coverage)
- Public hotspot design and implementation
- Support for dynamic end-user provisioning and real-time billing integration

4.5 INFORMATION SECURI TY RISKS

1. **Social Networking:** Sites such as Facebook, Bebo and MySpace offer cybercriminals a vast new world in which to target unsuspecting users. Malware can be cleverly disguised and can be distributed quickly and on a massive scale. The high levels of trust users place in social networking sites means they are an ideal target for the fraudsters, with a greatly likelihood they will succumb to an attack.
2. **Malware attacks:** Cyber criminals are using more creative means to package and deliver malware (viruses, worms, Trojans etc.). Increasingly, email is being used as the delivery mechanism containing seemingly innocent URL links shortened to disguise malicious site addresses, videos and pictures are all used to disguise and conceal malware. When activated, these software programs are designed to wreak havoc on a computer system and move on to infect more systems. The speed at which malware spreads and the damage caused continue to make malware rank highly as a security risk.
3. **Scareware:** Attackers and fraudsters use online pop-ups designed to look like messages from the operating system warning of a problem or virus infection to coerce users to download a program to "correct" the problem. In the worst cases, the program will itself be malicious and may damage the system or leave it vulnerable to attack/abuse. Ransomware enters a system through a security hole and encrypts personal files, making them inaccessible. The user is prompted to either buy a piece of decryption software or enter a code which can only be obtained by sending payment to the attacker.
4. **Microsoft:** Windows 7 is expected to be widely adopted by Microsoft users worldwide. This massive user base is a prime target for the opportunistic hacker looking to attack a new, unfamiliar operating system.
5. **The Insider Threat:** Information is stored in files and folders, accessible remotely by large numbers of users. Keeping it secure and safe from an internal breach, while allowing it to remain accessible to the majority of non-malicious employees, is an ongoing challenge.

If employees feel their employment is under threat they may see sensitive data as a valuable commodity that can be used for their own gain – always to the detriment of their employer.

6. **Localised attacks:** Often attempts to deceive victims fail because they are clearly fraudulent, text used is grammatically incorrect, spelling errors raise red flags and graphics are poor replicas. However, attacks are becoming more refined, not only in appearance, but in relevance to the target. Attackers are researching more to use local references including culture; sports, events to appear more authentic and better their chances of defrauding their targets.
7. **Smartphones:** The convergence of telecommunications and computing is creating a new target for hackers. Smartphones are as likely to be attacked as traditional computers. The risk to personal and corporate data is greater as the availability of security applications for these devices is low. As the number of users and volume of data transmitted increases and more financial transactions are done using these devices they become a more attractive and lucrative target for attack.
8. **Mac OS X:**There is a widespread misconception that relative to PCs, Macs are resistant to attack. This results in users deploying far fewer security measures and not updating systems with security patches. Hackers will continue to target the OS X platform and Apple continues to respond with regular security updates.
9. **Embedded Computing:** As society relies increasingly on Information and Communications Technology (ICT) across all aspects of life, national critical information infrastructures – such as energy, transport and telecommunications- will become more and more connected to and reliant on the Internet. As beneficial as this is to the provision of services and communications it also exposes critical devices to the same risks and threats that exist online.
10. **Virtualisation and Cloud Computing:** Lower budgets and improvements in distributed computing and high-speed internet access, are making Cloud Computing and Virtualization appealing alternatives to costly and complex conventional computing methods. Cloud computing offers capacity and functionality over the Internet that is scalable, subscription-based and fully managed by the provider. Virtualization has lower power and space requirements and simplifies management. However, businesses need to consider the regulatory and legal issues associated with managing data and the new kinds of security challenges that these alternatives bring. How and where the data is stored and who has access to it? The issues are more complex if the data includes payment card information, as PCI-DSS requirements come into play.

4.6 SECURITY IN MOBILE AND WIRELESS COMPUTING

Modern technologies are becoming ever more integrated with each other. Mobile phones are becoming increasing intelligent, and handsets are growing ever more like computers in functionality. And smart devices, such as PDAs, on-board car computers, and new generation household appliances are now equipped with communications functions. We are entering a new era the age of smart houses, global networks which encompass a wide range of devices, all of them exchanging data with each other via as cyberpunk authors say air saturated with bits and bytes. Such trends clearly open new horizons to malicious users, and the potential threats are self evident.

This wired world is still evolving. We should be grateful for the fact that it still requires a bit more than a laptop and a wireless connection to gain control over someone else's car. However, security for mobile devices is already an issue; and the first indication of trouble came, not surprisingly, in the form of a virus.

At first glance, the problem of malicious code appears only to be a part of the broader information security picture. However, malicious programs inevitably mutate from innocent amusements created by bored programmers and students who wish to show off their skills to professional solutions created expressly for financial gain. Today the boundary which previously existed between virus research on the one hand, and network security, program vulnerabilities, advertising software and criminal structures on the other, has effectively been eliminated. Therefore researching the techniques used by the authors of malicious code cannot be overestimated as an essential part of ensuring digital security.

Mobile devices have made securing organizations more challenging than ever. Computer networks are no longer confined to the office, even at small and medium-sized businesses (SMBs). However, SMBs can prevent and protect against mobile security vulnerabilities, even without a dedicated information security team. Existing IT and network staffs can follow these easy guidelines without increasing their workloads. The best practices listed below involve tweaks to systems and monitoring of networks, which you may already be doing. If not, add them to your daily routine and you'll be on your way to securing and protecting your mobile devices.

4.7 SECURITY ASPECTS OF MOBILE COMMUNICATION

Mobile communication faces all threats that does its' fixed counterpart: Masquerade, eavesdropping, authorization violation, loss or modification of transmitted information, repudiation of communication acts, forgery of information, sabotage, Thus, similar measures like in fixed networks have to be taken.

However, there are some specific issues arising out of mobility of users and / or devices:

Some already existing threats get more dangerous:

- Wireless communications is more accessible for eavesdropping
- The lack of a physical connection makes it easier to access services

Some new difficulties for realizing security services:

- Authentication has to be re-established when the mobile device moves
- Key management gets harder as peer identities can not be predetermined

One completely new threat:

- The location of a device / user becomes a more important information that is worthwhile to eavesdrop on and thus to protect

4.8 SECURING CHALLENGES IN MOBILE DEVICES

4.8.1 Mobile Devices

Mobile devices have become a plague for information security professionals. There are worms and other malware that specifically target these devices such as the iPhone worm that would steal banking data and enlist these devices in a botnet. Theft is still a major cause of data breaches as mobile devices, especially laptops, are the main culprits. Tens of thousands of laptops are stolen each year and often these have sensitive data that require public disclosure as a data breach.

Intelligent mobile devices are revolutionizing the way remote users connect to their business, and thus are presenting unique security opportunities for solution providers. Blackberrys, iPhones, and the emerging category of promising Mobile Internet Devices (MIDs) are exploding in popularity, fueled by the availability of easy-to-use application interfaces to access information (both business and personal) in non-traditional ways.

Solution providers would be wise to monetize their networking infrastructure experience by helping customers secure their mobile devices. Security Software as a Service (SaaS) opportunities exist for small and medium business markets that need to secure the professional use of personal devices. Ideas for security-related revenue include innovative approaches to configuration administration, secure remote access, compliance auditing and application delivery

There are different steps to take when securing mobile devices, depending on the type of device you have. USB keys and wireless access points (WAPs) are two very different creatures. What works for one may not work for the other.

1. **Choose Device Carefully:** Not all devices are created equally when it comes to security. For example, iPods are built for general consumers not as concerned by security and is therefore less inherently secure than a BlackBerry device designed for enterprise users.

   "The degree to which IT managers can control security on mobile devices is highly dependent upon the vendor that they select. You should try to get mobile devices that have the best possible control and security on them and then use those mechanisms and it will go a long way to locking down those mobile devices.

2. **Turn On Encryption:** Once you choose devices with stronger security controls, use those controls! Many organizations do not enforce or even set policies mandating the use of device encryption on mobile devices.

   "Many people don't go through the bother of doing the encryption. You always want to be careful and you always want to have a level of paranoia about what happens to your sensitive information. Mainstream enterprises need to lock it down and take it seriously like they do with a laptop and be really consistent with their policies and enforce them.

3. **Require Authentication:** A survey released by Credent Technologies in September 2008 found that in just a six month period more than 31,000 New Yorkers left behind mobile devices in a taxicab. The fact of the matter is that these devices are just too easy to lose to go without proper authentication. And yet, most enterprise users don't use the password function on their devices.

   "So imagine, you lose your phone in a cab and the next passenger gets in opens it up and then they immediate access to your device because you didn't put any authentication in there.

   It is critical that users be required to turn on device authentication so that lost devices can not be easily accessed by any person that finds or steals a device.

4. **Utilize Remote Wipe Capabilities:** Give IT staff the ability to remotely access and disable devices in the event of loss or theft. This could be very handy in a situation where, say, an executive loses his or her device at a conference along with yearly sales projections and strategies stored within. With the remote capability all it would take is a quick call to IT and they'll take care of it.

5. **Set Up a Lost Phone Hotline:** It is not good enough simply to have remote wipe capabilities. Organizations also need to have a procedure set for users who have lost their devices. Make it easy for them to call IT to alert staff that a device has been lost by setting up a direct line and publicize the procedure for IT notification in such an event.

   "If you're concerned about losing data, make sure your users have a contact point where they can get a hold of you so you can initiate that process to wipe them over the network and make sure that data isn't lost. They'll have an incentive to get a hold of you if they want another phone, but it's useful if they know who to call and that you can immediately start that process.

6. **Control Third-Party Apps:** Smart phones are so dangerous because they are essentially miniature computing platforms that can accept any nature of third-party applications. Cross recommends limiting the installation of unsigned third-party applications to prevent the bad guys from requisitioning control of your devices.

   "It makes sense to limit people's ability to install arbitrary third-party applications because that is exactly the how some of these Trojans will allow a bad guy to connect form the internet and get back out into your corporate VPN," Cross says. "That's how they work, they go out and say 'Here's this cool video game for your Blackberry! Install this, it's a lot of fun.' And people will install it and it will say 'This isn't signed,' and they'll say, 'That's OK.' And then their phone is now a gateway."

7. **Set Unique Firewall Policies:** Enterprises should set up unique firewall policies specifically for traffic coming from smartphones. The way Cross sees it, smart phone users don't necessarily need access to every bit of data on the network, so it makes sense to limit exposure by only offering access to the types of data they need.

   "There's stuff that they need access to, but they probably don't need access to your financial database. It probably doesn't work very well from a phone browser anyway," he says. "Stuff like that that has nothing to do with what people are doing from the phone, so you should firewall it off and traffic coming from the phone should only go to stuff that people would reasonably want to use."

8. **Use Intrusion Prevention Software:** As smart phones become more and more powerful, they're likely to become another weapon in the hacker toolbox. As a result, it makes sense to have your intrusion prevention software examining traffic coming through mobile devices.

   "It's possible that you could see attacks come in from phones; they're very sophisticated devices," Cross says. "I mean, you can run Metasploit on an iPhone. So that's something you need to think about."

9. **Keep an Open Mind About AV:** Cross says that he doesn't necessarily suggest enterprises go out today and buy host-based antivirus software for their smart phones, but he does believe they should be paying attention to advances in mobile device AV. He believes that it may be necessary in the coming years.

   "I don't know what the numbers are , but we've obviously seen a tremendous explosion in the sophistication of these devices and the number of these devices that are out there and i think that that's going to continue," he says. "It's my sort of futurist vision that in at some time maybe five or ten years from now there were actually be more smart phones on the Internet as client devices than there are PCs."

10. **Shore Up Bluetooth:** Bluetooth capabilities on today's smart phones may make it easy to talk on a hands-free headset, but they're also a target for hackers, who can take advantage of its default always-on, always-discoverable settings to launch attacks. In order to limit your exposure, US CERT recommends that users disable Bluetooth when it is not actively transmitting information. It also suggests switching Bluetooth devices to hidden mode. Organizations can limit exposure by making this company policy.

4.9 AUTHENTICATION SERVICE SECURITY

Authentication is the verification of the identity of a party who generated some data, and of the integrity of the data. A principal is the party whose identity is verified. The *verifier* is the party who demands assurance of the principal's identity. Data integrity is the assurance that the data received is the same as generated. Authentication mechanisms differ in the assurances they provide: some indicate that data was generated by the principal at some point in the past, a few indicate that the principal was present when the data was sent, and others indicate that the data received was freshly generated by the principal. Mechanisms also differ in the number of verifiers: some support a single verifier per message, while others support multiple verifiers. A third difference is whether the mechanism supports non-repudiation, the ability of the verifier to prove to a third party that the message originated with the principal.

Because these differences affect performance, it is important to understand the requirements of an application when choosing a method. For example, authentication for electronic mail may require support for multiple recipients and non-repudiation, but can tolerate greater latency.

In contrast, poor performance would cause problems for authentication to a server responding to frequent queries.

Other security services include confidentiality and authorization. Confidentiality is the protection of information from disclosure to those not intended to receive it. Most strong authentication methods optionally provide confidentiality. Authorization is the process by which one determines whether a principal is allowed to perform an operation. Authorization is usually performed after the principal has been authenticated, and may be based on information local to the verifier, or based on authenticated statements by others.

4.10 WEB SECURITY

4.10.1 What is Web

Web, is a system of interlinked hypertext documents accessed via the Internet. With a web browser, one can view web pages that may contain text, images, videos, and other multimedia and navigate between them by via hyperlinks.

4.10.2 Web Security and its Services

The term Web services describes a standardized way of integrating Web-based applications using the XML, SOAP, WSDL and UDDI open standards over an Internet protocol backbone. XML is used to tag the data, SOAP is used to transfer the data, WSDL is used for describing the services available and UDDI is used for listing what services are available. Used primarily as a means for businesses to communicate with each other and with clients, Web services allow organizations to communicate data without intimate knowledge of each other's IT systems behind the firewall.

Unlike traditional client/server models, such as a Web server/Web page system, Web services do not provide the user with a GUI. Web services instead share business logic, data and processes through a programmatic interface across a network. The applications interface, not the users. Developers can then add the Web service to a GUI (such as a Web page or an executable program) to offer specific functionality to users.

Web services allow different applications from different sources to communicate with each other without time-consuming custom coding, and because all communication is in XML, Web services are not tied to any one operating system or programming language. For example, Java can talk with Perl, Windows applications can talk with UNIX applications. Web services do not require the use of browsers or HTML. Web services are sometimes called application services.

4.10.3 Reason to Use Web Services

There are two main reasons to use web services, both remarkably straightforward: someone else has information you require, or you have information you wish to provide to others. When planning a new web service, remember that servers can either provide or accept information. Remember that web services can provide any level of security, from a completely open service open to all who request it, to a private service with transfers happening over SSL and client-side certificates to validate identities.

4.10.4 Convincing the Boss

Here are a few more tidbits that should help convince the boss (or you) that web services are a route to look into:

- Web services make use of technology you already have deployed you already have a web server, you already have a database, and so on. Why not provide another way to access the data?
- Web services fit into the security scheme you are already employing. Careful deployment will keep security concerns in line with regular web access.
- Technically savvy users will find a way to access the information they desire. Without web services they will need to resort to methods like screen scraping, which is more difficult to control and can be unreliable (and providing unreliable access to your information is worse than providing none at all).
- Web services can help manage costs; easy integration with companies (like FedEx) that offer services to you can result in lower variable costs for your transactions.
- Web services will allow your business to scale; allowing clients to integrate their systems with yours will help encourage continued relationships, and avoid devoting resources to creating systems for specific clients.

4.10.5 Role of Internet

With the use of internet, it is possible to transmit/receive information containing images, graphics, sound and videos. ISP industry can offer services as:

- Linking consumers and businesses via internet.
- Monitoring/maintaining customer's Web sites.
- Network management/systems integration.
- Backbone access services for other ISP's.
- Managing online purchase and payment systems.

The internet is designed to be indefinitely extendible and the reliability of internet primarily depends on the quality of the service providers' equipments.

Benefits of Internet

- Doing fast business.
- Trying out new ideas.
- Gathering opinions.

- Allowing the business to appear alongside other established businesses.
- Improving the standards of customer service/support resource.
- Supporting managerial functions.

Limitations

- Security
- Privacy

Threats: Hackers, viruses etc.

4.11 SECURITY ISSUES IN ELECTRONIC COMMERCE ON WEB

Most businesses that have made the move towards an online presence have experienced some kind of security threat to their business. Since the Internet is a public system in which every transaction can be tracked, logged, monitored and stored in many locations, it is important for businesses to understand possible security threats to their business.

There are many threats to E-Commerce that may come from sources within an organization or through some external channel. The following are the top corporate security threats categorized by internal and external threats.

- Unauthorized internal users who accesses confidential information by using a stolen passwords for the purpose of committing fraud or theft.
- Former employees of an organization that maintain access to information resources directly by creating alternative passwords, "back doors" into the computer system, or indirectly through former co-workers.
- Weak access points in information infrastructure and security that can expose company information and trade secrets.
- Management that undermines security is maybe the greatest risk to E-Commerce as there Contractors, partners, consultants, and temps who take advantage of even limited access to important systems.
- Peoples mentality on Internet security is changing this is evident through the increase in sales of antivirus software and subscriptions to email virus protection.
- Businesses may take Visa's lead of requiring its service providers and merchants to have firewalls, encryption, as well as testing and access policies as a condition of doing business with them. They feel that the security of their B2B partner is as important as their creditworthiness.

4.11.1 Security Risks in eBusiness

Security risks can include theft of data (credit card numbers from your database), distortion of data (changes to payment files or invoices so that people appear to owe you more or less than they do), destruction of data, or broadcasting of data (showing visitors" real names instead of their nicknames in a chat room or forum). All of these cost your business money in terms of data recovery and goodwill recovery.

4.11.2 Criminal vs. Civil Laws

One of the points that this white paper really brings home is that most problems businesses experience with hackers have to be resolved in a civil court, not a criminal court. The difference is that when a law that's broken is civil, the company being harmed must collect its own evidence of the crime and take the perpetrator to court on its own dime. With criminal laws, you can call and ask police or the FBI for assistance. This distinction matters immensely for planning purposes. If a business doesn't have a plan in place, with resources readily available, vital forensic evidence can be lost in the time it does take to find the appropriate resources. Usually the evidence is all digital and smart crackers know how to erase their tracks before you have a chance to get a copy of the server log or other files with which they've been tinkering. Without evidence you have no case. Companies need to have a culture of security to prevent abuse of computer systems by insiders and to be on the lookout for attempted hacking. According to the report, most companies will find evidence of attempted hacking in their server logs, if they look for it. One problem is that companies don't do anything about attempted hacking until it becomes effective hacking. The report suggests that any hacking attempts be prosecuted as vigorously as successful hacking to discourage it and to make clear that they're not easy pickings.

Annual employee training should include security training and cybercrime awareness so that all employees know that your company doesn't take it lightly. They should also be aware of what suspicious activities on their own and network computers looks like, so they can report it when they see it. Finally, your company should have clear procedures in place so that when someone reports unusual activity on a computer, a database, or a server, that person doesn't inadvertently destroy the forensic evidence, the IT team knows how to proceed, and management is both informed and involved in following through with the investigation.

4.11.3 Privacy and Security Issues in E-Commerce

As mentioned, security is also a major concern for E-Commerce sites and consumers alike. Consumers fear the loss of their financial data, and E-Commerce sites fear the financial losses associated with break-ins and any resulting bad publicity. Not only must E-Commerce sites and consumers judge security vulnerabilities and assess potential technical solutions, they must also assess, evaluate, and resolve the risks involved. We cover each in turn.

4.11.4 Security Vulnerabilities in Electronic Commerce

There are many points of failure, or vulnerabilities, in an E-Commerce environment. Even in a simplified E-Commerce scenario a single user contacts a single web site, and then gives his credit card and address information for shipping a purchase many potential security vulnerabilities exist. Indeed, even in this simple scenario, there are a number of systems and networks involved. Each has security issues:

A user must use a web site and at some point identify, or authenticate, himself to the site. Typically, authentication begins on the user's home computer and its browser. Unfortunately, security problems in home computers offer hackers other ways to steal E-Commerce data and identification data from users. Some current examples include a popular home-banking system that stores a user's account number in a Web "cookie" which hostile web-sites can crack ineffective encryption or lack of encryption for home wireless networks and, mail-borne viruses that can steal the user's financial data from the local disk .While these specific security problems will be fixed by some software developers and web-site administrators, similar problems will continue to occur. Alternatives to the home computer include Point-of- Sale (POS) terminals in brick-and-mortar stores, as well as a variety of mobile and handheld devices.

The user's web browser connects to the merchant front-end. When a consumer makes an online purchase, the merchant's web-server usually caches the order's personal information in an archive of recent orders. This archive contains everything necessary for credit-card fraud. Further, such archives often hold 90 days' worth of customers' orders.

The merchant back-end and database. A site's servers can weaken the company's internal network. This not easily remedied, because the web servers need administrative connections to the internal network, but web server software tends to have buggy security. Here, the cost of failure is very high, with potential theft of customers' identities or corporate data. Additionally, the back-end may connect with third party fulfillment centers and other processing agents. Arguably, the risk of stolen product is the merchant's least-important security concern, because most merchants' traditional operations already have careful controls to track payments and deliveries. However, these third parties can release valuable data through their own vulnerabilities.

In summary, privacy and security are still ongoing research problems. There have been some interesting and significant findings, however, in the last five years that bear important consequences for E-Commerce sites and consumers. Privacy is now understood, by many, to be social construction with expectations the largest consideration. Yet, privacy is also considered a public issue by regulators, who have nonetheless largely allowed technology to unfold to date.

Security is now understood to be largely imperfect, the continual cat-and-mouse game of security expert and hacker. Important technical developments have been deployed in the last five years; however, it is clear that organizational policies may play as an important a role in site security. Finally, detailed economics- and sociologically- based analyses are beginning to find their way into the published literature, and we expect that these studies will bring greater clarity and proficiency to admittedly murky areas.

4.12 SECURITY TECHNOLOGIES

There are many relevant technologies, including cryptographic technologies that can mitigate the above vulnerabilities. However, none is comprehensive or airtight by itself. Accordingly, we next present a brief overview of the major technologies, also considering the advantages and disadvantages of each.

4.12.1 Economic Issues

Again, an understanding of security would be incomplete without an analysis of the underlying economic issues. The above presented security either as a technical imperative or as a set of social and organizational issues; however, it must be stressed that security for both consumer and site requires an analysis with the proper weighing of potential risk. More importantly, as Anderson points out, security engineering is a matter of control and power as well as access. Security mechanisms can be used to govern compatibility and attempt to control network effects governing the adoption of new or potentially replacing technologies . Indeed, Anderson argues that security technologies are often deployed as much for risk reassignment as risk reduction.

4.12.2 E-Commerce Security: Attacks and Preventive Strategies

Web Sphere Commerce is business middleware that accelerates the development of any business transaction-oriented application, from the smallest online retailer to B2B portals, to supply chain management applications. For many of our clients, Web Sphere Commerce provides an integrated platform that runs both their customer facing online shopping sites, and their internal distributor or supplier portals as shown in Figure 3.2.

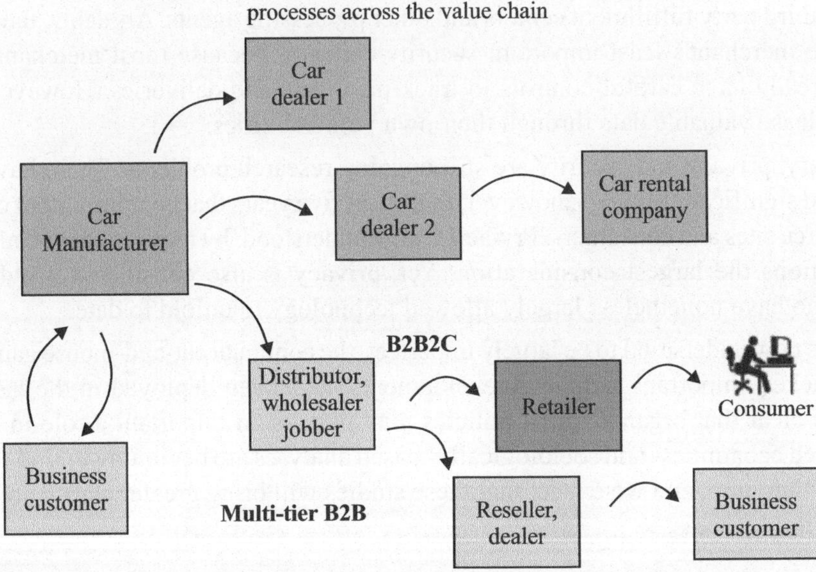

Fig. 3.2: Common WebSphere Commerce Business Model

4.13 SECURITY FEATURES

While security features do not guarantee a secure system, they are necessary to build a secure system. Security features have four categories:

- **Authentication:** Verifies who you say you are. It enforces that you are the only one allowed to logon to your Internet banking account.
- **Authorization:** Allows only you to manipulate your resources in specific ways. This prevents you from increasing the balance of your account or deleting a bill.
- **Encryption:** Deals with information hiding. It ensures you cannot spy on others during Internet banking transactions.
- **Auditing:** Keeps a record of operations. Merchants use auditing to prove that you bought a specific merchandise.

4.13.1 The Criminal Incentive

Attacks against E-Commerce Web sites are so alarming, they follow right after violent crimes in the news. Practically every month, there is an announcement of an attack on a major Web site where sensitive information is obtained. Why is E-Commerce vulnerable? Is E-Commerce software more insecure compared to other software? Did the number of criminals in the world increase? The developers producing E-Commerce software are pulled from the same pool of developers as those who work on other software. In fact, this relatively new field is an attraction for top talent. Therefore, the quality of software being produced is relatively the same compared to other products. The criminal population did not undergo a sudden explosion, but the incentives of an E-Commerce exploit are a bargain compared to other illegal opportunities.

Compared to robbing a bank, the tools necessary to perform an attack on the Internet is fairly cheap. The criminal only needs access to a computer and an Internet connection. On the other hand, a bank robbery may require firearms, a getaway car, and tools to crack a safe, but these may still not be enough. Hence, the low cost of entry to an E-Commerce site attracts the broader criminal population.

The payoff of a successful attack is unimaginable. If you were to take a penny from every account at any one of the major banks, it easily amounts to several million dollars. The local bank robber optimistically expects a windfall in the tens of thousands of dollars. Bank branches do not keep a lot of cash on hand. The majority is represented in bits and bytes sitting on a hard disk or zipping through a network.

While the local bank robber is restricted to the several branches in his region, his online counterpart can choose from the thousands of banks with an online operation. The online bank robber can rob a bank in another country, taking advantage of non-existent extradition rules between the country where the attack originated, and the country where the attack is destined.

An attack on a bank branch requires careful planning and precautions to ensure that the criminal does not leave a trail. He ensures the getaway car is not easily identifiable after the robbery. He cannot leave fingerprints or have his face captured on the surveillance cameras. If he performs his actions on the Internet, he can easily make himself anonymous and the source of the attack untraceable.

The local bank robber obtains detailed building maps and city maps of his target. His online counterpart easily and freely finds information on hacking and cracking. He uses different sets of tools and techniques everyday to target an online bank.

4.13.2 Points the Attacker Can Target

As mentioned, the vulnerability of a system exists at the entry and exit points within the system. Figure 4.2 shows an E-Commerce system with several points that the attacker can target:

- Shopper
- Shopper' computer
- Network connection between shopper and Web site's server
- Web site's server
- Software vendor

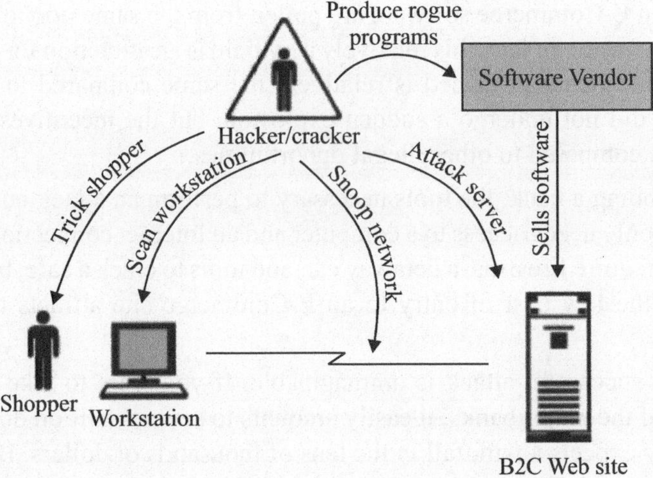

Figure 3.4: Points the attacker can target

These target points and their exploits are explored later in this article.

4.14 TOP FIVE SECURITY ISSUES

Small and medium-sized businesses use the Internet and networked applications to reach new customers and serve their existing ones more effectively. At the same time, new security threats and legislation puts increased pressure on business networks to be reliable and secure. Cisco® delivers comprehensive, affordable, integrated security solutions tailored for small and medium-sized businesses that help ensure business continuity, maintain customer privacy, and reduce operating costs. Businesses can confidently spend more time growing their business, and less time focusing on network security issues.

4.14.1 Business Challenges

Today's globally competitive business environment has small and medium-sized businesses focused on expanding their business and improving customer satisfaction while simultaneously controlling costs. Fortunately, the Internet and networked applications have leveled the playing field. Small and medium-sized businesses use their networks to extend their market reach and communicate with their customers and partners quickly and cost-effectively. But swift and agile e-business is a double-edged sword-access can also open up businesses to costly security breaches. It is more important than ever to have a reliable, secure, and available network.

4.14.2 Security Issues

According to recent studies, security is the biggest challenge facing small and medium-sized businesses. Ever-changing security threats from both inside and outside the business network can wreak havoc on business operations, affecting profitability and customer satisfaction. Small and medium-sized businesses must also comply with new regulations and laws created to protect consumer privacy and secure electronic information.

Security issues 1-worms and viruses

Computer worms and viruses remain the most common security threat, with 75 percent of small and medium businesses affected by at least one virus in the last year [Maritz Research, 2005]. Worms and viruses can have a devastating effect on business continuity and the bottom line. Smarter, more destructive strains are spreading faster than ever, infecting an entire office in seconds. Cleaning the infected computers takes much longer. The catastrophic results are lost orders, corrupted databases, and angry customers. As businesses struggle to update their computers with the latest operating system patches and antivirus software, new viruses can penetrate their defenses any day of the week. Meanwhile, employees spread viruses and spyware by unwittingly accessing malicious Websites, downloading untrustworthy material, or opening malicious e-mail attachments. These attacks are unintentionally invited into the organization, but still cause significant financial losses. Security systems must detect and repel worms, viruses, and spyware at all points in the network.

Security issue 2-information theft

Information theft is big business today. Malevolent hackers break into business networks to steal credit card or social security numbers for profit. Small and medium-sized businesses are at risk because they are seen as an easier mark than large corporations. Protecting the perimeter of the network is a good start, but it isn't enough, since many information thefts have help from a trusted insider, such as an employee or contractor.

Information theft can be costly to small and medium-sized businesses, since they rely on satisfied customers and a good reputation to help grow their business. Businesses that don't adequately protect their information could face negative publicity, government fines, or even lawsuits. For example, new consumer laws enacted in California require any business that suspects customer information has been viewed by unauthorized people must notify all their customers. Any security strategy must prevent theft of sensitive electronic information from both inside and outside the business.

4.15 FEATURES OF SECURITY IN TERMS OF INFORMATION SYSTEM

There are some feature of security as given below:

Authorization Manager. Authorization Manager gives application developers a flexible framework for integrating role-based access control into their applications, and it lets administrators who use those applications provide access in a natural, intuitive way: through assigned user roles relating to job function.

Stored user names and passwords. This utility provides secure storage for user names and credentials that are needed to access network or Internet resources.

Software restriction policies. This new security policy enables administrators to prevent software applications from running based on a hash algorithm of the software, the software's associated file path, the software publisher's certificate, or the Internet zone that hosts the software. Changes to existing technologies.

Certification authoritities. Numerous improvements and added features are included for certification authorities.

Constrained delegation. With this new security feature, you can specify what services you want to trust for delegation for a server.

Effective permissions tool. This tool calculates the permissions that are granted to a specified user or group.

Encrypting File System (EFS) no longer requires a recovery agent. Everyone membership. The built-in Everyone group includes Authenticated Users and Guests, but no longer includes members of the Anonymous group.

Operation-based auditing. Operation based auditing offers more descriptive auditing events and provides you with the opportunity to choose what operations you want to audit when auditing object accesses.

Reapplying security defaults. This procedure enables you to easily reapply the default security settings for the Windows Server 2003 family.

Every business, including yours, has valuable IT assets such as computers, networks, and data. And protecting those assets, requires that companies big and small conduct their own IT security audits in order to get a clear picture of the security risks they face and how to best deal with those threats.

4.15.1 What is the Security Perimeter

The security perimeter is both a conceptual and physical boundary within which your security audit will focus, and outside of which your audit will ignore. You ultimately decide for yourself what your security perimeter is, but a general rule of thumb is that the security perimeter should be the smallest boundary that contains the assets that you own and/or need to control for your own company's security.

4.16 TRANSACTION SECURITY

The tremendous increase in online transactions has been accompanied by an equal rise in the number and type of attacks against the security of online payment systems. Some of these attacks have utilized vulnerabilities that have been published in reusable third-party components utilized by websites, such as shopping cart software. Other attacks have used vulnerabilities that are common in any web application, such as SQL injection or cross-site scripting. This article discusses these vulnerabilities with examples, either from the set of known vulnerabilities, or those discovered during the author's penetration testing assignments. The different types of vulnerabilities discussed here are SQL injection, cross-site scripting, information disclosure, path disclosure, price manipulation, and buffer overflows.

Successful exploitation of these vulnerabilities can lead to a wide range of results. Information and path disclosure vulnerabilities will typically act as initial stages leading to further exploitation. SQL injection or price manipulation attacks could cripple the website, compromise confidentiality, and in worst cases cause the E-Commerce business to shut down completely.

Wherever examples of such vulnerabilities are given in advisories published by Bugtraq, we have given the Bugtraq ID in square brackets.

Electronic commerce, commonly known as **E-Commerce** or **eCommerce**, consists of the buying and selling of products or services over electronic systems such as the Internet and other computer networks. The amount of trade conducted electronically has grown extraordinarily with widespread Internet usage. The use of commerce is conducted in this way, spurring and drawing on innovations in electronic funds transfer, supply chain management, Internet marketing, online transaction processing, electronic data interchange (EDI), inventory management systems, and automated data collection systems. Modern electronic commerce typically uses the World Wide Web at least at some point in the transaction's lifecycle, although it can encompass a wider range of technologies such as e-mail as well.

A large percentage of electronic commerce is conducted entirely electronically for virtual items such as access to premium content on a website, but most electronic commerce involves the transportation of physical items in some way. Online retailers are sometimes known as e-tailers and online retail is sometimes known as **e-tail**. Almost all big retailers have electronic commerce presence on the World Wide Web.

Electronic commerce that is conducted between businesses is referred to as business-to-business or B2B. B2B can be open to all interested parties (e.g. commodity exchange) or limited to specific, pre-qualified participants (private electronic market). Electronic commerce that is conducted between businesses and consumers, on the other hand, is referred to as business-to-consumer or B2C. This is the type of electronic commerce conducted by companies such as Amazon.com. Online shopping is a form of electronic commerce where the buyer is directly online to the seller's computer usually via the internet. There is no intermediary service. The sale and purchase transaction is completed electronically and interactively in real-time such as Amazon.com for new books. If an intermediary is present, then the sale and purchase transaction is called electronic commerce such as eBay.com.

Electronic commerce is generally considered to be the sales aspect of e-business. It also consists of the exchange of data to facilitate the financing and payment aspects of the business transactions.

4.16.1 Policies

Nearly all parties agree that the Internet and E-Commerce will be led by business, with government playing a minimalist role.Nonetheless, it is important to recall that governments have played, and continue to play, a critical role in developing technology for these activities, and that they have an obligation to pursue broad societal goals. Conventional economic theory would suggest that governments should only subsidise basic research into ICT technologies. However, the experience of the past three decades shows that most of the major ICT innovations [*e.g.* timesharing, networking, routers, workstations, optic fibres, semiconductors (RISC, VLSI), parallel computing], many of which are more applied or developmental in nature, are the result of government- funded research or government programmes. This is also true of E-Commerce. The Internet's forerunner (ARPAnet), the World Wide Web (CERN), and the browser (government centre at the University of Illinois) were developed with government support. Government procurement and demonstration projects also play an important part. While governments should not intervene excessively in this area, neither should they simply be spectators. Governments will need to work closely with business to maximise the potential of this activity.

4.17 SECURITY THREAT

Identifying E-Commerce threats and vulnerabilities

It is important that you understand the risks facing your E-Commerce system, and the potential impact of any security incident.

4.17.1 What are the Threats

Threats to E-Commerce systems can be either malicious or accidental. The procedures and controls you put in place to protect your site should help minimize both.

Malicious threats could include:

- hackers attempting to penetrate a system to read or alter sensitive data
- burglars stealing a server or laptop that has unprotected sensitive data on its disk
- imposters posing as legitimate users and even creating a website similar to yours
- authorised users downloading a webpage or receiving an email with hidden active content that attacks your systems or sends sensitive information to unauthorised people

You should consider potential threats to sensitive information from three angles:

- Where (or who) are the potential sources of threats?

- What level of expertise is the hacker likely to possess? How much effort are they likely to expend in attempting to breach your security?
- What facilities and tools are available to them?

The real threat may not be the most obvious one. Attacks from authorised users (such as a disaffected employee or partner) are far more common than attacks by hackers.

4.17.2 E-Commerce Systems Risk Assessment

A risk assessment can be carried out to provide an organisation with a clear understanding of the risks facing its E-Commerce system and associated business processes, and the potential impact if a security incident arises.

A key part of a risk assessment is defining the business' **information access requirements.** This will cover the rules of access for different groups of users. For example, different rules may apply for employees, consultants, managed service providers, suppliers, customers, auditors and government agencies.

Any analysis should also take account of how electronic transactions are verified. How do you know that an order has actually come from a known customer? Where contracts are exchanged electronically, who can sign them and how can it be proved which is the signed version?

4.17.3 E-Commerce Security Issues

E-Commerce systems are based upon internet use, which provides open and easy communications on a global basis. However, because the internet is unregulated, unmanaged and uncontrolled, it poses a wide range of risks and threats to the systems operating on it.

The use of the internet means that your internal IT and E-Commerce systems are potentially accessible by anyone, irrespective of their location.

4.17.4 Threats from Hackers and the Risks to Business

Some of the more common threats that hackers pose to E-Commerce systems include:

- carrying out denial-of-service (DoS) attacks that stop access to authorised users of a website, so that the site is forced to offer a reduced level of service or, in some cases, ceases operation completely
- gaining access to sensitive data - such as price lists, catalogues and valuable intellectual property, and altering, destroying or copying it
- altering your website, thereby damaging your image or directing your customers to another site
- gaining access to financial information about your business or your customers, with a view to perpetrating fraud
- using viruses to corrupt your business data

4.17.5 Impact of a Security Incident on the Business

If your website is hacked into, it can have a significant impact upon a business running an E-Commerce service. The potential business implications of a security incident include the following:

- direct financial loss as a consequence of fraud or litigation
- subsequent loss as a result of unwelcome publicity
- criminal charges if you are found to be in breach of the Data Protection or Computer Misuse Acts, or other regulation on E-Commerce
- loss of market share if customer confidence is affected by a DoS attack

The image presented by your business, together with the brands under which you trade, are valuable assets. It is important to recognize that the use of E-Commerce creates new ways for both image and brands to be attacked.

4.18 NETWORK SECURITY

In the field of networking, the specialist area of **network security** consists of the provisions and policies adopted by the network administrator to prevent and monitor unauthorized access, misuse, modification, or denial of the computer network and network-accessible resources.

4.18.1 First Step to Information Security

The terms network security and information security are often used interchangeably. Network security is generally taken as providing protection at the boundaries of an organization by keeping out intruders (hackers). Information security, however, explicitly focuses on protecting data resources from malware attack or simple mistakes by people within an organization by use of data loss prevention (DLP) techniques. One of these techniques is to compartmentalize large networks with internal boundaries.

4.19 NETWORK SECURITY CONCEPTS

Network security starts from authenticating the user, commonly with a username and a password. Since this requires just one thing besides the user name, i.e. the password which is something you 'know', this is sometimes termed one factor authentication. With two factor authentication something you 'have' is also used (e.g. a security token or 'dongle', an ATM card, or your mobile phone), or with three factor authentication something you 'are' is also used (e.g. a fingerprint or retinal scan).

Once authenticated, a firewall enforces access policies such as what services are allowed to be accessed by the network users. Though effective to prevent unauthorized access, this component may fail to check potentially harmful content such as computer worms or Trojans being transmitted over the network. Anti-virus software or an intrusion prevention system (IPS)[3] help detect and inhibit the action of such malware. An anomaly-based intrusion detection system may also monitor the network and traffic for unexpected (i.e. suspicious) content or behavior and other anomalies to protect resources, e.g. from denial of service attacks or an employee accessing files at strange times. Individual events occurring on the network may be logged for audit purposes and for later high level analysis.

Communication between two hosts using a network could be encrypted to maintain privacy.

Honeypots, essentially decoy network-accessible resources, could be deployed in a network as surveillance and early-warning tools as the honeypot will not normally be accessed. Techniques used by the attackers that attempt to compromise these decoy resources are studied during and after an attack to keep an eye on new exploitation techniques. Such analysis could be used to further tighten security of the actual network being protected by the honeypot.

SUMMARY

Security is a branch of computer technology known as information security as applied to computers and networks. The objective of computer security includes protection of information and property from theft, corruption, or natural disaster, while allowing the information and property to remain accessible and productive to its intended users. The term computer system security means the collective processes and mechanisms by which sensitive and valuable information and services are protected from publication, tampering or collapse by unauthorized activities or untrustworthy individuals and unplanned events respectively. The strategies and methodologies of computer security often differ from most other computer technologies because of its somewhat elusive objective of preventing unwanted computer behavior instead of enabling wanted computer behavior.

EXERCISE

1. What do you mean by security?
2. What is security architecture?
3. Describe all the features of security.
4. What is web security?
5. What is security on web.
6. Write down a note on transaction security.
7. What do you mean by security threat?
8. What is network security?

Firewalls

5.1 FIREWALL AND ITS IMPORTANCE

A **firewall** is a part of a computer system or network that is designed to block unauthorized access while permitting authorized communications. It is a device or set of devices that is configured to permit or deny network transmissions based upon a set of rules and other criteria.

Firewalls can be implemented in either hardware or software, or a combination of both. Firewalls are frequently used to prevent unauthorized Internet users from accessing private networks connected to the Internet, especially intranets. All messages entering or leaving the intranet pass through the firewall, which inspects each message and blocks those that do not meet the specified security criteria.

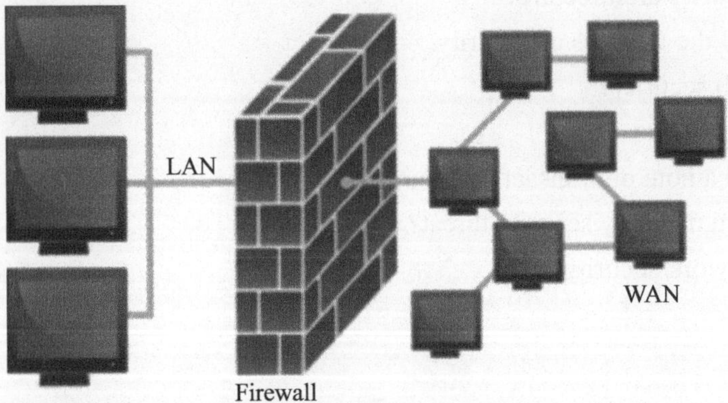

Fig. 5.15

There are several types of firewall techniques:

1. **Packet filter:** Packet filtering inspects each packet passing through the network and accepts or rejects it based on user-defined rules. Although difficult to configure, it is fairly effective and mostly transparent to its users. It is susceptible to IP spoofing.

2. **Application gateway:** Applies security mechanisms to specific applications, such as FTP and Telnet servers. This is very effective, but can impose a performance degradation.
3. **Circuit-level gateway:** Applies security mechanisms when a TCP or UDP connection is established. Once the connection has been made, packets can flow between the hosts without further checking.
4. **Proxy server:** Intercepts all messages entering and leaving the network. The proxy server effectively hides the true network addresses.

5.2 COMPONENT OF FIREWALL

A built-in firewall is provided for scenarios where servers (managers) are separated from destination clients (agents) by one or more intermediary networks because of firewall policies or address space concerns. The firewall components are used to tunnel traffic between network zones, and can be chained together to allow for multiple hops.

The following graphic is a high-level, functional overview of the firewall components:

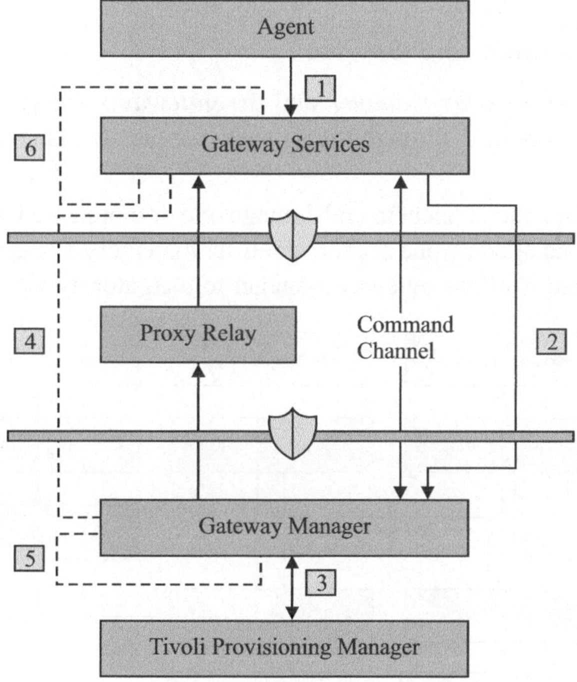

Fig. 5.2

1. An agent connects to gateway service and sends command to connect to the Agent Manager on the provisioning server.
2. The gateway service sends a command to gateway manager.
3. The gateway manager creates connection to manager.

4. The gateway creates a connection to the gateway service using the proxy relay.
5. The gateway manager ties connections 3 and 4 to form a virtual connection from the manager to the gateway service.
6. The gateway service ties connections 4 and 6 to form a virtual connection from the manager to the agent.

5.2.1 Proxy Relay

The firewall components operate by opening default port 1960 on the proxy relay system, and then listening on this port for routed traffic. When a connection is made to this port, the proxy relay expects control information to be sent, which instructs the relay to create a new TCP/IP connection to the specified address and port. Once the new connection is created, the two input and output stream connections are joined together using a thread that reads data from an input stream and writes data to another output stream.

Each proxy relay is configured with an access control list (ACL) which determines which incoming and outgoing connections to allow.

5.2.2 Gateway Manager and Service

The gateway includes the *gateway manager* and the *gateway service*. The gateway is used to tunnel TCP/IP traffic from point 1 through the gateway service and gateway manager to the final destination 2.

Each gateway manager can connect to and manage one or more gateway services. In turn, each gateway service can be managed by one or more gateway managers. For gateway communications, all connections are created from the gateway manager to the gateway service.

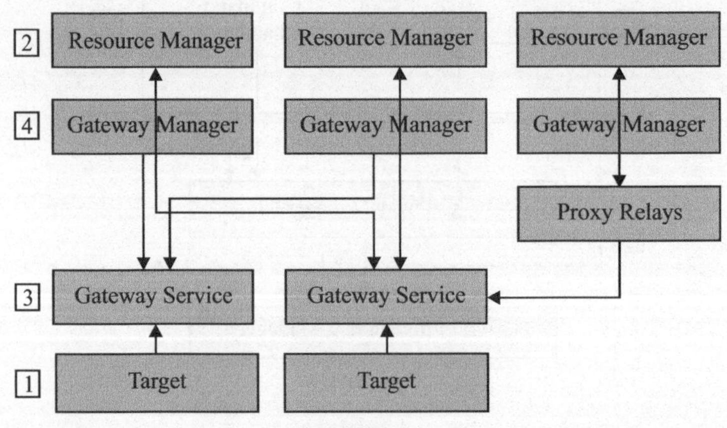

Fig. 5.3

For example, a target computer (1, illustrated in the preceding image) must create a TCP/IP connection to a resource (2). Because of unidirectional firewall rules, connections can only originate from the network where the resource (2) resides. Using the gateway, the target computer (1) creates a connection to the gateway service (3), which is allowed, as they are in the same network. A gateway manager (4) creates a connection to a resource (2), which resides in the same network. Next, the gateway manager (4) creates a new connection to the gateway service (3). Then, using the input and output streams, the original connection from the target computer (1) to the gateway service (3) acts as though it is connected directly to the resource (2). When the gateway manager and gateway service are operating correctly, there is a persistent TCP/IP from the gateway manager to the gateway service.

This "command channel" enables the gateway service to alert the gateway manager when it receives a new connection request. A periodic "heartbeat" signal is sent to keep the connection alive. If the "command channel" is closed, the gateway manager will attempt to reconnect periodically. The gateway service will automatically stop listening on that particular gateway manager's service ports when the connection is broken. The gateway service can be configured to advertise a particular service. To use this feature, user datagram protocol (UDP) broadcasting must be enabled for the local subnet. A target computer can discover a service by sending a broadcast UDP packet containing the service's name. If the gateway service receives the UDP packet and it currently advertises that service name, then it will respond back with an addressed UDP packet which contains the port number that service is listening on. The target computer can then use the source address of the UDP packet and the port contained within the packet to connect to the given service.

The primary components (or aspects) of a firewall are:

- network policy,
- advanced authentication mechanisms,
- packet filtering, and
- application gateways.

5.2.3 Network Policy

There are two levels of network policy that directly influence the design, installation and use of a firewall system. The higher-level policy is an issue-specific, network access policy that defines those services that will be allowed or explicitly denied from the restricted network, how these services will be used, and the conditions for exceptions to this policy. The lower-level policy describes how the firewall will actually go about restricting the access and filtering the services that were defined in the higher level policy.

5.2.4 Advanced Authentication

Advanced authentication measures such as smartcards, authentication tokens, biometrics, and software-based mechanisms are designed to counter the weaknesses of traditional passwords. While the authentication techniques vary, they are similar in that the passwords generated by advanced authentication devices cannot be reused by an attacker who has monitored a connection. Given the inherent problems with passwords on the Internet, an Internet-accessible firewall that does not use or does not contain the *hooks* to use advanced authentication makes little sense.

5.2.5 Packet Filtering

IP packet filtering is done usually using a *packet filtering router* designed for filtering packets as they pass between the router's interfaces. A packet filtering router usually can filter IP packets based on some or all of the following fields:

- source IP address,
- destination IP address,
- TCP/UDP source port, and
- TCP/UDP destination port.

Not all packet filtering routers currently filter the source TCP/UDP port, however more vendors are starting to incorporate this capability. Some routers examine which of the router's network interfaces a packet arrived at, and then use this as an additional filtering criterion. Some UNIX hosts provide packet filtering capability, although most do not.

Filtering can be used in a variety of ways to block connections from or to specific hosts or networks, and to block connections to specific ports. A site might wish to block connections from certain addresses, such as from hosts or sites that it considers to be hostile or untrustworthy. Alternatively, a site may wish to block connections from *all* addresses external to the site (with certain exceptions, such as with SMTP for receiving e-mail).

5.2.6 Application Gateways

To counter some of the weaknesses associated with packet filtering routers, firewalls need to use software applications to forward and filter connections for services such as TELNET and FTP. Such an application is referred to as a *proxy service*, while the host running the proxy service is referred to as an *application gateway*. Application gateways and packet filtering routers can be combined to provide higher levels of security and flexibility than if either were used alone.

As an example, consider a site that blocks all incoming TELNET and FTP connections using a packet filtering router. The router allows TELNET and FTP packets to go to one host only, the TELNET/FTP application gateway. A user who wishes to connect inbound to a site system would have to connect first to the application gateway, and then to the destination host, as follows:

1. A user first telnets to the application gateway and enters the name of an internal host,
2. The gateway checks the user's source IP address and accepts or rejects it according to any access criteria in place,
3. The user may need to authenticate herself (possibly using a one-time password device),
4. The proxy service creates a TELNET connection between the gateway and the internal host,
5. The proxy service then passes bytes between the two connections, and
6. The application gateway logs the connection

5.3 FIREWALL LIMITATIONS

Firewalls help protect your internal network from hackers. However, firewalls do have limitations. The top 10 firewall limitations include:

1. ***Monitoring*** - firewalls restrict traffic but can't notify you if someone has hacked into your network.
   Many organizations need additional security monitoring tools.
2. ***Architecture*** - firewalls reflect the overall level of security in the network. An architecture that depends upon one method of security or one security mechanism has a single point of failure and may open the organization to intruders.
3. ***Viruses*** - there are many ways to encode files and transfer them over the Internet. Not all firewalls offer protection against computer viruses.
4. ***Attacks*** - firewalls can't protect against attacks that don't go through the firewall. Your firewall may restrict access from the Internet, but may not protect your network from wireless and other access to your systems.
5. ***Encryption*** - firewalls and Virtual Private Networks (VPNs) don't provide formalized solutions to encrypt confidential documents and e-mail messages sent within your organization or to outside business contacts.
6. ***Traffic*** – many firewalls are configured to restrict inbound traffic. Firewalls should also be configured to restrict outbound traffic as well.
7. ***Masquerades*** - firewalls can't stop a hacker from masquerading as an employee. Hackers have a number of ways to acquire user ids and passwords.
8. ***Policies*** - firewalls are not a replacement for strong security policies and procedures. An organization's security is only as strong as its weakest link.
9. ***Employees*** - like a deadbolt lock on a front door, a firewall can't tell you if there are other vulnerabilities that allow your internal network to be compromised by a malicious employee.
10. ***Configuration*** – a firewall can't tell you if it has been incorrectly configured. Security audits provide an independent verification that a firewall has been correctly configured and is properly protecting you from Internet related threats.

5.4 DESIGN AND IMPLEMENTATION ISSUES

5.4.1 What are Some of the Basic Design Decisions in a Firewall

There are a number of basic design issues that should be addressed by the lucky person who has been tasked with the responsibility of designing, specifying, and implementing or overseeing the installation of a firewall.

The first and most important decision reflects the policy of how your company or organization wants to operate the system: is the firewall in place explicitly to deny all services except those critical to the mission of connecting to the Net, or is the firewall in place to provide a metered and audited method of "queuing" access in a non-threatening manner? There are degrees of paranoia between these positions; the final stance of your firewall might be more the result of a political than an engineering decision.

The second is: what level of monitoring, redundancy, and control do you want? Having established the acceptable risk level (i.e., how paranoid you are) by resolving the first issue, you can form a checklist of what should be monitored, permitted, and denied. In other words, you start by figuring out your overall objectives, and then combine a needs analysis with a risk assessment, and sort the almost always conflicting requirements out into a laundry list that specifies what you plan to implement.

The third issue is financial. We can't address this one here in anything but vague terms, but it's important to try to quantify any proposed solutions in terms of how much it will cost either to buy or to implement. For example, a complete firewall product may cost between $100,000 at the high end, and free at the low end. The free option, of doing some fancy configuring on a Cisco or similar router will cost nothing but staff time and a few cups of coffee. Implementing a high end firewall from scratch might cost several man-months, which may equate to $30,000 worth of staff salary and benefits. The systems management overhead is also a consideration. Building a home-brew is fine, but it's important to build it so that it doesn't require constant (and expensive) attention. It's important, in other words, to evaluate firewalls not only in terms of what they cost now, but continuing costs such as support.

On the technical side, there are a couple of decisions to make, based on the fact that for all practical purposes what we are talking about is a static traffic routing service placed between the network service provider's router and your internal network. The traffic routing service may be implemented at an IP level via something like screening rules in a router, or at an application level via proxy gateways and services.

The decision to make is whether to place an exposed stripped-down machine on the outside network to run proxy services for telnet, FTP, news, etc., or whether to set up a screening router as a filter, permitting communication with one or more internal machines. There are benefits and drawbacks to both approaches, with the proxy machine providing a greater level of audit and, potentially, security in return for increased cost in configuration and a decrease in the level of service that may be provided (since a proxy needs to be developed for each desired service). The old trade-off between ease-of-use and security comes back to haunt us with a vengeance.

5.4.2 What are the Basic Types of Firewalls

Conceptually, there are three types of firewalls:

1. Network layer
2. Application layer
3. Hybrids

They are not as different as you might think, and latest technologies are blurring the distinction to the point where it's no longer clear if either one is "better" or "worse." As always, you need to be careful to pick the type that meets your needs.

Which is which depends on what mechanisms the firewall uses to pass traffic from one security zone to another. The International Standards Organization (ISO) Open Systems Interconnect (OSI) model for networking defines seven layers, where each layer provides services that "higher-level" layers depend on. In order from the bottom, these layers are physical, data link, network, transport, session, presentation, application.

The important thing to recognize is that the lower-level the forwarding mechanism, the less examination the firewall can perform. Generally speaking, lower-level firewalls are faster, but are easier to fool into doing the wrong thing.

These days, most firewalls fall into the "hybrid" category, which do network filtering as well as some amount of application inspection. The amount changes depending on the vendor, product, protocol and version, so some level of digging and/or testing is often necessary.

5.4.3 Network Layer Firewalls

These generally make their decisions based on the source, destination addresses and ports in individual IP packets. A simple router is the "traditional" network layer firewall, since it is not able to make particularly sophisticated decisions about what a packet is actually talking to or where it actually came from. Modern network layer firewalls have become increasingly sophisticated, and now maintain internal information about the state of connections passing through them, the contents of some of the data streams, and so on. One thing that's an important distinction about many network layer firewalls is that they route traffic directly though them, so to use one you either need to have a validly assigned IP address block or to use a "private internet" address block. Network layer firewalls tend to be very fast and tend to be very transparent to users.

In Figure 5.4, a network layer firewall called a "screened host firewall" is represented. In a screened host firewall, access to and from a single host is controlled by means of a router operating at a network layer. The single host is a bastion host; a highly-defended and secured strong-point that (hopefully) can resist attack.

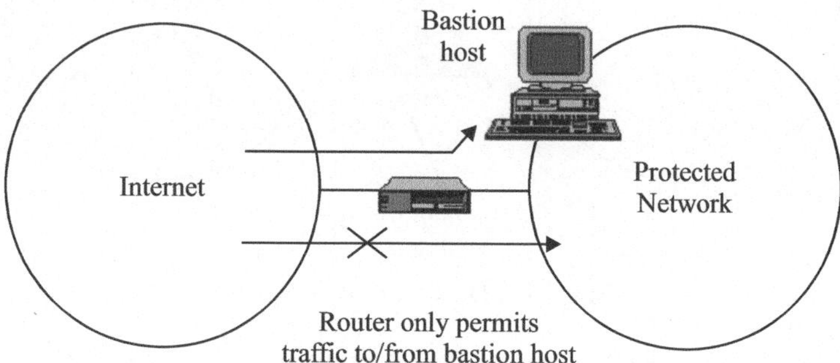

Fig. 5.4: Screened Host Firewall

Example Network layer firewall: In Figure 5.5, a network layer firewall called a "screened subnet firewall" is represented. In a screened subnet firewall, access to and from a whole network is controlled by means of a router operating at a network layer. It is similar to a screened host, except that it is, effectively, a network of screened hosts Application layer firewalls.

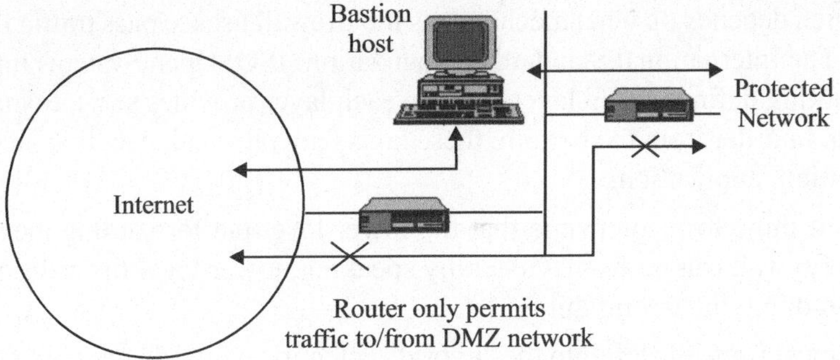

Fig. 5.5: Screened Subnet

These generally are hosts running proxy servers, which permit no traffic directly between networks, and which perform elaborate logging and auditing of traffic passing through them. Since the proxy applications are software components running on the firewall, it is a good place to do lots of logging and access control. Application layer firewalls can be used as network address translators, since traffic goes in one "side" and out the other, after having passed through an application that effectively masks the origin of the initiating connection. Having an application in the way in some cases may impact performance and may make the firewall less transparent. Early application layer firewalls such as those built using the TIS firewall toolkit, are not particularly transparent to end users and may require some training. Modern application layer firewalls are often fully transparent. Application layer firewalls tend to provide more detailed audit reports and tend to enforce more conservative security models than network layer firewalls.

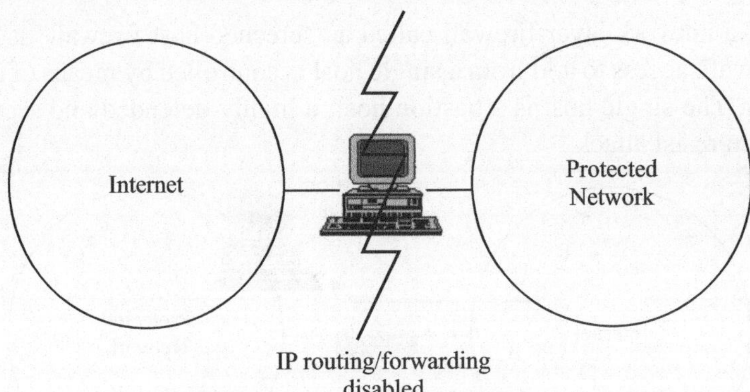

Fig. 5.18: Dual Homed Gateway

Example Application layer firewall: In Figure 5.18, an application layer firewall called a "dual homed gateway" is represented. A dual homed gateway is a highly secured host that runs proxy software. It has two network interfaces, one on each network, and blocks all traffic passing through it.

Most firewalls now lie someplace between network layer firewalls and application layer firewalls. As expected, network layer firewalls have become increasingly "aware" of the information going through them, and application layer firewalls have become increasingly "low level" and transparent. The end result is that now there are fast packet-screening systems that log and audit data as they pass through the system. Increasingly, firewalls (network and application layer) incorporate encryption so that they may protect traffic passing between them over the Internet. Firewalls with end-to-end encryption can be used by organizations with multiple points of Internet connectivity to use the Internet as a "private backbone" without worrying about their data or passwords being sniffed.

5.5 FIREWALL POLICY

A firewall is an appliance (a combination of hardware and software) or an application (software) designed to control the flow of Internet Protocol (IP) traffic to or from a network or electronic equipment. Firewalls are used to examine network traffic and enforce policies based on instructions contained within the Firewall's Ruleset. Firewalls represent one component of a strategy to combat malicious activities and assaults on computing resources and network-accessible information. Other components include, but are not limited to, antivirus software, intrusion detection software, patch management, strong passwords/passphrases, and spyware detection utilities.

Firewalls are typically categorized as either "Network" or "Host": a Network Firewall is most often an appliance attached to a network for the purpose of controlling access to single or multiple hosts, or subnets; a Host Firewall is most often an application that addresses an individual host (e.g., personal computer) separately. Both types of firewalls (Network and Host) can be and often are used jointly.

This policy statement is designed to:

- Provide guidance on when firewalls are required or recommended. A Network Firewall is required in all instances where Sensitive Data is stored or processed; a Host Firewall is required in all instances where Sensitive Data is stored or processed and the operating environment supports the implementation. Both the Network and Host Firewalls afford protection to the same operating environment, and the redundancy of controls (two separate and distinct firewalls) provides additional security in the event of a compromise or failure.
- Raise awareness on the importance of a properly configured (installed and maintained) firewall.

5.6 EMERGING CLIENT/SERVER NETWORKS

Server based networks, or client/server networks as they are properly called, has a machine at the heart of its operations called the server. A server is a machine that provides services over a network by responding to client requests. Servers rarely have individuals operating it, and even then, it is usually to install, configure or manage its capabilities. The server's essential role on the network is to be continuously available to handle the many requests generated by its clients.

Server-based networks provide centralised control of the entire network environment. The computer systems used for this role are generally more powerful than end-user machines, incorporating faster CPUs, more memory, larger disk drives and other drive types installed, like a tape drive for backup purposes. These are required, because servers are dedicated to handling multiple simultaneous requests from their client communities.

Server based networks provide centralised verification of user accounts and passwords. Only valid account name and password combinations are allowed access to the network. Client/Server networks typically require a single login to the network itself, meaning that users need to remember long password lists to access various resources. Concentrations of resources on a single server, mean that they are easier to find, as opposed to the peer-to-peer model, were resources were distributed throughout the network since they were attached to multiple machines. The server being a central data repository, means that not only is data more accessible to users, but it also makes life much easier in terms of performing backups, since the data is in a location know to the administrator.

Server-based networks are easier to scale. Peer-to-peer networks bog down seriously as they grow beyond ten users, and serious slow up with 20 users. On the other hand, client/server networks can handle a few users, up to a thousand users as such networks grow to keep pace with an organisations growth and expansion.

Unlike peer-to-peer networks, client/server networks don't come cheap. The server machine itself may cost several thousands of pounds, along with the software to make it run; another thousand pounds. Because of the complex nature of this kind of networking environment, a dedicated administrator is required to be on site at all times to be involved in the day to day running of the network. Hiring an individual of this nature adds considerably to the cost of client/server networks.

Lastly, because the networks operability is so dependant upon the server, this introduces a single point of failure, if the server goes down the network goes down. There are measures available, that can legislate for such failures, however these techniques add even more cost to this solution.

Advantages

- Centralised user accounts, security and access controls simplify network administration.
- More powerful equipment means more efficient access network resources.
- Single password login, means access to all resources.
- Supports greater numbers of users, or networks where resources are heavily used.

Disadvantages

- More costly to install and maintain.
- Single point of failure, server goes down, the network goes down.
- Complex special-purpose software requires appointment of expert staff, increasing costs.
- Dedicated hardware and software increases costs.

SUMMARY

A firewall is a part of a computer system or network that is designed to block unauthorized access while permitting authorized communications. It is a device or set of devices that is configured to permit or deny network transmissions based upon a set of rules and other criteria.

Firewalls can be implemented in either hardware or software, or a combination of both. Firewalls are frequently used to prevent unauthorized Internet users from accessing private networks connected to the Internet, especially intranets. All messages entering or leaving the intranet pass through the firewall, which inspects each message and blocks those that do not meet the specified security criteria.

EXERCISE

1. What is firewall?
2. Write down the importance of firewall.
3. What are different component of firewall?
4. What is emerging client server technology?
5. What are the different limitations of firewall?
6. What are the factors to consider in firewall design?
7. Write down all the type of firewall.

UNIT – 4

6. Encryption Techniques
7. Virtual Private Network

CHAPTER

6

Encryption Techniques

6.1 INTRODUCTION

Cryptography is the science of using mathematics to encrypt and decrypt data. Cryptography enables you to store sensitive information or transmit it across insecure networks (like the Internet) so that it cannot be read by anyone except the intended recipient.

Cryptography is a study of how to scramble data so that:

1. Anyone who steals it will be unable to scramble it.
2. Your intended recipients will be able to unscramble it with ease.

6.1.1 Important Terms in Cryptography

The transformation of actual message into coded form (scrambling) is known as encryption or Enciphering and reverse of this (unscrambling) is known as Decryption or Deciphering. The message to be encrypted is known as Plaintext or Message text. The output of encryption Process is known as Cipher text or Cryptogram. The person who sends a message text is known as Sender and person who intends to receive the message text is known as Receiver. Sending a message in plaintext rather in cipher text to receiver is termed as sending in the Clear text. The person who intends to hack/steal the cipher text between sender and receiver is known as Intruder or Attacker. The set of data transformation used to do encryption or workhouse of cryptography is known as Cryptographic Algorithm or simply a Cipher, normally the transformation is parameterized by one or more s. The art of breaking ciphers is known as Cryptanalysis and the art of developing and breaking cipher is collectively known as Cryptology.

6.1.2 Types of Cryptography

There are two types of encryption techniques.

- Symmetric or Conventional encryption
- Asymmetric or Public key encryption

In the world where information and communication is the indispensable composition of human activities, where men and technology must communicate or share information in order to make decisions; it therefore behooves that this composite essence of humans should be protected and managed to ensure its sustainability, integrity, accuracy.

6.2 WHAT IS ENCRYPTION

Data that can be read and understood without any special measures is called plaintext or clear text. The method of disguising plaintext in such a way as to hide its substance is called encryption. Encrypting plaintext results in unreadable gibberish called cipher text. You use encryption to ensure that information is hidden from anyone for whom it is not intended, even those who can see the encrypted data. The process of reverting cipher text to its original plaintext is called decryption.

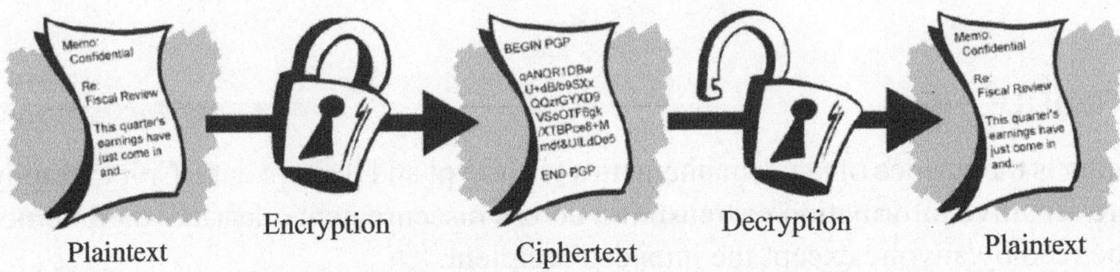

Fig. 6.1: Encryption and Decryption

6.3 ENCRYPTION TECHNIQUES

Encryption techniques have become the immediate solution to protect information against third parties. These techniques required that data and information should be encrypted with some sort of mathematical algorithm where only the party that shares the information could possible decrypt to use the information. This phenomenon has long existed and is not fully reliable which pose danger to the information sharing. However, many method of encryption emerge to serve the need of the emergent trend of rapid technological advancement. These emergent techniques were more reliable and are fast in operation and performance wise.

However, as this new trend of fast and reliable cryptography emerged, there is a very big concern on that issue of using to hide proof of violent scheme as many government authorities see it as impending danger. Since Cryptography has become so powerful that messages scrambled with so-called strong cryptography are virtually undecipherable. Like many powerful technologies, this is a double-edged sword. For good, we know that Encryption can keep email and financial transactions over the Internet secure and private, but law enforcement officials worry those criminals and terrorists could use the same tools to conceal incriminating evidence and violent plots.

This concern has convoked many viewpoint and argument, which has alerted the formation of policies by some law enforcement agencies to regulate the encryption techniques.

In this view, we will be discussing popular encryption system, types of cryptography, issues of regulating Encryption technology, social and legal implication, computer ciphers and encryption and other cryptosystems, which will aid the understanding of Encryption Techniques and its advantages and challenges in the electronic age.

6.3.1 Definiton and Origin of Encryption Technique

Encryption, process of converting messages or data into a form that cannot be read without decrypting or deciphering it. The root of the word encryption crypt comes from the Greek word kryptos, meaning "hidden" or "secret." The study and practice of encryption and decryption is called the science of cryptography.

Scientists who study different ways to protect and ensure the confidentiality, integrity, and authenticity of information are called cryptologists. Cryptologists also engage in cryptanalysis to find ways to break encryption methods.

For centuries before the age of electronic communication and computers, individuals, militaries, and other groups coded written information. As electronic forms of communication and information storage and processing have developed, the opportunities to intercept, modify, use, disclose, and read confidential information has grown, and the need for powerful encryption techniques has increased.

Government agencies, banks, and many corporations now routinely send a great deal of confidential information from one computer to another. Such data are usually transmitted via telephone lines or other non-private channels, such as the Internet. Continuing development of secure computer systems and networks will ensure that confidential information can be securely transferred across computer networks.

6.3.2 Basic Vocabulary of Classical Encryption

Plaintext: This is what you want to encrypt.

Ciphertext: The encrypted output.

Enciphering or encryption: The process by which plaintext is converted into ciphertext.

Encryption algorithm: The sequence of data processing steps that go into transforming plaintext into ciphertext. Various parameters used by an encryption algorithm are derived from a secret key. In classical cryptography for commercial and other civilian applications, the encryption algorithm is made public.

Secret key: A secret key is used to set some or all of the various parameters used by the encryption algorithm. The important thing to note is that the same secret key is used for encryption and decryption in classical cryptography. It is for this reason that classical cryptography is also referred to as symmetric key cryptography.

Deciphering or decryption: Recovering plaintext from ciphertext decryption algorithm: The sequence of data processing steps that go into transforming ciphertext back into plaintext. Various parameters used by a decryption algorithm are derived from the same secret key that was used in the encryption algorithm.

In classical cryptography for commercial and other civilian applications, the decryption algorithm is made public.

Cryptography: The many schemes available today for encryption cipher processes a block of input data at a time and produces a ciphertext block of the same size.

Stream cipher: A stream cipher encrypts data on the fly, usually one byte at a time.

Cryptanalysis: Means "breaking the code". Cryptanalysis relies on a knowledge of the encryption algorithm (that for civilian applications should be in the public domain) and some knowledge of the possible structure of the plaintext (such as the structure of a typical inter-bank financial transaction) for a partial or full reconstruction of the plaintext from ciphertext. Additionally, the goal is to also infer the key for decryption of future messages.

6.3.3 How Encryption Works

Encryption uses a systematic or step-by-step procedure called an algorithm to convert data or the text of an original message, known as plaintext, into ciphertext, its encrypted form.

Cryptographic algorithms normally require a string of characters called a key to encrypt or decrypt data. Those who possess the key and the algorithm can encrypt the plaintext into ciphertext and then decrypt the ciphertext back into plaintext.

Cryptologists engage in an unending competition to create stronger cryptographic techniques and to break them. Many recent cryptography techniques are nearly unbreakable even with the most powerful computers. These systems produce ciphertext that appears to be random characters. These systems resist most existing methods for deciphering back into plaintext.

The many different types of new cryptosystems use highly complex mathematical language and resist breaking even though cryptologists may know the techniques used in creating them.

6.3.4 Pretty Good Privacy (PGP)

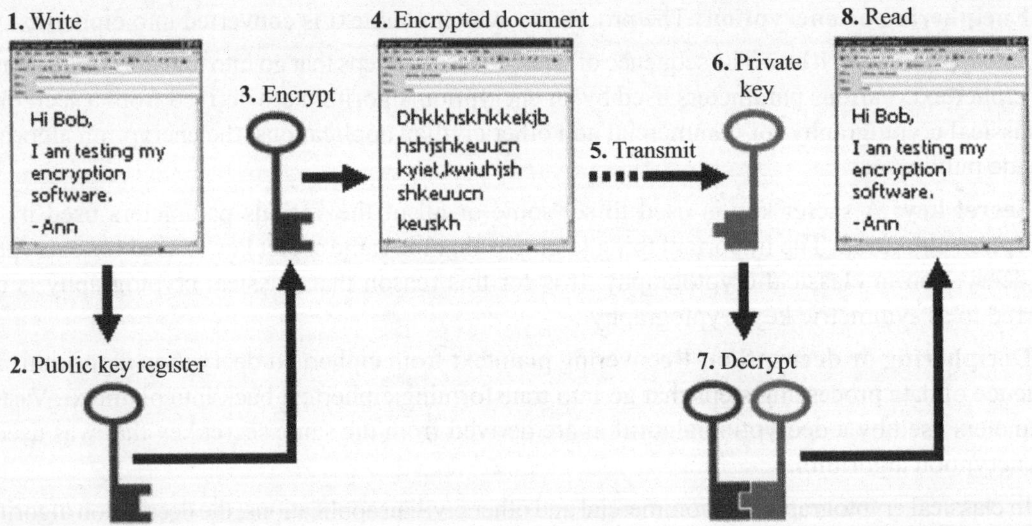

Fig. 6.2

Pretty Good Privacy (PGP) helps users of e-mail keep their communications private. In this two-key system, also known as the public key system, the computer sending an encrypted message uses a chosen private key that is never shared and so is known only to the sender.

All computers authorized to receive and decrypt the message are given the matching public key. This method also establishes who sent the message. If a sending computer first encrypts the message with the intended receiver's public key and again with the sender's secret, private key, then the receiving computer may decrypt the message, first using its secret key and then the sender's public key. Using this public-key cryptographic method, the sender and receiver are able to authenticate one another as well as protect the secrecy of the message. The use of the keys is done.

6.3.5 Popular Encryption Systems

Three of the most popular cryptography systems used are the Data Encryption Standard (DES), Pretty Good Privacy (PGP), and the Rivest, Shamir, Adleman (RSA) system. Most of this has been shortly describe above, however, We will elaborate it below.

DES uses a single key for both encrypting and decrypting. In private-key cryptography. A secret key may be held by one person or exchanged between the sender and the receiver of a message. For example, if you encrypt data for storage on a hard drive, you remember the key and usually do not give it to another person. But if you want to send secure messages to a business partner using symmetric cryptography, you need to make sure your partner knows the key that will decrypt the messages The secret (or private) key in a public-key cryptographic system is never transmitted or shared. For example, when using this method for client-side authentication, the server sends some data to your client program. The client uses your private key to encrypt that data. Using your public key, the server will attempt to decrypt the returned data, and, if successful, know that it has established communication with you.

If private -key cryptography is used to send secret messages between two parties, both the sender and receiver must have a copy of the secret key. However, the key may be compromised during transit. If you know the party you are exchanging messages with, you can give them the key in advance. However, if you need to send an encrypted message to someone, you have never met; you will need to figure out a way to exchange keys in a secure way. One method is to send it via another secure channel.

The Rivest, Shamir, Adleman (RSA) algorithm is a popular encryption method that uses two keys. Unlike symmetric cryptography, the keys are mathematically related, yet it is computationally infeasible to deduce one from the other. Anyone with the public key can encrypt a message but not decrypt it. Only the person with the private key can decrypt the message. One of the most common uses of public-key technology is to provide a secure communication channel between computer programs, although private-key techniques can be used for this, too.

Public key infrastructure also provides the foundation for secure emails because public key cryptography is used to distribute symmetric keys, which are then used to encrypt and decrypt actual messages. For example, in using a public-key system for personal authentication or secure messaging, you keep one key secret. The second (public) key can then be distributed to anyone.

The typical example of public key infrastructure is SSL (Secure Socket Layer) protocol. SSL is often used to protect information sent between Web browsers and web servers; this is commonly used in E-Commerce systems.

In the two-key system, also known as the public key system, one key encrypts the information and another, mathematically related key decrypts it. The computer sending an encrypted message uses a chosen private key that is never shared and so is known only to the sender. All computers authorized to receive and decrypt the message are given the matching public key. This method also establishes who sent the message. If a sending computer first encrypts the message with the intended receiver's public key and again with the sender's secret, private key, then the receiving computer may decrypt the message, first using its secret key and then the sender's public key. Using this public-key cryptographic method, the sender and receiver are able to authenticate one another as well as protect the secrecy of the message. Single key methods, in contrast, require great secrecy in conveying a key from sender to recipient.

6.3.6 Building Blocks of Classical Encryption Techniques

Two building blocks of all classical encryption techniques are substitution and transposition.

- Substitution means replacing an element of the plaintext with an element of ciphertext.
- Transposition means rearranging the order of appearance of the elements of the plaintext.
- Transposition is also referred to as permutation.

6.3.7 Caesar Cipher

- This is the earliest known example of a substitution cipher.
- Each character of a message is replaced by a character three position down in the alphabet.
  plaintext: are you ready
  ciphertext: DUH BRX UHDGB
- If we represent each letter of the alphabet by an integer that corresponds to its position in the alphabet, the formula for replacing each character 'p' of the plaintext with a character 'C' of the ciphertext can be expressed as

$$C = E(3, p) = (p + 3) \bmod 26$$

- A more general version of this cipher that allows for any degree of shift would be expressed by

$$C = E(k, p) = (p + k) \bmod 26$$

- The formula for decryption would be

$$p = D(k, C) = (C - k) \bmod 26$$

- In these formulas, 'k' would be the secret key. The symbols 'E' and 'D' represent encryption and decryption.

6.3.8 Problems of Encryption Techniques

Although, encryption mechanisms make information unreadable. Therefore, no third parties, including server administrators and others, have access to plain text version of transmitted information through public networks such as internet, but the following are the problems encountered or associated with encryption techniques.

6.4 SYMMETRIC ENCRYPTION

Symmetric or **Conventional** encryption is one of the very old encryption schemes used in very early days and also known as encryption. In this scheme both the sender and the receiver shares the same encryption and decryption secret key Obviously, this scheme uses old substitutions and permutations functions of mathematics to replace one character of plaintext with other to do encryption and decryption and that is why it given the name as symmetric encryption scheme. This scheme is shown in figure below

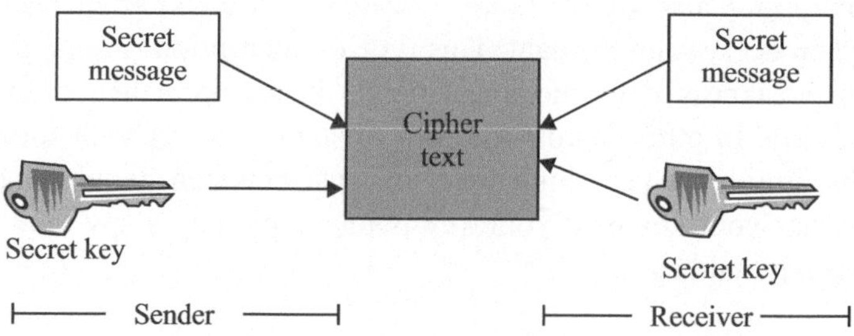

Fig. 6.3: How symmetric encryption works

NET Framework provides us with the following secret key encryption algorithms:

- DES CryptoServiceProvider
- RC2 CryptoServiceProvider
- Rijndael Managed / AES (Advance encryption Standard)
- TripleDESCryptoServiceProvider

6.4.1 Block Cipher

Block Ciphers operates in a purely combinational fashion with a fixed transformation applied to a large block of plaintext on block by block basis the most common block size is eight bytes. Because each block is heavily processed, block ciphers provide a higher level of security. However, block cipher algorithms tend to execute more slowly.

Block ciphers use the same encryption algorithm for each block. Because of this, a block of plain text will always return the same cipher text when encrypted with the same key and algorithm. Because this behavior can be used to crack a cipher, cipher modes are introduced that modify the encryption process based on feedback from earlier block encryption. The resulting encryption provides a higher level of security than a simple block encryption

6.4.2 Block Cipher Modes

- **Cipher Block chaining** mode (CBC) introduces feedback. Before each plain text block is encrypted, it is combined with the cipher text of the previous block by a bitwise exclusive OR operation. This ensures that even if the plain text contains many identical blocks, they will each encrypt to a different cipher text block. The initialization vector is combined with the first plain text block by a bitwise exclusive OR operation before the block is encrypted.
- The **Cipher Feedback** (CFB) mode processes small increments of plain text into cipher text, instead of processing an entire block at a time. This mode uses a shift register that is one block in length and is divided into sections. For example, if the block size is eight bytes, with one byte processed at a time, the shift register is divided into eight sections.

The Electronic Codebook (ECB) mode encrypts each block individually. This means that any blocks of plain text that are identical and are in the same message, or in a different message encrypted with the same key will be transformed into identical cipher text blocks.

In *symmetric encryption also known as the* Private Key Method or encryption, a single key is used for encrypting and decrypting the data. This type of encryption is quite fast, but has a severe problem. The inherent weakness of this method is mostly the requirement of a key exchange between communications partners. In other words, in order to share a secret with someone, they have to know your key. This implies a very high level of trust between people sharing secrets, if an unscrupulous person has your key or if your key is intercepted by a spy they can decrypt all the messages you send using that key.

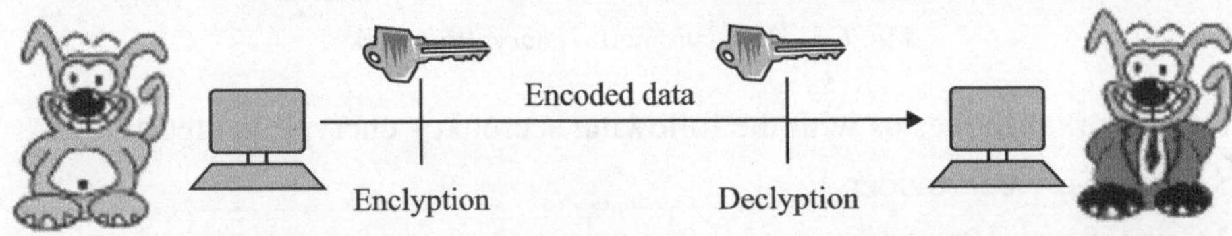

Fig. 6.4

However, Asymmetric encryption solves the trust problem inherent in symmetric encryption by using two different keys: a public key for encrypting messages, and a private key for decrypting messages. This makes it possible to communicate in secrecy with people you don't fully trust. If an unscrupulous person has your public key, who cares? The public key is only good for encryption; it's useless for decryption. They can't decrypt any of your messages! However, asymmetric encryption is very slow. It's not recommended for use on more than roughly 1 kilobyte of data.

6.4.3 Key Management

One of the big challenges in using cryptography on a widespread basis especially public-key encryption--is the management of private and public keys. Key management deals with the secure generation, distribution, and storage of keys. Secure methods of key management are extremely important. Once a key is randomly generated, it must remain secret to avoid unfortunate mishaps.

Most attacks on public-key systems will probably be aimed at the key management level, rather than at the cryptographic algorithm itself.

Users must be able to securely obtain a key pair suited to their efficiency and security needs. There must be a way to look up other people's public keys and to publicize one's own public key. Users must be able to legitimately obtain others' public keys; otherwise, an intruder can either change public keys listed in a directory, or impersonate another user.

If someone's private key is lost or compromised, others must be made aware of this, so they will no longer encrypt messages under the invalid public key nor accept messages signed with the invalid private key. Users must be able to store their private keys securely, so no intruder can obtain them, yet the keys must be readily accessible for legitimate user. Keys need to be valid only until a specified expiration date but the expiration date must be chosen properly and publicized in an authenticated channel.

6.4.4 Digital Certificates

A digital certificate is an attachment to an electronic message used for security purposes. It is commonly used to verify that a user is who he/she claims to be and to provide the receiver with the means to encode a reply.

When you obtain a certificate by applying to a certificate authority (CA). Once the CA verifies you are who you say you are, it creates a certificate—a digital document for you.

The certificate contains:

- A name that is unique to you
- The length of time the certificate is valid
- Your public key
- Your key's purpose: to sign messages or to encrypt data

Certificates do the following for your system:

- Backed up and recoverable
- Protected against theft
- Matched with encrypted data
- Accessible from many systems
- Accessible only to the authorized user

In order for you to manage your certificate to be used with applications, you will need to do the followings:

- Production and maintenance of a very large standards-based directory
- Support for a highly distributed computing environment
- Methodologies supporting transparent access by applications
- Private and public key storage and access issues

- Incompatibility of browser vendors' certificate formats
- Issues that Certificate Authority deals with are as follows:
- Maintenance of a certificate repository
- Methodology for verifying individuals and departments
- Management of certificate revocation lists (CRLs)
- Renewal of key pairs and certificates
- Support for trust relationships with other certificate authorities
- Secure messaging is the principal driver for using personal certificates.

Other alternatives can be used to address security problems in online systems, including Web-based transaction systems. However, the technical, policy, and management issues mentioned previously must be resolved before any wide scale deployment of a public-key infrastructure is reasonable.

6.4.5 Data Encryption Standard

A commonly accepted definition of a good symmetric key algorithm, such as the DES, is that there exists no attack better than key exhaustion to read an encrypted message. Critics argued that the 56-bit DES key was too short for long-term security, and that expected increases in computer power would soon make a 56-bit key vulnerable to attack by exhaustion.

DES uses a sequence of operations, including several substitution and permutation primitives, to encrypt a data block. The DES algorithm is a block cipher that uses the same binary key both to encrypt and decrypt data blocks, and thus is called a symmetric key cipher. DES operates on 64-bit "plaintext" data blocks, processing them under the control of a 56-bit key to produce 64 bits of encrypted ciphertext. Similarly, the DES decryption process operates on a 64-bit ciphertext block using the same 56-bit key to produce the original 64-bit plaintext block.

6.4.6 DES Explanation

Data Encryption Standard (DES) is a widely-used method of data encryption using a private (secret) key that was judged so difficult to break by the U.S. government that it was restricted for exportation to other countries. There are 72,000,000,000,000,000 (72 quadrillion) or more possible encryption keys that can be used. For each given message, the key is chosen at random from among this enormous number of keys. Like other private key cryptographic methods, both the sender and the receiver must know and use the same private key.

It was developed in the 1970s by the National Bureau of Standards with the help of the National Security Agency. Its purpose is to provide a standard method for protecting sensitive commercial and unclassified data. IBM created the first draft of the algorithm, calling it LUCIFER. DES officially became a federal standard in November of 1976.

To understand this implementation, you'll first need to understand bit operations and read some more general explanations of DES.

In general, DES takes as input a 64 bit key, of which only 56 bits are used. From these 56 bits, 16 48 bit subkeys are created. The message is split into 64 bit chunks, and a complex series of steps enciphers the message using each subkey. As Javascript only supports 32 bit integers, all 48 or 64 bit integers are represented by two 32 bit integers in an array.

Creating the Keys - PC1

DES must first create the 16 subkeys. First, the 8 character string representing the key is turned into two integers which are passed to the des_createKeys function. The bits of these two integers are then reorganised according to PC1 (permuted choice 1). The bits end up in the following places:

57	49	41	33	25	17	9	1
58	50	42	34	26	18	10	2
59	51	43	35	27	19	11	3
60	52	44	36	0	0	0	0
63	55	47	39	31	23	15	7
62	54	46	38	30	22	14	6
61	53	45	37	29	21	13	5
28	20	12	4	0	0	0	0

This means that the first 57th bit of the original key becomes the first bit, etc. The permuting is done using a permutation sequence, which is a clever way of rotating and switching bits between 2 integers. For instance, temp = ((left >>> 4) ^ right) & 0x0f0f0f0f; right ^= temp; left ^= (temp << 4); rotates 4x4 blocks of bits:

33	34	35	36	1	2	3	4
41	42	43	44	9	10	11	12
49	50	51	52	17	18	19	20
57	58	59	60	25	26	27	28
37	38	39	40	5	6	7	8
45	46	47	48	13	14	15	16
53	54	55	56	21	22	23	24
61	62	63	64	29	30	31	32

6.4.7 Triple Encryption

In cryptography, **Triple DES** is the common name for the Triple Data Encryption Algorithm (TDEA) block cipher, which applies the Data Encryption Standard (DES) cipher algorithm three times to each data block. Because of the availability of increasing computational power, the key size of the original DES cipher was becoming subject to brute force attacks; Triple DES was designed to provide a relatively simple method of increasing the key size of DES to protect against such attacks, without designing a completely new block cipher algorithm.

6.4.8 Secret Key Encryption

Secret-key encryption uses one key, the secret key, to both encrypt and decrypt messages. This is also called symmetric encryption. The term "private key" is often used inappropriately to refer to the secret key. A private key is one of the keys in the public/private key pair for asymmetric cryptography. In this scheme, a user has two keys, one that is made public and one that is held privately.

In secret-key cryptography schemes, a single key is used to encrypt data. A secret key may be held by one person or exchanged between the sender and the receiver of a message. For example, if you encrypt data for storage on a hard drive, you remember the key and usually don't give it to someone else. But if you want to send secure messages to a business partner using symmetric cryptography, you need to make sure your partner knows the key that will decrypt the messages.

If secret-key cryptography is used to send secret messages between two parties, both the sender and receiver must have a copy of the secret key. However, the key may be compromised during transit. If you know the party you are exchanging messages with, you can give them the key in advance. However, if you need to send an encrypted message to someone you have never met, you'll need to figure out a way to exchange keys in a secure way. One method is to send it via *another secure channel* or even via overnight express, but this may be risky in some cases.

As mentioned, secret-key cryptography is often used to encrypt data on hard drives. The person encrypting the data holds the key privately and there is no problem with key distribution. Secret-key cryptography is also used for communication devices like bridges that encrypt all data that cross the link. A network administrator programs two devices with the same key, and then personally transports them to their physical locations.

6.5 ASYMMETRIC KEY ENCRYPTION

Asymmetric key encryption uses different keys for encryption and decryption. These two keys are mathematically related and they form a key pair. One of these two keys should be kept private, called private-key, and the other can be made public (it can even be sent in mail), called public-key. Hence this is also called Public Key Encryption.

A private key is typically used for encrypting the message-digest; in such an application private-key algorithm is called message-digest encryption algorithm. A public key is typically used for encrypting the secret-key; in such a application private-key algorithm is called key encryption algorithm.

Popular private-key algorithms are RSA (invented by Rivest, Shamir and Adlemen) and DSA (Digital Signature Algorithm). While for an ordinary use of RSA, a key size of 768 can be used, but for corporate use a key size of 1024 and for extremely valuable information a key size of 2048 should be used.

Asymmetric key encryption is much slower than symmetric key encryption and hence they are only used for key exchanges and digital signatures.

6.5.1 Asymmetric Encryption

Asymmetric encryption also known as the Public Key Method, it uses two different keys: the private key and public key. The public key is distributed freely and the private key is known only to the owner of a key. The two keys have a (mathematical) relationship. However, for obvious reasons, calculation of a private key on the basis of the public key must be impossible or at least not feasible.

Both keys have different functions depending on the application at hand. In the case of data encryption, data is encoded using the public key. The private key is required in order to decrypt the message. The private key can also be used to generate digital signatures, which can later be verified using the public key.

The disadvantage or problem of this method compared to symmetric encryption is the greater amount of processing time required for the calculation or a process. This is why usually the so-called hybrid technology, which is a mix of both asymmetric and symmetric encryption, is used when dealing with a greater amount of data. In this case, symmetric encryption is used to encode the data but the symmetric key is communicated on a previously determined frequency using asymmetric encryption.

6.5.2 Public Key vs. Secret Key Encryption

Definition: The purpose of a key in encryption systems is to ensure privacy by keeping information hidden from whom it is not intended. There are two types of encryption systems: secret-key and public-key systems.

Encryption is the transformation of data, the plaintext, into a form that is as close to impossible as possible to read, the ciphetext, without the appropriate knowledge (a key). Its purpose is to ensure privacy by keeping information hidden from anyone for whom it is not intended, even those who have access to the encrypted data, the ciphetext.

There are two types of encryption systems: secret-key and public-key systems. In secret-key encryption, also referred to as symmetric cryptography, the same key is used for both encryption and decryption. The most popular secret-key cryptosystem in use today is the Data Encryption Standard (DES, see). In general, the security of a secret-key system depends on the strength of the algorithm and the length of the key. In a brute-force attack, an N bits long key, which implies 2 N possible keys, will take 2 N attempts for the hacker to find the correct key. That is, the longer the key is, the longer it will take for a certain computer to find the correct key among the 2 N possible keys. Besides the key, there is another factor to determine the interval of a successful brute force attack: the speed of each test which relies on the speed of the computer and the computational complexity of the encryption algorithm. Unfortunately in most cases, the longer the key is, the longer it takes to encrypt/decrypt the message, and the more one need to pay for it in terms of cost. To determine the length of a proper key for a certain application, one needs to look at several aspects: the intended security, the current and future computer power, and the speed of the state-of-the-art factoring algorithms. That is, you need a key long enough to be secure but short enough to be computationally feasible and low cost.

On the other hand, in a public-key system, each user has a public key and a private key. The public key maybe made public while the private key remains secret. Encryption is performed with the one key while decryption is done with the other. Today's dominant public key encryption algorithms are factorization based. That is, the algorithms are based on the difficulty of factoring large numbers that are the product of two large prime numbers. One of the most popular public-key encryption algorithms, the RSA public-key cryptosystem, is a typical factorization based algorithm. To break such systems, one need to factor out the large number. Intuitively, the large the number is, the harder it is for a hacker to factor it.

6.6 MODEL OF CRYPTOGRAPHIC SYSTEMS

Cryptography can be used to provide:

- **Confidentiality:** ensure data is read only by authorized parties,
- **Data integrity:** ensure data wasn't altered between sender and recipient,
- **Authentication:** ensure data originated from a particular party.

A cryptographic system (or a cipher system) is a method of hiding data so that only certain people can view it. Cryptography is the practice of creating and using cryptographic systems. Cryptanalysis is the science of analyzing and reverse engineering cryptographic systems. The original data is called plaintext. The protected data is called ciphertext. Encryption is a procedure to convert plaintext into ciphertext. Decryption is a procedure to convert ciphertext into plaintext. A cryptographic system typically consists of algorithms, keys, and key management facilities.

There are two basic types of cryptographic systems: symmetric ("private key") and asymmetric ("public key").

Symmetric key systems require both the sender and the recipient to have the same key. This key is used by the sender to encrypt the data, and again by the recipient to decrypt the data. Key exchange is clearly a problem. How do you securely send a key that will enable you to send other data securely? If a private key is intercepted or stolen, the adversary can act as either party and view all data and communications. You can think of the symmetric crypto system as akin to the Chubb type of door locks. You must be in possession of a key to both open and lock the door.

Asymmetric cryptographic systems are considered much more flexible. Each user has both a public key and a private key. Messages are encrypted with one key and can be decrypted only by the other key. The public key can be published widely while the private key is kept secret. If Alice wishes to send Bob a secret, she finds and verifies Bob's public key, encrypts her message with it, and mails it off to Bob. When Bob gets the message, he uses his private key to decrypt it. Verification of public keys is an important step. Failure to verify that the public key really does belong to Bob leaves open the possibility that Alice is using a key whose associated private key is in the hands of an enemy. Public Key Infrastructures or PKI's deal with this problem by providing certification authorities that sign keys by a supposedly trusted party and make them available for download or verification. Asymmetric ciphers are much slower than their symmetric counterparts and key sizes are generally much larger. You can think of a public key system as akin to a Yale type door lock. Anyone can push the door locked, but you must be in possession of the correct key to open the door.

Cryptography enables you to store sensitive information or transmit it across insecure networks (like the Internet) so that it cannot be read by anyone except the intended recipient.

While cryptography is the science of securing data, cryptanalysis is the science of analyzing and breaking secure communication. Classical cryptanalysis involves an interesting combination of analytical reasoning, application of mathematical tools, pattern finding, patience, determination, and luck. Cryptanalysts are also called attackers.

6.6.1 How Does Cryptography Work

A cryptographic algorithm, or cipher, is a mathematical function used in the encryption and decryption process. A cryptographic algorithm works in combination with a key a word, number, or phrase to encrypt the plaintext.

The same plaintext encrypts to different cipher text with different keys. The security of encrypted data is entirely dependent on two things: the strength of the cryptographic algorithm and the secrecy of the key.

A cryptographic algorithm, plus all possible keys and all the protocols that make it work comprise a cryptosystem. PGP is a cryptosystem.

6.6.2 Symmetric Cryptography

Symmetric cryptography uses a single private key to both encrypt and decrypt data. Any party that has the key can use it to encrypt and decrypt data. They are also referred to as block ciphers.

Symmetric cryptography algorithms are typically fast and are suitable for processing large streams of data.

The disadvantage of symmetric cryptography is that it presumes two parties have agreed on a key and been able to exchange that key in a secure manner prior to communication. This is a significant challenge. Symmetric algorithms are usually mixed with public key algorithms to obtain a blend of security and speed.

6.6.3 Asymmetric, or Public Key, Cryptography

Public-key cryptography is also called asymmetric. It uses a secret key that must be kept from unauthorized users and a public key that can be made public to anyone. Both the public key and the private key are mathematically linked; data encrypted with the public key can be decrypted only by the private key, and data signed with the private key can only be verified with the public key.

The public key can be published to anyone. Both keys are unique to the communication session.

Public-key cryptographic algorithms use a fixed buffer size. Private-key cryptographic algorithms use a variable length buffer. Public-key algorithms cannot be used to chain data together into streams like private-key algorithms can. With private-key algorithms only a small block size can be processed, typically 8 or 16 bytes.

6.7 KEYS

A key is a value that works with a cryptographic algorithm to produce a specific ciphertext. Keys are basically really, really, really big numbers. Key size is measured in bits; the number representing a 1024-bit key is darn huge.

In public key cryptography, the bigger the key, the more secure the ciphertext. However, public key size and conventional cryptography's secret key size are totally unrelated. A conventional 80-bit key has the equivalent strength of a 1024-bit public key. A conventional 128-bit key is equivalent to a 3000-bit public key. Again, the bigger the key, the more secure, but the algorithms used for each type of cryptography are very different and thus comparison is like that of apples to oranges.

While the public and private keys are mathematically related, it's very difficult to derive the private key given only the public key; however, deriving the private key is always possible given enough time and computing power. This makes it very important to pick keys of the right size; large enough to be secure, but small enough to be applied fairly quickly. Additionally, you need to consider who might be trying to read your files, how determined they are, how much time they have, and what their resources might be.

Larger keys will be cryptographically secure for a longer period of time. If what you want to encrypt needs to be hidden formany years, you might want to use a very large key. Of course, who knows how long it will take to determine your key using tomorrow's faster, more efficient computers? There was a time when a 56-bit symmetric key was considered extremely safe. Keys are stored in encrypted form. PGP stores the keys in two files on your hard disk; one for public keys and one for private keys. These files are called keyrings. As you use PGP, you will typically add the public keys of your recipients to your public keyring. Your private keys are stored on your private keyring. If you lose your private keyring, you will be unable to decrypt any information encrypted to keys on that ring.

6.7.1 Key Management and Conventional Encryption

Public key cryptography

The problems of key distribution are solved by public key cryptography, the concept of which was introduced by Whitfield Diffie and Martin Hellman in 1975. (There is now evidence that the British Secret Service invented it a few years before Diffie and Hellman, but kept it amilitary secret and did nothing with it.)

Public key cryptography is an asymmetric scheme that uses a pair of keys for encryption: a public key, which encrypts data, and a corresponding private, or secret key for decryption. You publish your public key to the world while keeping your private key secret. Anyone with a copy of your public key can then encrypt information that only you can read. Even people you have never met. It is computationally infeasible to deduce the private key from the public key.

Anyone who has a public key can encrypt information but cannot decrypt it. Only the person who has the corresponding private key can decrypt the key.

Fig. 6.5: Public key encryption

The primary benefit of public key cryptography is that it allows people who have no preexisting security arrangement to exchange messages securely. The need for sender and receiver to share secret keys via some secure channel is eliminated; all communications involve only public keys, and no private key is ever transmitted or shared. Some examples of public-key cryptosystems are Elgamal (named for its inventor, Taher Elgamal), RSA (named for its inventors, Ron Rivest, Adi Shamir, and Leonard Adleman), Diffie-Hellman (named, you guessed it, for its inventors), and DSA, the Digital Signature Algorithm (invented by David Kravitz).

Because conventional cryptography was once the only available means for relaying secret information, the expense of secure channels and key distribution relegated its use only to those who could afford it, such as governments and large banks (or small children with secret decoder rings).

Public key encryption is the technological revolution that provides strong cryptography to the adult masses. Remember the courier with the locked briefcase handcuffed to his wrist? Public-key encryption puts him out of business (probably to his relief).

6.8 DIGITAL SIGNATURES

A digital signature is a code or verification used to uniquely identify you. By entering in certain information to validate yourself, the code or token is created, allowing it to be used instead of an actual signature.

A major benefit of public key cryptography is that it provides a method for employing digital signatures. Digital signatures enable the recipient of information to verify the authenticity of the information's origin, and also verify that the information is intact. Thus, public key digital signatures provide authentication and data integrity. A digital signature also provides non-repudiation, which means that it prevents the sender from claiming that he or she did not actually send the information. These features are every bit as fundamental to cryptography as privacy, if not more.

A digital signature serves the same purpose as a handwritten signature. However, a handwritten signature is easy to counterfeit. A digital signature is superior to a handwritten signature in that it is nearly impossible to counterfeit, plus it attests to the contents of the information as well as to the identity of the signer.

Some people tend to use signatures more than they use encryption. For example, you may not care if anyone knows that you just deposited $1000 in your account, but you do want to be darn sure it was the bank teller you were dealing with.

The basic manner in which digital signatures are created is illustrated in Figure 5.6. Instead of encrypting information using someone else's public key, you encrypt it with your private key. If the information can be decrypted with your public key, then it must have originated with you.

Fig. 6.6: Simple digital signatures

6.8.1 What are Digital ID's

Digital ID signature or certificate is an installed file resident on a computer validates who you are. Digital signatures are used by programs on the internet and local to the machines to confirm your identity to any third party concerned. Digital signatures have been confused with electronic signatures. Electronic signatures are scanned copies of a physical written signature.

6.8.2 When do We Need to Verify Identity

New ways of verification are being developed daily. Biometrics and other methods keep getting formulated and incorporated into the information technology industry. One interesting biometric authentication mechanism developed by a leading Japanese biometric company has found a way to get your DNA into a pen. You sign a document and it is digitally scanned. This document then can be scanned in the future to verify its authenticity. Identity should be verified when ever there is doubt of the 3rd party being whom they say they are or when there is personal information at risk. Personal information like credit card details and banking information should be kept safe using digital certification as one of the security layers. Some banking institutions require that a user verifies his/her identity by validating identification credentials using a digital certificate. Important e-mail can also use Digital signatures that verify that the e-mail is from the originating sender and that it has not been tampered with. On many occasions users are unsure if they are dealing with reputable suppliers of institutions. Digital certification gives the user a sense of legitimacy and formalizes the process. It ensure that the company that the user is dealing with has a registration with a trusted authority and that the transaction is guaranteed to be done with the intended parties.

6.8.3 Reasons for Using Digital Security

- It insures by means of verification and validation that the user is whom he/she claims to be. This is done by combine the users credential to the digital certificate and in turn this method uses one point of authentication.
- Digital certificates insure data Integrity giving the user piece of mind that the message or transaction has not been accidentally or maliciously altered. This is done cryptographically.
- Digital certificates ensure confidentiality and ensure that messages can only be read by authorized intended recipients.
- Digital certificates also verify date and time so that senders or recipients can not dispute if the message was actually sent or received.

The components that a digital signature comprise of.

1. **Your public key:** This is the part that any one can get a copy of and is part of the verification system.
2. **Your name and e-mail address:** This is necessary for contact information purposes and to enable the viewer to identify the details.
3. **Expiration date of the public key:** This part of the signature is used to set a shelf life and to ensure that in the event of prolonged abuse of a signature eventually the signature is reset.

Fig. 6.7(a)

4. **Name of the company:** This section identifies the company that the signature belongs too.
5. **Serial number of the Digital ID:** This part is a unique number that is bundled to the signature for tracking ad extra identification reasons.
6. **Digital signature of the CA (certification Authority):** This is a signature that is issued by the authority that issues the certificates.

User A is depicted above and has two keys a public key, this key is available to the public for download, and a private key, this key is not available to the public. All keys are used to lock the information in an encrypted mode. The same keys are required to decrypt the data.

Another user can encrypt the data using users A's Public Key. User A will use the Private Key to decrypt the message. Without user A's Private Key the data can not be decrypted. Figure B below depicts the encryption method and decryption method and witch keys are used.

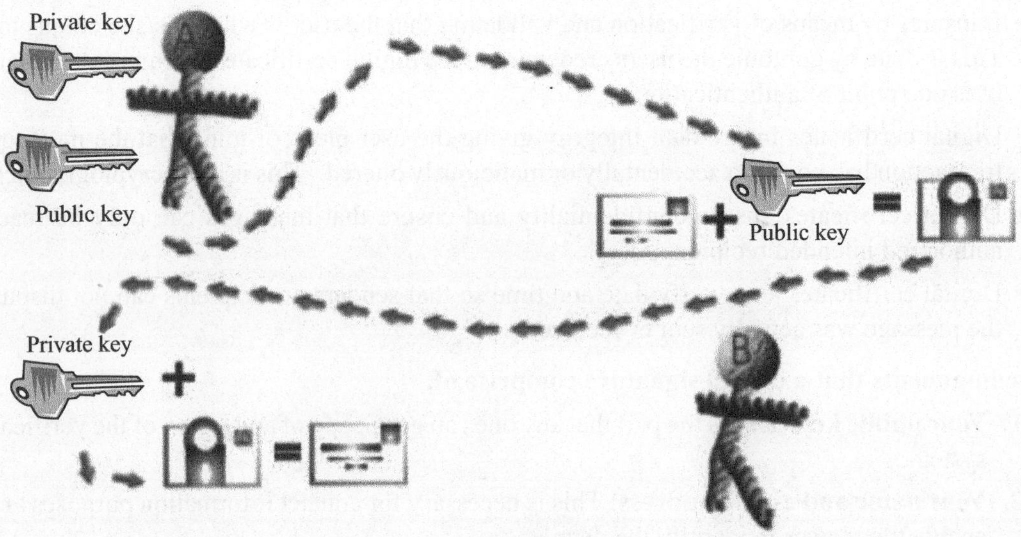

Fig. 6.7(b)

Digital signature can be used to make document e-mails and other data private. Big brother is out there and choosing a high encryption mechanism ensures that any one attempting to decrypt the data would find it unviable to attempt decryption.

User A's machine digests the data into a simple string of code after user A's software has encrypted the message digest with his private key. The result is the digital signature. User A's software then appends the digital signature to document. All of the data that was hashed has been signed. User A then passes the digitally signed document to user B.

First user B's software decrypts the signature, using User A's public key then changing it back into a message digest. After the decryption if it has decrypted the data to digest level then verifies that user A in fact did sign the data. To stop fraud certificate authorities have been introduced. Certificate authorities can sign User A's public key, ensuring that no one else uses Bobs information or impersonated his key.

If a user is uncertain of the digital signature it is possible to verify the digital signature with the certificate authority. Signatures can also be revoked if they are abused or if it is suspected that they are abused. When a digital signature is compromised the user that suspects that the certificate is compromised should report the incident to the certificate authority.

The process of checking the validity of digital signature.

- User A sends a signed document to User B.
- To verify the signature on the document, user B's application first uses the certificate authority's public key to check the signature on user A's certificate.
- Successful de-encryption of the certificate proves that the certificate authority created it.
- After the certificate is de-encrypted, user B's software can check if user A is in good standing with the certificate authority and that all of the certificate information concerning user A's identity has not been altered.
- User B's software then takes user A's public key from the certificate and uses it to check user A's signature. If user A's public key de-encrypts the signature successfully, then user B is assured that the signature was created using user A's private key, for the certificate authority has certified the matching public key.
- If the signature is found to be valid, then we know that an intruder didn't try to change the signed content.

6.8.4 The Importance of Private Key Revocation

At times there may be grounds for believing that a private key may have been compromised. This will then result in the key pair being revoked. When a digital signature is revoked the user that is requesting the revoke needs to be verified. If a key is wrongfully revoked legal action can follow.

Digital signatures deliver assurances in the role that the other party will keep their part of the bargain. Knowing the identity of the other party is one way of gaining that assurance. Keys used for digital signatures are very long series of bits, which can be represented as long series of alphanumeric characters. This makes digital signatures unfeasible for an individual to remember. They must consequently be stored in a method which is suitable, portable and protected. The most likely current technology to support such storage is a chip. Smart cards, bios chips, e-prom ships found in cable modems and other types of descrambles are all examples or primitive forms of digital signatures that act as away of identifying user. No form of identification to this date is used more than digital signature to verify the existence of a user and confirmation of credential over the internet. Digital signatures in some form or other are her to stay.

6.8.5 Advantages and Disadvantages of Digital Signatures

Just as with any technology, there will be plus and minuses. This is the way it is with anything, whether it is technology related or not. The advantages of using digital signatures include:

- **Imposter prevention:** By using digital signatures you are eliminating the possibility of committing fraud by an imposter signing the document. Since the digital signature cannot be altered, this makes forging the signature impossible.
- **Message integrity:** By having a digital signature you are in fact proving the document to be valid. You are assuring the recipient that the document is free from forgery or false information.
- **Legal requirements:** Using a digital signature satisfies some type of legal requirement for the document in question. A digital signature takes care of any formal legal aspect of executing the document.

The disadvantages of using digital signatures involve the primary avenue for any business: money. This is because the business may have to spend more money than usual to work with digital signatures including buying certificates from certification authorities and getting the verification software.

6.8.6 Uses of Digital Signatures

As organizations move away from paper documents with ink signatures or authenticity stamps, digital signatures can provide added assurances of the evidence to provenance, identity, and status of an electronic document as well as acknowledging informed consent and approval by a signatory. The United States Government Printing Office (GPO) publishes electronic versions of the budget, public and private laws, and congressional bills with digital signatures. Universities including Penn State, University of Chicago, and Stanford are publishing electronic student transcripts with digital signatures.

Below are some common reasons for applying a digital signature to communications:

Authentication

Although messages may often include information about the entity sending a message, that information may not be accurate. Digital signatures can be used to authenticate the source of messages. When ownership of a digital signature secret key is bound to a specific user, a valid signature shows that the message was sent by that user. The importance of high confidence in sender authenticity is especially obvious in a financial context. For example, suppose a bank's branch office sends instructions to the central office requesting a change in the balance of an account. If the central office is not convinced that such a message is truly sent from an authorized source, acting on such a request could be a grave mistake.

Integrity

In many scenarios, the sender and receiver of a message may have a need for confidence that the message has not been altered during transmission. Although encryption hides the contents of a message, it may be possible to change an encrypted message without understanding it. (Some encryption algorithms, known as nonmalleable ones, prevent this, but others do not.) However, if a message is digitally signed, any change in the message after signature will invalidate the signature. Furthermore, there is no efficient way to modify a message and its signature to produce a new message with a valid signature, because this is still considered to be computationally infeasible by most cryptographic hash functions (see collision resistance).

Non-repudiation

Non-repudiation, or more specifically non-repudiation of origin, is an important aspect of digital signatures. By this property an entity that has signed some information cannot at a later time deny having signed it. Similarly, access to the public key only does not enable a fraudulent party to fake a valid signature. This is in contrast to symmetric systems, where both sender and receiver share the same secret key, and thus in a dispute a third party cannot determine which entity was the true source of the information.

6.8.7 Requirements for Digital Signatures

To establish these conditions, the content creator must digitally sign the content by using a signature that satisfies the following criteria:

- The digital signature is valid. A CA that is trusted by the operating system must sign the digital certificate on which the digital signature is based.
- The certificate that is associated with the digital signature is not expired.
- The signing person or organization (known as the publisher) is trusted by the recipient.
- The certificate associated with the digital signature is issued to the signing publisher by a reputable CA.

Microsoft Office Word 2007, Microsoft Office Excel 2007, and Microsoft Office PowerPoint 2007 detect these criteria for you and warn you if there appears to be a problem with the digital signature. Information about problematic certificates is easily viewed in a certificate task pane that appears in the 2007 Microsoft Office system application. 2007 Office system applications let you add multiple digital signatures to the same document.

6.8.8 How It Works

Assume you were going to send the draft of your business data to your close business partner in another place. You want to give your partner the assurance that it was unchanged from what you sent and that it is really from you.

The sender

You copy-and-paste the data into an e-mail note.

Using special software, you obtain a message hash (mathematical summary) of the data.

You then use a private key that you have previously obtained from a public-private key authority to encrypt the hash.

The encrypted hash becomes your digital signature of the message which will be different each time you send a message.

At the other end, your business partner receives the message.

The-receiver

To make sure it's intact and from you, your business partner makes a hash of the received message.

He then uses your public key to decrypt the message hash or summary.

If the hashes match, the received message is valid.

How A digital certificate looks like

-------BEGIN SIGNATURE------

IQB1AwUBMVSiA5QYCuMfgNYjAQFAKgL/

ZkBfbeNEsbthba4BlrcnjaqbcKgNv+a5kr4537y8RCd+RHm

75yYh5xxA1ojELwNhhb7cltrp2V7LlOnAelws4S87UX80cL

BtBcN6AACf11qymC2h+Rb2j5SSU+rmXWru+=QFMx

-------END SIGNATURE------

SUMMARY

Cryptography is the science of using mathematics to encrypt and decrypt data. Cryptography enables you to store sensitive information or transmit it across insecure networks (like the Internet) so that it cannot be read by anyone except the intended recipient.

Cryptography is a study of how to scramble data so that:

1. Anyone who steals it will be unable to scramble it.
2. Your intended recipients will be able to unscramble it with ease.

EXERCISE

1. What is encryption techniques?
2. What are keys, write down all the type of keys available for encryption technique?
3. What do you mean by DES?
4. What is triple encryption?
5. What is secret key encryption?
6. What do you mean by asymmetric encryption?
7. What is public and private key encription?
8. What is digital signature?
9. What are the advantages of digital signature.

CHAPTER
7

Virtual Private Network

7.1 INTRODUCTION

A virtual private network (VPN) is the extension of a private network that encompasses links across shared or public networks like the Internet. A VPN enables you to send data between two computers across a shared or public internetwork in a manner that emulates the properties of a point-to-point private link. The act of configuring and creating a virtual private network is known as virtual private networking.

To emulate a point-to-point link, data is encapsulated, or wrapped, with a header that provides routing information allowing it to traverse the shared or public transit internetwork to reach its endpoint. To emulate a private link, the data being sent is encrypted for confidentiality. Packets that

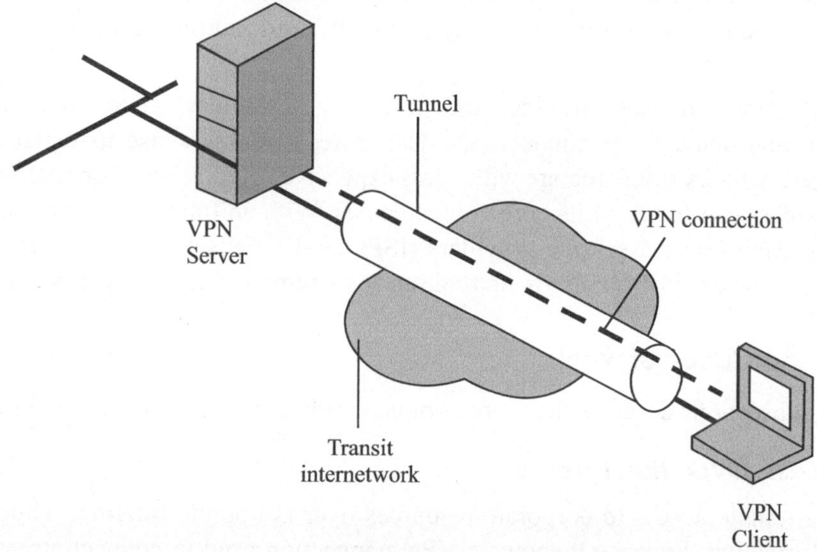

Fig. 7.1: Virtual Private Network Connection

are intercepted on the shared or public network are indecipherable without the encryption keys. The portion of the connection in which the private data is encapsulated is known as the tunnel. The portion of the connection in which the private data is encrypted is known as the virtual private network (VPN) connection.

VPN connections allow users working at home or on the road to connect in a secure fashion to a remote corporate server using the routing infrastructure provided by a public internetwork (such as the Internet). From the user's perspective, the VPN connection is a point-to-point connection between the user's computer and a corporate server. The nature of the intermediate internetwork is irrelevant to the user because it appears as if the data is being sent over a dedicated private link.

VPN technology also allows a corporation to connect to branch offices or to other companies over a public internetwork (such as the Internet), while maintaining secure communications. The VPN connection across the Internet logically operates as a wide area network (WAN) link between the sites.

In both of these cases, the secure connection across the internetwork appears to the user as a private network communication despite the fact that this communication occurs over a public internetwork hence the name virtual private network.

VPN technology is designed to address issues surrounding the current business trend toward increased telecommuting and widely distributed global operations, where workers must be able to connect to central resources and must be able to communicate with each other.

To provide employees with the ability to connect to corporate computing resources, regardless of their location, a corporation must deploy a scalable remote access solution. Typically, corporations choose either an MIS department solution, where an internal information systems department is charged with buying, installing, and maintaining corporate modem pools and a private network infrastructure; or they choose a value-added network (VAN) solution, where they pay an outsourced company to buy, install, and maintain modem pools and a telecommunication infrastructure.

Neither of these solutions provides the necessary scalability, in terms of cost, flexible administration, and demand for connections. Therefore, it makes sense to replace the modem pools and private network infrastructure with a less expensive solution based on Internet technology so that the business can focus on its core competencies. With an Internet solution, a few Internet connections through Internet service providers (ISPs) and VPN server computers can serve the remote networking needs of hundreds or thousands of remote clients and branch offices.

7.1.1 Common Uses of VPNs

The next few subsections describe the more common VPN configurations in more detail.

Remote Access Over the Internet

VPNs provide remote access to corporate resources over the public Internet, while maintaining privacy of information. Figure 6.9 shows a VPN connection used to connect a remote user to a corporate intranet.

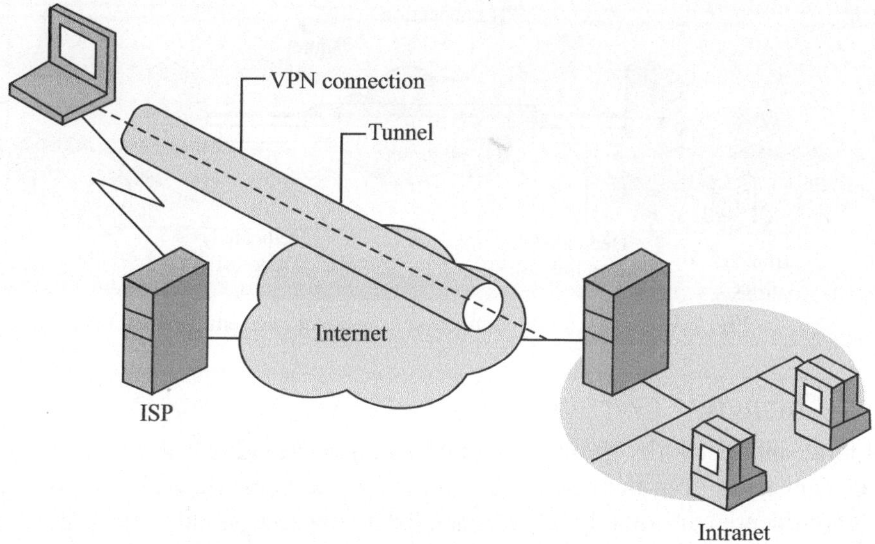

Fig. 7.2: Using a VPN connection to connect a remote client to a private intranet

Rather than making a long distance (or 1-800) call to a corporate or outsourced network access server (NAS), the user calls a local ISP. Using the connection to the local ISP, the VPN software creates a virtual private network between the dial-up user and the corporate VPN server across the Internet.

Connecting Networks Over the Internet

There are two methods for using VPNs to connect local area networks at remote sites:

- **Using dedicated lines to connect a branch office to a corporate LAN**. Rather than using an expensive long-haul dedicated circuit between the branch office and the corporate hub, both the branch office and the corporate hub routers can use a local dedicated circuit and local ISP to connect to the Internet. The VPN software uses the local ISP connections and the Internet to create a virtual private network between the branch office router and corporate hub router.
- **Using a dial-up line to connect a branch office to a corporate LAN.** Rather than having a router at the branch office make a long distance (or 1-800) call to a corporate or outsourced NAS, the router at the branch office can call the local ISP. The VPN software uses the connection to the local ISP to create a VPN between the branch office router and the corporate hub router across the Internet.

In both cases, the facilities that connect the branch office and corporate offices to the Internet are local. The corporate hub router that acts as a VPN server must be connected to a local ISP with a dedicated line. This VPN server must be listening 24 hours a day for incoming VPN traffic.

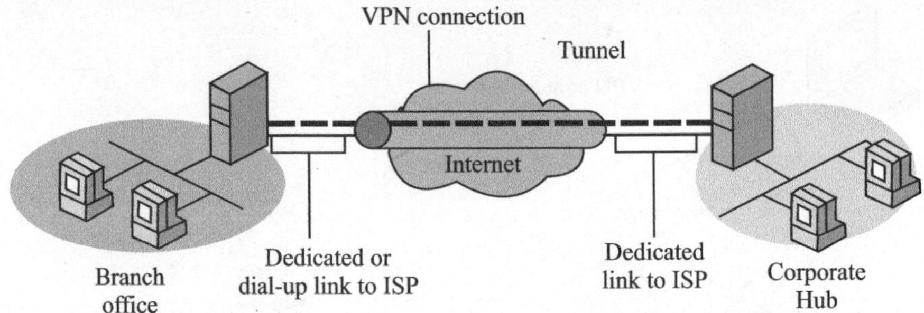

Fig. 7.3: Using a VPN connection to connect two remote sites

Connecting Computers over an Intranet

In some corporate internetworks, the departmental data is so sensitive that the department's LAN is physically disconnected from the rest of the corporate internetwork. Although this protects the department's confidential information, it creates information accessibility problems for those users not physically connected to the separate LAN.

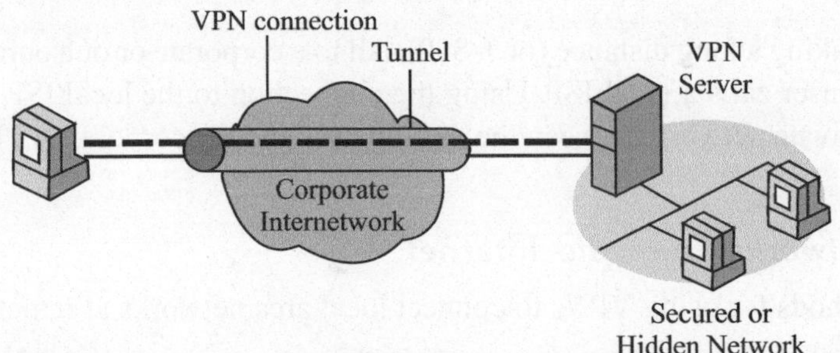

Fig. 7.4: Using a VPN connection to connect to a secured or hidden network

VPNs allow the department's LAN to be physically connected to the corporate internetwork but separated by a VPN server. The VPN server is not acting as a router between the corporate internetwork and the department LAN. A router would connect the two networks, allowing everyone access to the sensitive LAN. By using a VPN, the network administrator can ensure that only those users on the corporate internetwork who have appropriate credentials (based on a need-to-know policy within the company) can establish a VPN with the VPN server and gain access to the protected resources of the department. Additionally, all communication across the VPN can be encrypted for data confidentiality. Those users who do not have the proper credentials cannot view the department LAN.

7.1.2 Basic VPN Requirements

Typically, when deploying a remote networking solution, an enterprise needs to facilitate controlled access to corporate resources and information. The solution must allow roaming or remote clients to connect to LAN resources, and the solution must allow remote offices to connect to each other to share resources and information (router-to-router connections). In addition, the solution must ensure the privacy and integrity of data as it traverses the Internet. The same concerns apply in the case of sensitive data traversing a corporate internetwork.

Therefore, a VPN solution should provide at least all of the following:

- **User Authentication.** The solution must verify the VPN client's identity and restrict VPN access to authorized users only. It must also provide audit and accounting records to show who accessed what information and when.
- **Address Management.** The solution must assign a VPN client's address on the intranet and ensure that private addresses are kept private.
- **Data Encryption.** Data carried on the public network must be rendered unreadable to unauthorized clients on the network.
- **Key Management.** The solution must generate and refresh encryption keys for the client and the server.
- **Multiprotocol Support.** The solution must handle common protocols used in the public network. These include IP, Internetwork Packet Exchange (IPX), and so on.

An Internet VPN solution based on the Point-to-Point Tunneling Protocol (PPTP) or Layer Two Tunneling Protocol (L2TP) meets all of these basic requirements and takes advantage of the broad availability of the Internet. Other solutions, including Internet Protocol Security (IPSec), meet only some of these requirements, but remain useful for specific situations.

7.2 NEED OF VPN

As internal corporate networks grow and telecommuting/remote offices become more commonplace, companies are turning to virtual private networks (VPNs) to provide access to internal corporate resources. A VPN is a collection of private data and voice networks utilizing the public communications infrastructure. VPNs operate on the premise of tunnels, which protect the data inside from external threats, utilizing predetermined parameters.

The goal of a VPN is to offer the same services to both internal and authorized external personnel, while at the same time minimizing overhead costs. The need for point-to-point leased lines can be virtually eliminated when a VPN is implemented properly.

There are numerous vendors that offer a variety of VPN capable equipment. Several offer a variety of routers, firewalls, remote access clients and concentrators that support very scalable VPN implementations. IP Security (IPSec) is the most dominant of all secure VPN technologies and is a standards-based method of providing integrity to data transmitted over IP. IPSec provides layer 3 encryption of data packets and utilizes various checks and balances to ensure data integrity. Key management and security associations, the IPSec parameters between devices, are negotiated utilizing the Internet key exchange.

The Internet offers a wide variety of opportunities and resources, but they do not come without inherent risks. These risks, as well as the need to protect sensitive information, are what drives the need for VPNs. The following three items may explain the need of VPN.

1. **Data privacy:** Traffic traversing the Internet is unencrypted and can be viewed by unauthorized parties between the source and destination. This may be acceptable in many instances, but there are times when confidential information may be compromised.
2. **Data integrity:** While it may not be detrimental if unauthorized persons or entities could read your general e-mail, it could be problematic if they could access and possibly modify more sensitive documents, bank transactions, etc.
3. **Identity theft:** Hackers are becoming more creative in their techniques, and identity theft is becoming more prevalent. No secure data such as credit card numbers.

Social Security numbers and bank account numbers may give people the information they need to take on your identity and, in turn, gain access to your confidential information. The solution needs to be planned and implemented diligently. Defining exactly what types of information need to be secured is the first step. Certain traffic, such as remote file and mail requests, may need to access the corporate Internet, whereas World Wide Web (WWW) requests do not.

VPNs reference a series of permit-and deny statements to determine which traffic should and should not traverse the VPN. If traffic is marked as interesting, it follows the IPSec encapsulation and encryption process and is forwarded to the other end of the tunnel for validation, de-encapsulation and decryption. Traffic that is not interesting will be routed in clear text, based on current implemented policies.

Another popular implementation is the use of remote access clients. These clients have software installed on PCs, laptops or PDAs and are able to securely access internal resources. Typically the software is very inexpensive and is a more-than-adequate solution for remote salespersons, managers, IT staff and executives.

Network and information security are becoming increasingly more important in corporate environments. VPNs offer another level of defense against unauthorized access to confidential information while still maintaining flexibility and scalability.

There are still instances in which point to- point links make sense and are necessary, but in many cases, having a virtual point-to-point network is both cost effective and secure.

7.2.1 How does VPN work

Virtual private networks (VPN) are a secure way for businesses and companies to communicate via the Internet. They assure the tightest of security and are not open to traffic from the public. Remote users and multiple sites of users can be connected through a direct private pathway. The installation of a VPN alters the need for a WAN (wide area network), simplifies the companies' network needs, provides extended telecommute opportunities and opens up the possibility for global networking. Building a secure VPN requires reliability, scalability and management of the network and policies designed to run the network. VPN's can be managed by the company or contracted to a VPN provider.

The world has changed a lot in the last couple of decades. Instead of simply dealing with local or regional concerns, many businesses now have to think about global markets and logistics. Many companies have facilities spread out across the country or around the world, and there is one thing that all of them need: A way to maintain fast, secure and reliable communications wherever their offices are.

Until fairly recently, this has meant the use of **leased lines** to maintain a **wide area network** (WAN). Leased lines, ranging from ISDN (integrated services digital network, 128 Kbps) to OC3 (Optical Carrier-3, 155 Mbps) fiber, provided a company with a way to expand its private network beyond its immediate geographic area. A WAN had obvious advantages over a public network like the Internet when it came to reliability, performance and security. But maintaining a WAN, particularly when using leased lines, can become quite expensive and often rises in cost as the distance between the offices increases.

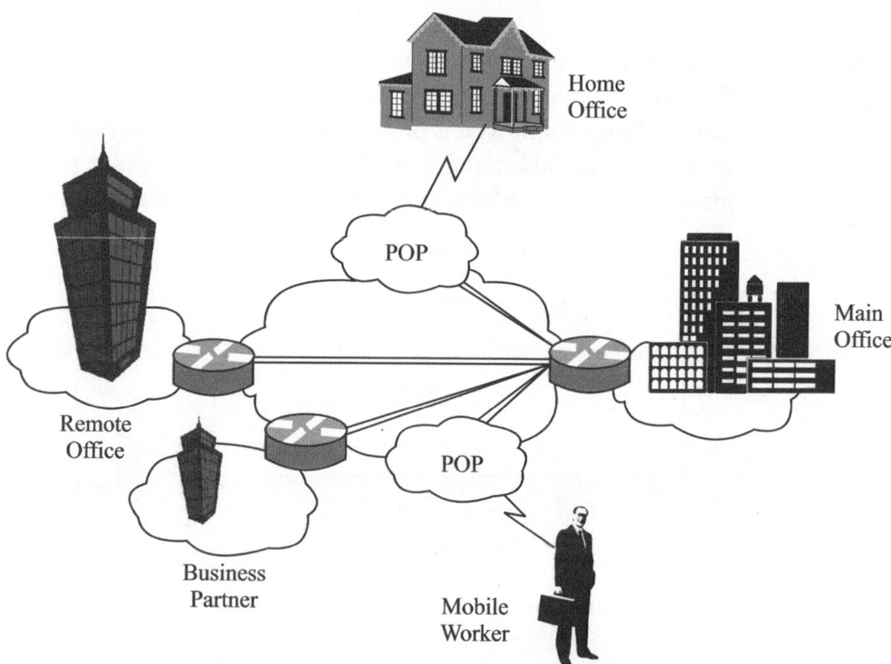

Fig. 7.5: Image courtesy Cisco Systems, Inc.

As the popularity of the Internet grew, businesses turned to it as a means of extending their own networks. First came intranets, which are password-protected sites designed for use only by company employees. Now, many companies are creating their own **VPN (virtual private network)** to accommodate the needs of remote employees and distant offices.

A typical VPN might have a main LAN at the corporate headquarters of a company, other LANs at remote offices or facilities and individual users connecting from out in the field.

Basically, a VPN is a private network that uses a public network (usually the Internet) to connect remote sites or users together. Instead of using a dedicated, real-world connection such as leased line, a VPN uses "virtual" connections routed through the Internet from the company's private network to the remote site or employee. In this article, you will gain a fundamental understanding of VPNs, and learn about basic VPN components, technologies,tunneling and security.

7.3 USE OF TUNNELING WITH VPN

Tunneling is the transmission of data intended for use only within a private, usually corporate network through a public network in such a way that the routing nodes in the public network are unaware that the transmission is part of a private network. Tunneling is generally done by encapsulating the private network data and protocol information within the public network transmission units so that the private network protocol information appears to the public network as data. Tunneling allows the use of the Internet, which is a public network, to convey data on behalf of a private network

Tunneling is a method of using an internetwork infrastructure to transfer data for one network over another network. The data to be transferred (or payload) can be the frames (or packets) of another protocol. Instead of sending a frame as it is produced by the originating node, the tunneling protocol encapsulates the frame in an additional header. The additional header provides routing information so that the encapsulated payload can traverse the intermediate internetwork.

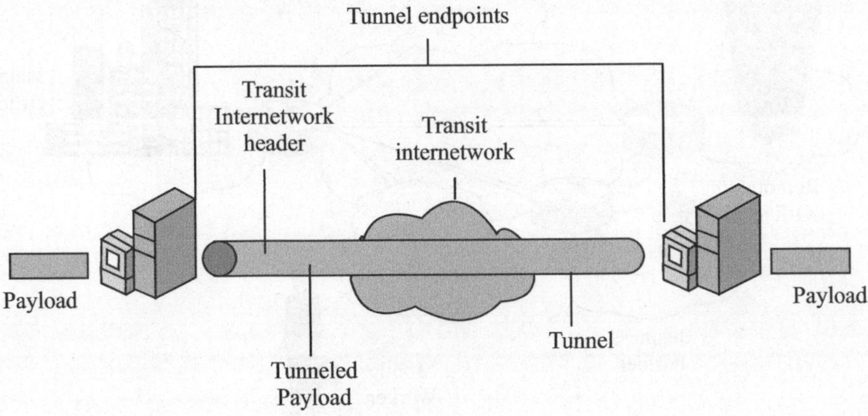

Fig. 7.6: Tunneling

The encapsulated packets are then routed between tunnel endpoints over the internetwork. The logical path through which the encapsulated packets travel through the internetwork is called a tunnel. Once the encapsulated frames reach their destination on the internetwork, the frame is decapsulated and forwarded to its final destination. Tunneling includes this entire process (encapsulation, transmission, and decapsulation of packets).

The transit internetwork can be any internetwork-the Internet is a public internetwork and is the most widely known real world example. There are many examples of tunnels that are carried over corporate internetworks. And while the Internet provides one of the most pervasive and cost-effective internetworks, references to the Internet in this paper can be replaced by any other public or private internetwork that acts as a transit internetwork.

Tunneling technologies have been in existence for some time. Some examples of mature technologies include:

- **SNA tunneling over IP internetworks:** When System Network Architecture (SNA) traffic is sent across a corporate IP internetwork, the SNA frame is encapsulated in a UDP and IP header.
- **IPX tunneling for Novell NetWare over IP internetworks:** When an IPX packet is sent to a NetWare server or IPX router, the server or the router wraps the IPX packet in a UDP and IP header, and then sends it across an IP internetwork. The destination IP-to-IPX router removes the UDP and IP header and forwards the packet to the IPX destination.

New tunneling technologies have been introduced in recent years. These newer technologies-which are the primary focus of this paper-include:

- Point-to-Point Tunneling Protocol (PPTP). PPTP allows IP, IPX, or NetBEUI traffic to be encrypted, and then encapsulated in an IP header to be sent across a corporate IP internetwork or a public IP internetwork such as the Internet.
- Layer Two Tunneling Protocol (L2TP). L2TP allows IP, IPX, or NetBEUI traffic to be encrypted, and then sent over any medium that supports point-to-point datagram delivery, such as IP, X.25, Frame Relay, or ATM.
- IPSec tunnel mode. IPSec tunnel mode allows IP packets to be encrypted, and then encapsulated in an IP header to be sent across a corporate IP internetwork or a public IP internetwork such as the Internet.

7.3.1 Virtual Network Types

You can create virtual networks on the server running Hyper-V to define various networking topologies for virtual machines and the virtualization server. Using Virtual Network Manager (accessed from Hyper-V Manager), you have three different types of virtual networks to choose from.

- **External virtual networks:** Use this type when you want to allow virtual machines to communicate with externally located servers and the management operating system (sometimes referred to as the parent partition). This type also allows virtual machines on the same physical server to communicate with each other.
- **Internal virtual networks:** Use this type when you want to allow communication between virtual machines on the same physical server and virtual machines and the management operating system. An internal virtual network is a virtual network that is not bound to a physical network adapter. It is commonly used to build a test environment where you need to connect to the virtual machines from the management operating system.
- **Private virtual networks:** Use this type when you want to allow communication only between virtual machines on the same physical server. A private virtual network is a virtual network without a virtual network adapter in the management operating system. Private virtual networks are commonly used when you want to isolate virtual machines from network traffic in the management operating system and in the external networks.

You can use VPN connections whenever you need a secure point-to-point connection to connect users or networks. Typical VPN connections are either Internet-based or intranet-based. This section covers:

- Internet-based VPNs
- Intranet-based VPNs

7.3.2 Internet-based VPNs

By using an Internet-based VPN connection, you can avoid long-distance and 1-800 telephone charges while taking advantage of the global availability of the Internet.

Remote access over the Internet

Rather than making a long distance or 1-800 call to a corporate or outsourced network access server (NAS), a remote access client can call a local ISP. By using the established physical connection to the local ISP, the remote access client initiates a VPN connection across the Internet to the organization's VPN server. Once the VPN connection is created, the remote access client can access the resources of the private intranet. The following illustration shows remote access over the Internet.

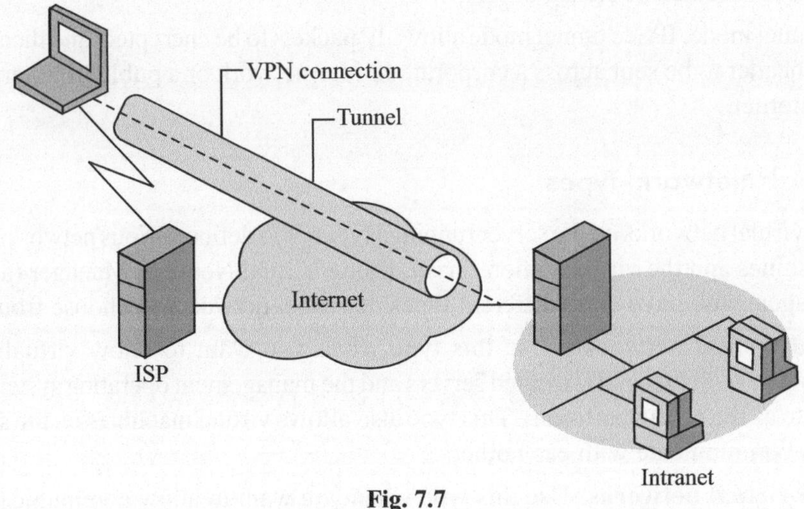

Fig. 7.7

For more information on deploying remote access VPN connections across the Internet, see **Deploying VPNs for Remote Access**. For an example implementation of a remote access VPN connection across the Internet, see Virtual Private Network Implementation Examples.

Connecting networks over the Internet

When networks are connected over the Internet, a router forwards packets to another router across a VPN connection. This is known as a router-to-router VPN connection. To the routers, the VPN operates as a data-link layer link.

The following illustration shows connecting networks over the Internet.

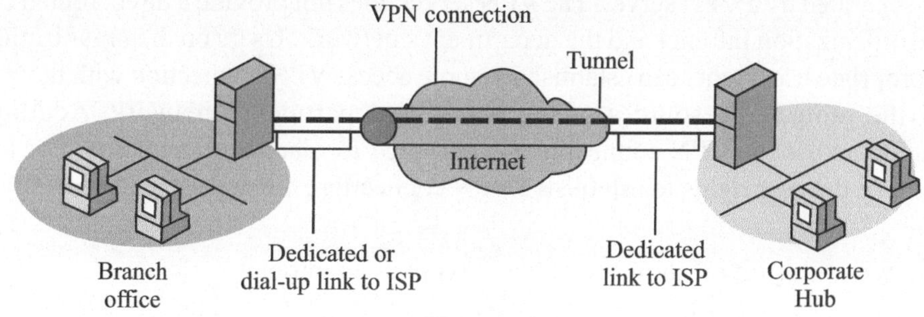

Fig. 7.8

Using dedicated WAN links

Rather than using an expensive long-distance dedicated WAN link between branch offices, the branch office routers are connected to the Internet by using local dedicated WAN links to a local ISP. A router-to-router VPN connection is then initiated by either router across the Internet. Once connected, routers can forward directed or routing protocol traffic to each other by using the VPN connection.

Using dial-up WAN links

Rather than making a long distance or 1-800 call to a corporate or outsourced NAS, a branch office router can call a local ISP. By using the established connection to the local ISP, a router-to-router VPN connection is initiated by the branch office router to the corporate office router across the Internet. The corporate office router acts as a VPN server and must be connected to a local ISP by using a dedicated WAN link.

It is possible to have both the corporate office and the branch office connected to the Internet by using a dial-up WAN link. However, this is only feasible if the ISP supports demand-dialing routing to customers--the ISP calls the customer router when an IP datagram is to be delivered to the customer. Demand-dial routing to customers is not widely supported by ISPs.

For more information on deploying router-to-router VPN connections across the Internet, see **Deploying Router-to-Router VPNs**. For an example implementation of router-to-router VPN connections across the Internet, see Virtual Private Network Implementation Examples.

7.3.3 Intranet-based VPNs

The intranet-based VPN connection takes advantage of IP connectivity on an organization intranet.

Remote access over an intranet

On some organization intranets, the data of a department, such as a human resources department, is so sensitive that the department's network is physically disconnected from the rest of the organization's intranet. While this protects the department's data, it creates information accessibility problems for those users who are not physically connected to the separate network.

With a VPN connection, the department's network is physically connected to the organization intranet but separated by a VPN server. The VPN server does not provide a direct routed connection between the organization intranet and the department's network. Users on the organization intranet with the appropriate user rights can establish a remote access VPN connection with the VPN server and access the protected resources of the sensitive department's network. Additionally, all communication across the VPN connection is encrypted for data confidentiality. For those users who do not have the user rights to establish a VPN connection, the department's network is hidden from view.

The following illustration shows remote access over an intranet.

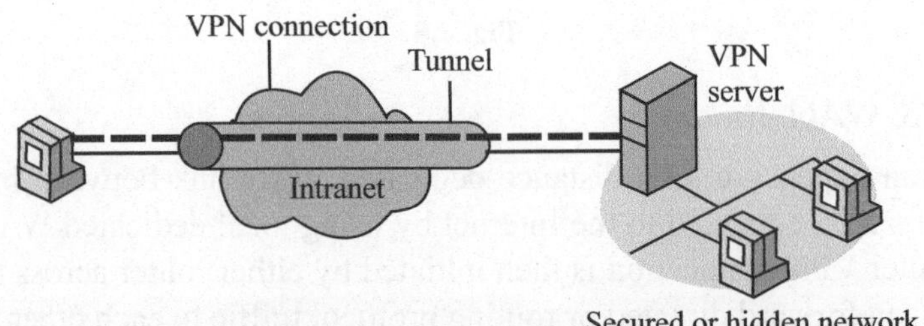

Fig. 7.9

For more information on deploying remote access VPN connections across an intranet, see Deploying VPNs for Remote Access.

Connecting networks over an intranet

You can also connect two networks over an intranet by using a router-to-router VPN connection. Organizations with departments in separate locations, whose data is highly sensitive, may use a router-to-router VPN connection to communicate with each other.

For example, the finance department might need to communicate with the human resources department to exchange payroll information. The finance department and the human resources department are connected to the common intranet with computers that can act as VPN routers. Once the VPN connection is established, users on computers on either network can exchange sensitive data across the corporate intranet.

The following illustration shows connecting networks over an intranet.

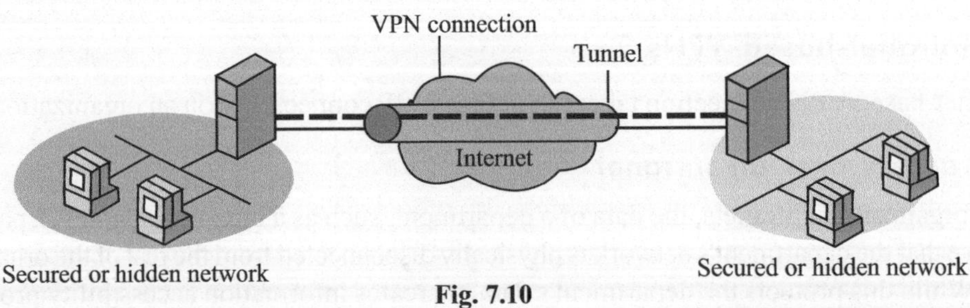

Fig. 7.10

For more information on deploying router-to-router VPN connections across an intranet, see Deploying Router-to-Router VPNs.

Why should I use VPN? Nowadays most corporate offices operate through a computer network. Most offices also use the Internet, whether for research, e-mail or other communications. Although network firewalls prevent most attacks from outsiders seeking to breach into the network using the Internet, they also prevent remote users to access essential data. That's where VPN comes in. By ensuring that only properly configured and authenticated users can access network data, and that this data is secure because encrypted, companies can implement mobile network access and telecommuting from any Internet-enabled location.

7.4 AUTHENTICATION-MECHANISM (VPN)

VPN involves two parts: the protected or "inside" network that provides physical security and administrative security sufficing to protect transmission (sometimes it is not always the case), and a less trustworthy or "outside" network or segment (the internet is the biggest "jungle"). Generally, a Firewall sits between a remote user's workstation or Client and the host Network or Server . As the user's client establishes the communication with the firewall, the client may pass Authentication data to an authentication service inside the perimeter. A known trusted person, sometimes only when using trusted devices, can be provided with appropriate security privileges to access resources not available to general users.

Many VPN client programs can be configured to require that all IP traffic must pass through the tunnel while the VPN is active, for better security. From the user's perspective, this means that while the VPN client is active, all access outside their employer's secure network must pass through the same firewall as would be the case while physically connected to the office ethernet. This reduces the risk that an attacker might gain access to the secured network by attacking the employee's laptop: to other computers on the employee's home network, or on the public internet, it is as though the machine running the VPN client simply does not exist. Such security is important because other computers local to the network on which the client computer is operating may be untrusted or partially trusted. Even with a home network that is protected from the outside internet by a firewall, people who share a home may be simultaneously working for different employers over their respective **VPN** connections from the shared home network. Each employer would therefore want to ensure their proprietary data is kept secure, even if another computer in the local network gets infected with Malware . And if a travelling employee uses a VPN client from a Wi-Fi access point in a public place, such security is even more important. However, the use of IPX/SPX is one way users might still be able to access local resources.

7.4.1 VPN Authentication - Secure Remote Access with eToken

Virtual Private Networks (VPNs) have changed the way people do business. Employees and business partners can now access sensitive business resources through the internet anytime, anywhere. But how can organizations be sure that the users gaining access are indeed who they claim to be?

VPNs ensure privacy by providing a private tunnel through the Internet for remote access to the network. For full security, your VPN must be enhanced with a reliable user authentication mechanism, securing the end points of the VPN.

User name and password authentication is not enough - this method is weak and highly susceptible to hacking, cracking, keyloggers, and other attacks. It only takes one compromised password for your organization to lose control over who gains network access. Strong user authentication with a VPN provides true secure remote access for today's world.

7.4.2 eToken Provides the Best Secure Access to Your VPN

Together with our world class solution partners, eToken provides a highly robust and secure VPN solution, enabling:

- Strong user VPN authentication using varied methods, including certificates and one-time passwords
- Secure access from any platform, including unparalleled support for certificate-based access on Windows, Linux, and Mac OS platforms
- Rapid and easy deployment with Token Management System (TMS): a single system managing the entire solution

7.5 FOUR TYPES OF VPN SECURE DIALOG

The most important part of a VPN solution is security. The very nature of VPNs putting private data on public networks raises concerns about potential threats to that data and the impact of data loss. A Virtual Private Network must address all types of security threats by providing security services in the areas of:

7.5.1 Authentication (Access Control)

Authentication is the process of ensuring that a user or system is who the user claims to be. There are many types of authentication mechanisms, but these mechanisms all work off of one or more of the following principles: something you know (a login name, a password), something you have (a token, a card key), something you are (fingerprint, retinal scan). Weak authentication makes use of one of these components, usually a simple login/password sequence. Strong authentication combines at least two authentication components from different areas.

7.5.2 Presentation (Privacy /Encryption)

Encryption is based on two components: an algorithm and a key. A cryptographic algorithm is a mathematical function that combines data with the string of digits contained in a key to produce encrypted text. There are several major types of encryption of varying degrees of complexity, as measured by lengths (bits) of cryptographic keys. Examples: Advanced Encryption Standard (AES), RSA, Elliptic Curve Cryptosystems (ECC).

7.5.3 Transportation (Data Integrity)

The modification of data packets in a network is an attack on data integrity. Message authentication is the procedure used to verify that received messages come from the alleged source and have not been altered.

7.5.4 Non repudiation (Correct Message Reception)

Non-repudiation is a means to verify that an electronic message has been sent and received by the specified parties. This protects both parties to ensure that neither the sender nor the recipient can later claim the transaction did not take place. This is vital not only when dealing with contracts, but also for online sales of digital goods such as music.

7.6 SECURITY CONCERN IN VPN

A firewall provides a strong barrier between your private network and internet. You can set firewalls to restrict the number of open ports, what type of packets are passed through and which protocols are allowed through.

While the potential savings and employee productivity increases that come with a remote-access VPN is significant and attractive to business, advance consideration must be given to the initial efforts required to plan, implement and monitor the technology. These considerations should be documented and addressed within security policy and additionally it is recommended by cisco that security policies be in place prior to be deployment of any security technology and also supporting the implementation of security policy to address VPN. It is important to note that while the VPN connection offers secure connectivity between the client PC and the corporate n/w it does not offer personal security features to the client, or protect it from outside attack from sources such as internet.

The VPN connection is in place to provide data confidentiality and integrity as well as authentication services. To reduce exposure to the corporate network, VPN users should be prevented from opening a VPN session to the corporate office, and leaving the connection established. This is of particular concern to remote users with broadband internet access due to the always on nature of the connection.

Security policy should address the VPN session connect time of the VPN clients and require that a session be terminated after a prescribed period of idle time has elapsed.

VPNs serve as gateways into corporate infrastructure and as such, security is a critical component of any SSL VPN offering. So important are the security-related capabilities of SSL VPN products that the differences in the security features set across products often determine which SSL VPN an enterprise will choose to deploy.

VPN security falls into three categories:

1. **Authentication and Authorization:** Users gain access to valuable information and systems through the SSL VPN. Because of this, it is critical to ensure that only authorized users access resources through the SSL VPN and that individual users access only those resources that they are supposed to access.

2. **Endpoint Security:** Endpoint security is sometimes known as Client-Side Security or Browser-Side Security. It refers to technology implemented to prevent any security-related problems occurring on devices used to access resources via the SSL VPN. It is important to realize that as opposed to earlier remote-access technologies, SSL VPN technology allows access from machines not known to be secure and as such, the endpoint concerns are different from the endpoint issues present in older remote-access scenarios.
3. **Server-Side Security:** Server-Side security, sometimes known as Network Security, refers to protecting internal corporate resources including the SSL VPN server itself from falling victim to any form of compromise.

Throughout our detailed review of these areas, it is important to keep in mind that SSL VPN products differ widely on how security is implemented. Each product does not necessarily offer all the features discussed, and due to product design and capability differences, some of the security issues may not even be pertinent when certain products are deployed. One should also be aware that some of the security functions described below are often implemented through the integration of third-party products with the core SSL VPN offering sometimes by the SSL VPN vendor and sometimes by the implementer. In any case, the remainder of this chapter describes the security concerns associated with SSL VPN technology and some approaches to addressing them.

Authentication is generally required to access secure data or enter a secure area. The requestor for access or entry shall authenticate himself based on proving authentically his identity by means of

- What are requestor individually knows as a secret, such as a password or a Personal Identification Number (PIN), or
- What the requesting owner uniquely has, such as a passport or an ID-card, or
- What the requesting bearer individually is, such as biometric data, like a fingerprint or the face geometry.

Two-factor authentication means using any independent two of these authentication methods (password + PIN) to increase the assurance that the bearer has been authorized to access secure systems. The owner of secure data or the operator of such secure systems is implementing two-factor authentication for laptops first because of the inherent security risks in mobile computers, to make it more difficult for unauthorized persons to use a "found" laptop to access secure data or systems. With mobile phones or smart phones, the quality of the problem does not change: A lost or left phone shall not be activated to enable the finder for unauthorised access to secure data or system. Multi-factor authentication hence means two or more of the authentication factor required for being authenticated.

Types of Two-factor Authentication

1. **Tokens:** One form of 'something you have' is the smart cad and USB tokens. Difference between the smart card and USB token are diminishing; both technologies include a microcontroller, an OS, a security application, and a secured storage area.
2. **Wireless tokens:** A new quality of tokens has been developed to ease the authentication process without keying character sequences and with automatic pairing of authentication

factors. Presumed the bearer of the authentication factors prepares himself in good separation from other similar entities, the achieved pairing status may be maintained for all the daytime and especially during worktime without repetition of the pairing process.

SUMMARY

A virtual private network (VPN) is the extension of a private network that encompasses links across shared or public networks like the Internet. A VPN enables you to send data between two computers across a shared or public internetwork in a manner that emulates the properties of a point-to-point private link. The act of configuring and creating a virtual private network is known as virtual private networking.

To emulate a point-to-point link, data is encapsulated, or wrapped, with a header that provides routing information allowing it to traverse the shared or public transit internetwork to reach its endpoint. To emulate a private link, the data being sent is encrypted for confidentiality. Packets that are intercepted on the shared or public network are indecipherable without the encryption keys. The portion of the connection in which the private data is encapsulated is known as the tunnel. The portion of the connection in which the private data is encrypted is known as the virtual private network (VPN) connection.

EXERCISE

1. What is virtual private network?
2. Why we have need to use VPN?
3. What are the uses of tunneling with VPN?
4. What is the authentication mechanism?
5. What are security concern in VPN?

UNIT – 5

8. Set Protocol
9. E-Commerce Applications
10. Implementation of Ecommerce

CHAPTER

8

Set Protocol

8.1 INTRODUCTION TO SET

SET (Secure Electronic Transaction) is a protocol that was developed by Visa and MasterCard and that uses the SSL standard.

SET is based on the use of an electronic signature from the buyer and a transaction involving not only the buyer and the seller, but also their respective banks.

Internet has been one of the most dominant technologies in the field of computers in the last decade. The domain of internet usage ranges from sharing information, enabling communication between people, sharing resources, remote education, distributed computation, online shopping, etc. The advent of Internet led to the beginning of a whole new set of technologies. One such technology that redefined the manner in which business was conducted is Electronic Commerce (E-Commerce).

E-Commerce or E-Business is the method of conducting business and transactions through networks and computers. E-Commerce involves buying and selling of goods, business-to-business exchange of data and trading with the participating entities in remote locations. Indeed, this was a very convenient way of doing business and soon business through E-Commerce was a norm. But this convenience also brought along with it some serious security concerns.

All the transactions carried out through E-Commerce are monetary and it involves the flow of money in some form from one remote place to another through networks. The most common way in which money is transferred in E-Commerce is using a credit card. Since the networks are inherently insecure it is possible for the malicious intruder to break into a network and gain access to secure data (Ex. reading credit card number).

This requires securing communication channels by encrypting data, identifying and authorizing participating entities, limiting access to resources and by implementing security protocols to provide the needed security.

Transport Layer Security (TLS), Secure Sockets Layer (SSL) and Secure Electronic Transaction (SET) are some of the popular security protocols. Transport Layer Security (TLS) is a protocol that ensures privacy between communicating applications and their users on the Internet. Secure Socket Layer (SSL) is a protocol developed by Netscape for transmitting private documents or data via the Internet. SET (Secure Electronic Transaction) is a system for ensuring the security of financial transactions on the Internet.

The security protocols are a collection of algorithms that facilitate the secure communication of data. Immaterial of the environment these protocols are used, the users of these protocols depend highly on the correctness of these protocols. Any minor flaw in these protocols could compromise the security of the data which these security protocols are intended to protect.

Due to the critical nature of data, documents or applications these security protocols protect, it is doubly important to prove the correctness of these protocols. Formal methods have been used in a wide variety of environments to verify whether complex systems accomplish their intended functionality. One area where formal methods received wide attention is in the area of security protocol verification.

8.1.1 How SET Works?

When a secure transaction is made with SET, data are sent by the customer to the seller's server, but the latter receives only the order. The bank card number is directly sent to the merchant's bank, which will be able to read the buyer's bank account details and contact his bank to verify them in real time.

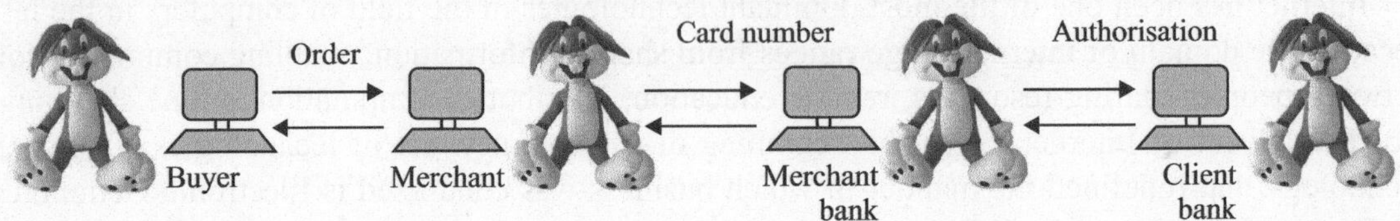

Fig. 8.1

This type of method requires an electronic signature from the card's user to certify he is the card's owner.

Secure Electronic Transactions (SET) is an open protocol which has the potential to emerge as a dominant force in the securing of electronic transactions. Jointly developed by Visa and MasterCard, in conjunction with leading computer vendors such as IBM, SET is an open standard for protecting the privacy, and ensuring the authenticity, of electronic transactions. This is critical to the success of electronic commerce over the Internet; without privacy, consumer protection cannot be guaranteed, and without authentication, neither the merchant nor the consumer can be sure that valid transactions are being made.

Technology

Secure Electronic Transactions (SET) relies on the science of cryptography – the art of encoding and decoding messages. Cryptography dates back many centuries – even in the time of Julius Caesar, encryption was used to preserve the secrecy of messages. Preserving the secrecy of transactions is no different, though stronger encryption algorithms are used, as well as significantly stronger encryption keys. Encryption advancements have come about through its application by the military, and by advances in computing power and mathematics.

The SET protocol relies on two different encryption mechanisms, as well as an authentication mechanism. SET uses symmetric encryption, in the form of the aging Data Encryption Standard (DES), as well as asymmetric, or public-key, encryption to transmit session keys for DES transactions. Rather than offer the security and protection afforded by public-key cryptography, SET simply uses session keys (56 bits) which are transmitted asymmetrically – the remainder of the transaction uses symmetric encryption in the form of DES. This has disturbing connotations for a "secure" electronic transaction protocol – because public key cryptography is only used only to encrypt DES keys and for authentication, and not for the main body of the transaction. The computational cost of asymmetric encryption is cited as reason for using weak 56 bit DES, however other reasons such as export/ import restrictions, and the perceived need by law enforcement and government agencies to access the plain-text of encrypted SET messages may also play a role.

8.1.2 Overview of Symmetric and Asymmetric Cryptography

Modern cryptography uses encryption keys, which can encode (lock) and decode (unlock) messages when an encryption algorithm is used. Symmetric encryption works by using a single key, which must be known by all parties wishing to unlock the message.

Fig. 8.2: Symmetric encryption with a single key

If we apply a specific key to a message, using a good encryption algorithm, then it will be unreadable by unauthorized parties. If we then apply the same key to the encrypted message, then the message will be restored to its original form. However, this presents a problem, because we must find a secure means of transmitting the key to all parties.

Asymmetric encryption, also known as public-key encryption, frees us from this limitation. Asymmetric algorithms use two keys – a public and a private key. These keys are completely independent – a private key cannot be easily deduced from a public one. When we sign a message using someone's public key, only the holder of the private key can read it. We can place our public key out in the open, and rest assured that only the private key holder can read messages encrypted for him or her.

A protocol designed to ensure the security and integrity of online communications and purchases, Secure Electronic Transaction (SET) uses digital certificates, issued to merchants and other businesses and customers, to perform a series of security checks verifying that the identity of a customer or sender of information is valid. SET provides the basic framework within which many of the various components of securing digital transactions function. Digital certificates, digital signatures, and digital wallets all function according to the SET protocol.

To meet the business requirements, SET incorporates the following features:

- Confidentiality of information
- Integrity of data
- Cardholder account authentication
- Merchant authentication

There are several components for the SET protocol.

- The Cardholder Application, also referred to as a digital wallet, is held by an online consumer and packages a digital signature and credit card information that ensures his or her identity and safeguards his or her financial information through a complex encryption system.
- The Merchant Server component is the verification product held by the merchant to process the online card payment.
- The Payment Gateway component is held by an acquiring bank or other trusted third party that accepts and processes the merchant's verification and the customer's payment information and filters them to their appropriate financial institutions.
- The Certificate Authority component, usually run by a financial institution, is the trusted agent that issues the digital certificates and is responsible for ensuring that all users of digital certificates are in fact secure and trustworthy customers.

Once a security product for any of these components has passed the SET Compliance Testing, it bears the SET Mark, ensuring all users that it meets the SET standards.

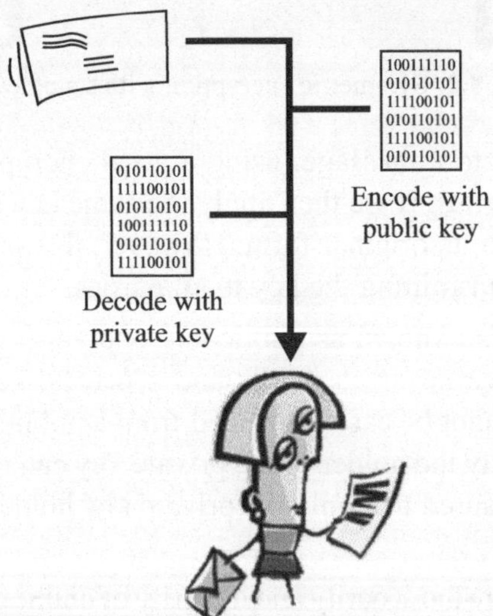

Fig. 8.3: Asymmetric encryption with a public and a private key

SET is an open standard available to anyone engaged in electronic commerce. MasterCard International and Visa International, recognizing that security was the key to the widespread use of credit cards for E-Commerce, developed the SET protocol, which was launched on February 1, 1996. The first version of the SET Specification was published in May 1997. In December of that year, the credit-card giants and other major players in the E-Commerce world, including Microsoft, Netscape, and IBM, set up a company called SET Secure Electronic Transaction LLC (SETCo) to maintain and implement the SET specification, administer compliance testing, and foster the increased global adoption of the SET standard.

8.1.3 Symmetric and Asymmetric Encryption in SET

In the SET protocol, two different encryption algorithms are used – DES and RSA. The DES algorithm has been used since the 1970's. It is believed by some that the National Security Agency (NSA) of America played "an invisible hand in the development of the algorithm" (Schneier, 1996), and that they were responsible for reducing its key size from the original 128-bits to 56. DES quickly became a federal standard in 1976, and has been used ever since.

In the SET protocol, a DES 56-bit key is used to encrypt transactions. This level of encryption, using DES, can be easily cracked using modern hardware. In 1993, a brute-force DES cracking machine was designed by Michael Wiener – one which was massively parallel. For less than a million dollars (well within the budget of many large companies), a 56-bit DES key could be cracked in average time of 3.5 hours. For a billion dollars, which might be considered small change for a military or security organisation such as the NSA or a foreign power, a parallel machine can be constructed that cracks 56-bit DES in a second (Schneier, 1996). Clearly, this is of great concern, since DES encrypts the majority of a SET transaction. As the power of computers grows, and the cost diminishes, such code-crackers may become more and more common.

One may wonder why such crippled cryptography would be used in a "secure" transaction protocol. One possible reason may be that the organizations involved recognise the desire by government organizations (both foreign and domestic to the US) to observe and monitor financial transactions conducted over the Internet. "Governments tend to look favorably upon SET based cryptography" (IBM, 1998), and the prospect that any government with enough resources to build a code cracker could have access to people's financial transactions is disturbing. While many people believe that it is legitimate for a government to observe the financial transactions of its citizens, it is unthinkable that a "secure" protocol would allow those same transactions to be observed by foreign, and possibly hostile, governments.

8.1.4 Transaction Authenticity

Authentication is an important issue for users of electronic commerce. Consumers must have faith in the authenticity of the merchant, and merchants must have faith in the authenticity of the consumer. Without authentication, any individual could pose as a merchant, and besmirch a merchant's good name by failing to deliver goods and billing up credit card bills. Without authentication, any individual could pose as a consumer, ordering costly goods to an abandoned house or apartment, and defrauding the merchant. Without authentication, an individual could pose as a willing buyer, accept the goods, and then repudiate the transaction. Authentication is critical to achieving trust in electronic commerce.

Authentication is achieved through the use of digital signatures. Using a hashing algorithm, SET can sign a transaction using the sender's private key. This produces a small message digest, which is a series of values that "sign" a message. By comparing the transaction message and the message digest, along with the sender's public key, the authenticity of the transaction can be verified. Digital signatures are aimed at achieving the same level of trust as a written signature has in real life. This helps achieve non-repudiation, as the consumer cannot later establish that the message wasn't sent using his private key[1].

8.1.5 Importance of Secure Transactions

Secure electronic transactions will be an important part of electronic commerce in the future. Without such security, the interests of the merchant, the consumer, and the credit or economic institution cannot be served. Privacy of transactions, and authentication of all parties, is important for achieving the level of trust that will allow such transactions to flourish. However, it is important that the encryption algorithms and key-sizes used, will be robust enough to prevent observation by hostile entities (either criminal or foreign powers). The ideal of the secure electronic transactions protocol (SET) is important for the success of electronic commerce. However, it remains to be seen whether the protocol will be widely used because of the weakness of the encryption that it uses.

8.2 PAYMENT GATEWAY

A payment gateway is a separate service and acts as an intermediary between the merchants' shopping cart and all the financial networks involved with the transaction, including the customers' credit card issuer and your merchant account. Think of it as a EFTPOS terminal in cyberspace. It checks for validity, encrypts transaction details, ensures they are sent to the correct destination and then decrypts the responses which are sent back to the shopping cart.

This is a seamless process and your customer does not directly interact with the gateway; as data is forwarded to the gateway via your shopping cart and a secure (SSL) connection. The shopping cart is configured via plugins to send information in a format that is acceptable to the particular gateway.

The proper choice of payment gateway is another vital element which will contribute to your success or failure as an online business

Since the payment gateway is the secure connection and transmission of the orders through to banking networks, it is independent of the interface (point of sale software or catalog/cart) that you use to transmit the order information through the payment gateway.

A **payment gateway** is an E-Commerce application service provider service that authorizes payments for e-businesses, online retailers, bricks and clicks, or traditional brick and mortar. It is the equivalent of a physical point of sale terminal located in most retail outlets. Payment gateways protect credit card details by encrypting sensitive information, such as credit card numbers, to ensure that information is passed securely between the customer and the merchant and also between merchant and the payment processor.

When using a payment gateway system in connection with the cart, you will receive all of your orders via e-mail. As a merchant you will receive 2 e-mail messages, the first is generated by the cart, and supplies you with the necessary information to fulfill the order, such as names, addresses, and items ordered. The second will come from your payment gateway, and will tell you the status of the order approval. You should wait to ship a product until you have received this order status message.

If you receive a declined message from your gateway regarding an order, you will need to contact the customer and ask for alternative payment. The customer will not receive notification via e-mail of the approval status.

8.2.1 How Payment Gateways Work

A payment gateway facilitates the transfer of information between a payment portal (such as a website, mobile phone or IVR service) and the Front End Processor or acquiring bank. When a customer orders a product from a payment gateway-enabled merchant, the payment gateway performs a variety of tasks to process the transaction:

- A customer places order on website by pressing the 'Submit Order' or equivalent button, or perhaps enters their card details using an automatic phone answering service.
- If the order is via a website, the customer's web browser encrypts the information to be sent between the browser and the merchant's webserver. This is done via SSL (Secure Socket Layer) encryption.
- The merchant then forwards the transaction details to their payment gateway. This is another SSL encrypted connection to the payment server hosted by the payment gateway.
- The payment gateway forwards the transaction information to the payment processor used by the merchant's acquiring bank.
- The payment processor forwards the transaction information to the card association (i.e., Visa/MasterCard)
- If an American Express or Discover Card was used, then the processor acts as the issuing bank and directly provides a response of approved or declined to the payment gateway.
- Otherwise, the card association routes the transaction to the correct card issuing bank.
- The credit card issuing bank receives the authorization request and sends a response back to the processor (via the same process as the request for authorization) with a response code. In addition to determining the fate of the payment, (i.e. approved or declined) the response code is used to define the reason why the transaction failed (such as insufficient funds, or bank link not available)
- The processor forwards the response to the payment gateway.

- The payment gateway receives the response, and forwards it on to the website (or whatever interface was used to process the payment) where it is interpreted as a relevant response then relayed back to the cardholder and the merchant.
- The entire process typically takes 2–3 seconds
- The merchant submits all their approved authorizations, in a "batch", to their acquiring bank for settlement.
- The acquiring bank deposits the total of the approved funds in to the merchant's nominated account. This could be an account with the acquiring bank if the merchant does their banking with the same bank, or an account with another bank.
- The entire process from authorization to settlement to funding typically takes 3 days.

Many payment gateways also provide tools to automatically screen orders for fraud and calculate tax in real time prior to the authorization request being sent to the processor. Tools to detect fraud include geolocation, velocity pattern analysis, delivery address verification, computer finger printing technology, identity morphing detection, and basic AVS checks.

Payment gateways are necessary for online transactions to provide the secure connection for the transaction to take place. It is the payment gateway that allows you to submit a credit card and within a few seconds be told whether it was declined or accepted. LinkPoint API is one the most sophisticated levels of this service, enabling software companies, commerce service providers (CSPs), Internet service providers (ISPs) or cyber-wise merchants to add secure sockets layer (SSL) payment capabilities to their products, services or custom storefronts. Using the LinkPoint APIs, the Miva storefront product line has developed modules to support a seamless integration with their shopping carts. What this means to you the customer is a simple to configure payment gateway that is both powerful and affordable.

For the merchant who wants to get online fast with limited startup expenses and who currently does not have any form of online merchant account, then Cardservice International (which includes LinkPoint API) is the best choice. Since LinkPoint is already packaged in with the Cardservice International offering, it gives you the best ability to have your online store accepting credit cards quickly and affordably. If you already have your own online merchant account and only need a payment gateway, then VeriSign Pay Flow Pro is the way go.

8.2.2 Payment Gateway Issues

As with any other ecommerce element, shop around, compare prices and read the fine print. Here are some of the major points to consider when selecting a payment gateway service.

- If you have already purchased a shopping cart package, ensure that the payment gateway service is compatible. If a service is not listed, contact the shopping cart vendor for clarification. Many vendors would be happy to support other payment gateway services if there is a demand for it.
- If you haven't yet selected a shopping cart, get a list of supported applications from the payment gateway service provider. A payment gateway may offer great pricing, but if the range of shopping carts or storefront software it supports is limited, the whole process of

setting up for taking online payments may cost a lot more than you think. I've noticed some gateways only support horribly expensive and restrictive shopping cart software packages and services.

- Ensure the gateway at least offers AVS protection. The Address Verification System (AVS) AVS decreases the incidence of accepting fraudulent transactions by verifying the cardholder's billing address with the card issuer. Using AVS on your transactions may also benefit you by a reduction in fees charged by your Merchant Bank.
- Check to see what other types of transaction protection are offered to you as a merchant. These will probably be 'premium' services, the charges added to the basic servicing fees, but dependent on your products may be absolutely necessary. If you are engaged in the sale of anything that is youth or technology oriented, it's probably a wise move to pay for the extra service as chargeback rates on fraudulent transactions can cost you around US$30 per incident

8.2.3 What Kinds of Payment Alternatives Exist

While credit cards are the leading method of payment for online purchases, offering multiple payment alternatives will bring improved convenience to your customers and increased confidence in your online business. The kinds of payment methods you provide will depend on your web site, your customers and your markets. For instance, in some countries, credit cards are not a common way to purchase online. Therefore, it is important to consider different payment alternatives for your international clients.

There are a number of alternative payment methods that exist, including the following:

8.2.4 Person-to-Person (P-to-P)

This transaction method enables payments to be made to an individual's e-mail address without any need to send cash, cheque or use a credit card or chequing account. If you wanted to pay back a friend, that friend would only need an e-mail account to accept the payment. On the other hand, as a merchant, you require software that accepts P-to-P payments in order to receive funds. For instance, your customer has a P-to-P account, where he or she has deposited a certain amount of funds. The customer buys a product from your site and uses funds from his or her P-to-P account to pay for the purchase. Your web site will provide the customer with an option to pay through this method.

8.2.5 Electronic Cash/Digital Cash

E-cash is money that is converted to an electronic equivalent, and present either on a smart card, or on a consumer's personal computer. The cash is normally used for making small purchases over the Internet.

8.2.6 Smart Cards

The smart card looks like a credit card, the biggest difference being it holds a chip that enables applications and data to be downloaded. Since it can store and process information, the card has the capacity to collect customer information as well as E-cash.

To use the card, the cardholder needs a PIN. To read the information on the card, a smart card reader is required. The reader is connected to the Internet, and enables the cardholder to transfer information from his or her computer to an online merchant's site or from a point-of-sale terminal at retail stores. It also enables the card to capture data from other sources, such as the cardholder's bank account. As a merchant, you require a smart card reader on your site to access payments from customers.

8.2.7 Digital Wallets

A digital wallet enables consumers to store their personal information online such as credit card and shipping details so they can carry their identity with them as they browse between sites.

A digital wallet comes in two forms—client-based or server-based. A client-based wallet requires that consumers download and install software on their computer. They input personal information into the wallet, which is secured and protected locally on their computer's hard drive. When using a digital wallet, consumers will not be required to fill out order forms on each site they purchase from as the information required is readily available from their hard drive and automatically entered into the order fields of the online site.

A server-based wallet is acquired from a merchant's site. When consumers complete a merchant's Web form to make a purchase they are invited to sign up for a free wallet where they provide a username and password. The information they add to the Web form, including credit card number and shipping information, is stored on the merchant's server or the merchant's payment processor's server. When consumers go to the same site to make a purchase in the future, their personal information is easily extracted for the purchase. The servers will have encryption security. As well, since certificates are used to verify the identity of all parties, the merchant is protected against fraud.

8.2.8 E-Cheque

An E-cheque is essentially an electronic version of the paper cheque, except it is created on a computer and processed via the Internet. To issue a cheque, a consumer uses an electronic chequebook issued by his or her bank, which displays all the same fields as a paper cheque. Before it is sent to the merchant, the consumer enters a PIN in addition to other required information and signs the E-cheque with his or her digital signature. The digital signature is stored with a bank so that the E-cheque can be verified as it moves through the payment process.

What types of payment gateways are there

Payment gateways can be implemented through two methods. As a merchant, you can either house the gateway on your server, which requires installation of software, or you can choose to implement the payment gateway on your payment processing company's server i.e. financial institution.

Housing the payment gateway on your site requires you to have appropriate security measures in place to encrypt and protect customer information. If you implement a payment gateway separate from the rest of your shopping cart solution, all the components will require configuration to ensure they work properly together, which can require high level technical capabilities. The advantage of housing your own gateway is that customer information can be collected in your database, enabling you to better manage your customers and site.

If a payment processing company houses your payment gateway, then customer information will not be at your easy disposal. As well, since you do not gain access to customers' credit card information, it is more difficult to track charge backs.

However, since the gateway is out of your hands, problems that occur are the responsibility of the payment gateway provider.

8.2.9 Explanation of Credit Card Processing Solutions

In order to process credit and debit cards through your merchant account, you need to decide which processing solution is right for you.

Retail Swipe Terminal

This particular solution is for retail and storefront merchants who see their customers face-to-face. This type of solution incurs the lowest merchant account processing fees since you actually are able to swipe the customers credit card through the terminal. It is believed that orders that are swiped have a lower fraud risk, hence the reason for the lower processing fees.

Real-Time Processing

This is the solution for businesses on the Internet. Real-Time allows you to automatically process credit card orders through your merchant account with no assistance needed on your end. Everything is automated, and the funds transferred into the merchant account, from the cardholder, is deposited into your business checking account, within a few days. All Real-Time solutions are secure and the purchase of a secure certificate is not usually required.

Virtual Terminal

If you are a merchant on the Internet and expect to receive orders via phone, fax or mail then getting a Virtual Terminal solution (along with a Real-Time processing solution) is the best route to go. The Virtual Terminal is a secure website where you login and manually type in a customers credit card information. Once the information is submitted, it is securely processed and funds are then deposited into your merchant account within a few days. A Virtual Terminal can be accessed securely from any computer connected to the Internet. Most all Real-Time processing solutions also come with a Virtual Terminal at little or no additional cost.

8.3 ELECTRONIC PAYMENT

The emergence of E-Commerce has created new financial needs that in many cases cannot be effectively fulfilled by the traditional payment systems. Recognizing this, virtually all interested parties are exploring various types of electronic payment system and issues surrounding electronic payment system and digital currency. Broadly electronic payment systems can be classified into four categories: Online Credit Card Payment System, Online Electronic Cash System, Electronic Cheque System and Smart Cards based Electronic Payment System. Each payment system has its advantages and disadvantages for the customers and merchants. These payment systems have numbers of requirements: e.g. security, acceptability, convenience, cost, anonymity, control, and traceability. Therefore, instead of focusing on the technological specifications of various electronic payment systems, the researcher have distinguished electronic payment systems based on what is being transmitted over the network; and analyze the difference of each electronic payment system by evaluating their requirements, characteristics and assess the applicability of each system.

As payment is an integral part of mercantile process, electronic payment system is an integral part of E-Commerce. The emergence of E-Commerce has created new financial needs that in many cases cannot be effectively fulfilled by traditional payment systems. For instance, new types of purchasing relationships-such as auction between individuals online-have resulted in the need for peer-to-peer payment methods that allows individuals to e-mail payments to the other individual. Recognizing this, virtually all interested parties (i.e. academicians, government, business community and financial service providers) are exploring various types of *electronic payment system and issues* surrounding electronic payment system and digital currency. Some proposed electronic payment systems are simply electronic version of existing payment systems such as cheques and credit cards, while, others are based on the digital currency technology and have the potential for definitive impact on today's financial and monetary system. While popular developers of electronic payment system predict fundamental changes in the financial sector because of the innovations in electronic payment system, Therefore, electronic payment systems and in particular, methods of payment being developed to support electronic commerce cannot be studied in an isolation. A failure to take place these developments into the proper context is likely to result in undue focus on the various experimental initiatives to develop electronic forms of payment without a proper reflection on the broader implications for the existing payment system.

8.3.1 Concept and Size of Electronic Payment

Payment systems that use electronic distribution networks constitute a frequent practice in the banking and business sector since 1960s, especially for the transfer of big amounts of money. In the four decades that have passed since their appearance, important technological developments have taken place, which on the one hand have expanded the possibilities of electronic payment systems and on the other hand they have created new business and social practice, which make the use of these systems necessary. These changes, naturally, have affected the definition of electronic payments, which is evolving depending on the needs of each period. In its, most general form, the term electronic payment includes any payment to businesses, bank or public services from citizens or businesses, which are executed through a telecommunications or electronic networks using modern technology. It is obvious that based on this definition, the electronic payments that will be the objects of present result, are the payment that are executed by the payer himself, whether the latter is a consumer or a business, without the intervention of the another natural person. Furthermore, the payment is made from distance, without the physical presence of the payer and naturally it does not include cash. By providing such definition for the electronic payment system, researcher include the transfer of information concerning the accounts of the parties involved in the E-Commerce transactions, as well as the technological means of distribution channels through which the transactions is executed.

8.3.2 Size of Electronic Payments

Electronic payment system is conducted in different E-Commerce categories such as Business-to-Business (B2B), Business-to-Consumer (B2C), Consumer-to-Business (C2B) and Consumer-to-Consumer (C2C). Each of which has special characteristics that depend on the value of order. Danial, (2002) classified electronic payment systems as follows:

- Micro Payment (less than $ 10) that is mainly conducted in C2C and B2C E-Commerce.
- Consumer Payment that has a value between $ 10 and $ 500. It is conducted mainly in B2C transactions.

Business Payment that has the value more than $ 500. it is conducted mainly in B2B E-Commerce. B2B transactions account about 95% of E-Commerce transactions, while others account about 5% (Turban et al, 2004). P2P, which is related to the C2C category transactions, is relatively small due to its stiff usability. Further, Cavarretta and de Silva (1995), identify three classes of typical electronic transactions:

- Tiny value transactions: below $1.
- Medium value transactions: between $ 1 and $ 1,000
- Large value transactions: above $ 1,000.

Systems that can support tiny value transactions have to trade-off between conveniences of transactions (the major part of a cost in an extremely cheap transaction) vs. the security or durability of transactions. On the other side of the amount range, large value transactions will require highly secure protocols whose implementations are costly: be on-line and/or carry traceability information. Finally, nearly all the system can perform medium value transactions.

8.3.3 Conventional vs. Electronic Payment System

To get into the depth of electronic payment process, it is better to understand the processing of conventional or traditional payment system. A conventional process of payment and settlement involves a buyer-to-seller transfer of cash or payment information (i.e., cheque and credit cards). The actual settlement of payment takes place in the financial processing network. A cash payment requires a buyer's withdrawals form his/her bank account, a transfer of cash to the seller, and the sellers deposit of payment to his/her account. Non-cash payment mechanisms are settled by adjusting i.e. crediting and debiting the appropriate accounts between banks based on payment information conveyed via cheque or credit cards.

Figure 8.4 is simplified diagram for both cash and non-cash transactions. Cash moves from the buyers? bank to sellers? bank through face-to-face exchange in the market. If a buyer uses a non-cash method of payment, payment information instead of cash flows from the buyer to the seller, and ultimate payments are settled between affected banks, who notation ally adjust accounts based on payment information.

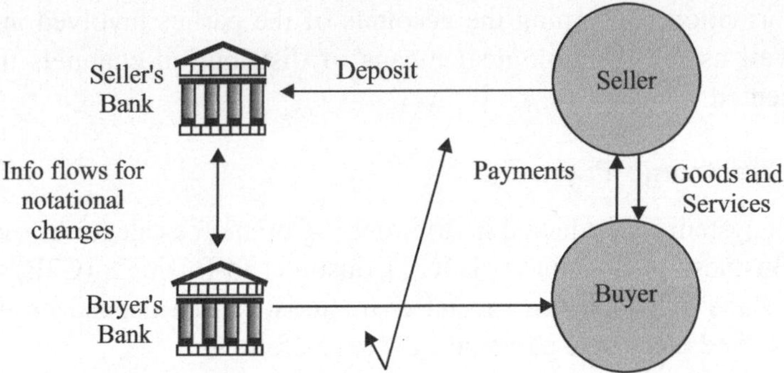

Fig. 8.4: Conventional/Traditional Payment System

8.3.4 Process of Electronic Payment System

Electronic payment systems have been in operations since 1960s and have been expanding rapidly as well as growing in complexity. After the development of conventional payment system, EFT (Electronic Fund Transfer) based payment system came into existence. It was first electronic based payment system, which does not depend on a central processing intermediary. An electronic fund transfer is a financial application of EDI (Electronic Data Interchange), which sends credit card numbers or electronic cheques via secured private networks between banks and major corporations. To use EFT to clear payments and settle accounts, an online payment service will need to add capabilities to process orders, accounts and receipts. But a landmark came in this direction with the development of digital currency. The nature of digital currency or electronic money mirrors that of paper money as a means of payment. As such, digital currency payment systems have the same advantages as paper currency payment, namely anonymity and convenience. As in other electronic payment systems (i.e. EFT based and intermediary based) here too security during the transaction and storage is a concern, although from the different perspective, for digital currency systems double spending, counterfeiting, and storage become critical issues whereas eavesdropping and the issue of liability (when charges are made without authorizations) is important for the notational funds transfer. Figure 8.5 shows digital currency based payment system.

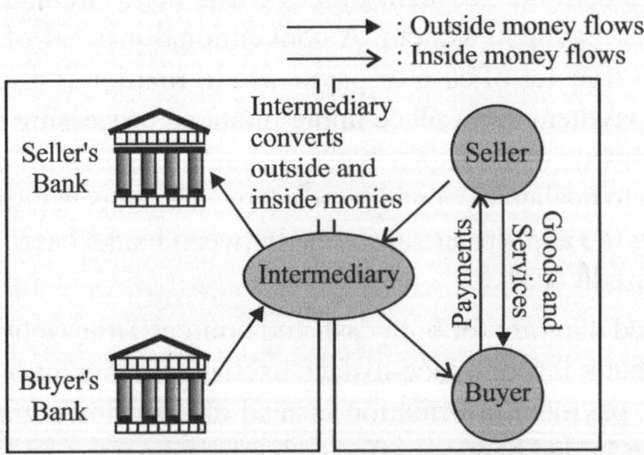

Fig. 8.5: Electronic Payment System

In this figure, it is shown that intermediary acts as an electronic bank, which converts outside money (e.g. Rupees or US $), into inside money (e.g. tokens or e-cash), which is circulated within online markets. However, as a private monetary system, digital currency has wide ranging impact on money and monetary system with implications extending far beyond more transactional efficiency.

8.3.5 Payment Instructions

A payment instruction is the instance of a payment method with the details necessary to perform payment actions. For example, if a payment method name is Visa, then the payment instruction consists of Visa, the payment amount, cardholder's name, billing address, account number, and expiration date.

A shopper adds a payment instruction during the checkout flow. When the payment instruction is added, the PIAdd command runs and persists payment information to the payment tables. A payment instruction is created in the EDPPAYINST and PPCPAYINST tables. The protocol data is stored in the PPCEXTDATA table.

Payment methods

Payment methods are the means by which payments are made. Payment methods include credit card brands, electronic checks, gift certificates, and manufacturers' coupons. The shopper selects the payment method on the Order Summary page.

Payment methods have the following properties: payment method name, priority, ability to be edited (whether the amount can be changed by an administrator, or by the system), and amount limits. The payment policy is specified in the POLICY and POLICYDESC database tables. The properties are defined in the PaymentMethodConfigurations.xml file.

A shopper can use more than one payment method to pay for an order. The priority determines which payment method should be used first. For example, if a gift certificate has a high priority and a credit card has a medium priority, the gift certificate is used first.

By default, the following payment methods are available:

Credit cards

- AMEX
- MasterCard
- VISA

BillMeLater: Offline transaction, customer is billed

Check: Electronic check or automated clearing house (ACH) transaction

COD: Cash on delivery

LOC: Line of credit

8.4 TYPES OF ELECTRONIC PAYMENT SYSTEMS

With the growing complexities in the E-Commerce transactions, different electronic payment systems have appeared in the last few years. At least dozens of electronic payment systems proposed or already in practice are found (Murthy, 2002). The grouping can be made on the basis of what information is being transferred online. Murthy explained six types of electronic payment systems: (1) PC-Banking (2) Credit Cards (3) Electronic Cheques (i-cheques) (4) Micro payment (5) Smart Cards and (6) E-Cash. Kalakota and Whinston (1996) identified three types of electronic payment systems: (1) Digital Token based electronic payment systems, (2) Smart Card based electronic payment system and (3) Credit based electronic payment systems. Dennis (2001) classified electronic payment system into two categories: (1) Electronic Cash and (2) Electronic Debit-Credit Card Systems. Thus, electronic payment system can be broadly divided into four general types (Anderson, 1998):

- Online Credit Card Payment System
- Electronic Cheque System
- Electronic Cash System and
- Smart Card based Electronic Payment System

8.5 ONLINE CREDIT CARD PAYMENT SYSTEM

Credit card is made of plastic whose holder has been granted a revolving credit lines. This enables the holder to make purchase and/ or cash advances upto a pre arranged limits. The credit granted can be settled in full by the end of a specific period or in part, with the balance taken as extended credit. Interest may be charged on the transaction amounts from the date of each transaction or only the extended credit where the credit granted has not been settled in full.

The card normally contains the cardholders name and account number and many other information encoded on the magnetic strip. Some credit cards may be used in ATM. Credit cards began in the late 40's when banks began giving out paper certificates that could be used like cash in local stores. Frankline National Bank of New York used the first real credit card in 1951.

It seeks to extend the functionality of existing credit cards for use as online shopping payment tools. This payment system has been widely accepted by consumers and merchants throughout the world, and by far the most popular methods of payments especially in the retail markets (Laudon and Traver, 2002). This form of payment system has several advantages, which were never available through the traditional modes of payment. Some of the most important are: privacy, integrity, compatibility, good transaction efficiency, acceptability, convenience, mobility, low financial risk and anonymity. Added to all these, to avoid the complexity associated with the digital cash or electronic-cheques, consumers and vendors are also looking at credit card payments on the internet as one of possible time-tested alternative. But, this payment system has raised several problems before the consumers and merchants. Online credit card payment seeks to address several limitations of online credit card payments for merchant including lack of authentication, repudiation of charges and credit card frauds. It also seeks to address consumer fears about using credit card such as having to reveal credit information at multiple sites and repeatedly having to communicate sensitive information over the Internet. Basic process of Online Credit Card Payment System is very simple. If consumers want to purchase a product or service, they simply send their credit card details to the service provider involved and the credit card organization will handle this payment like any other. This can be understood very easily with the format (Figure 8.6) of Credit Card Payment Form.

Credit Card Type: Fraud Protection Guaranteed Click Here | VISA | MASTERCARD | DISCOVER | AMERICAN EXPRESS

Expiration date: ....

Card number: ....

Card holder's name (on card): ....

....

Full billing address of credit card :.

....

Your email address: ....

Comment/Description: ....

In the comment field please enter the service you are ordering, the domain or username this information should be applied to, or further information to help up speed and assist your order.

Fig. 8.6: Credit card payment form (Sample)

8.6 ELECTRONIC CHEQUE PAYMENT SYSTEM

Electronic cheque also known as e-cheque and I-cheque are used to make electronic payment between two parties through an intermediary and not very much different from the traditional or current cheque processing system. Electronic cheques are generated and exchanged online. The intermediary will debit the customer account and credit the merchant account. Electronic cheque is different from the electronic fund transfer (EFT) in several ways. For electronic chequing, electronic versions of cheques are issued, received and processed. So, the payee issues an electronic cheque for each payment. For EFT, automatic withdrawals are made for monthly bills or other fixed payments; no charges are issues. Thus, a complete electronic cheque transaction may consist of several basic steps and these steps are executed in three distinct and optionally separate phases. In the first phase, the consumer makes a purchase; in the second phase, the merchant sends the electronic cheques to its bank for the redemption. In the third phase, the merchant's bank approaches the clearinghouse or consumer's bank to cash the electronic cheques.

Electronic cheques address the electronic needs of millions of businesses, which today exchange traditional paper cheques with the other vendors, consumers and government. The e-cheque method was deliberately created to work in much the same way as conventional paper cheque. An account holder will issue an electronic document that contains the name of the financial institution, the payer's account number, the name of payee and amount of cheque. Most of the information is in uncoded form. Like a paper cheques e-cheques also bear the digital equivalent of signature: a computed number that authenticates the cheque from the owner of the account. Digital chequing payment system seeks to extend the functionality of existing chequing accounts for use as online shopping payment tools. Electronic cheque system has many advantages: (1) they do not require consumers to reveal account information to other individuals when setting an auction (2) they do not require consumers to continually send sensitive financial information over the web (3) they are less expensive than credit cards and (4) they are much faster than paper based traditional cheque. But, this system of payment also has several disadvantages. The disadvantage of electronic cheque system includes their relatively high fixed costs, their limited use only in virtual world and the fact that they can protect the users' anonymity. Therefore, it is not very suitable for the retail transactions by consumers, although useful for the government and B2B operations because the latter transactions do not require anonymity, and the amount of transactions is generally large enough to cover fixed processing cost. The process of electronic chequing system can be described using (Figure 8.7) the following steps.

Step 1: A purchaser fills a purchase order form, attaches a payment advice (electronic cheque), signs it with his private key (using his signature hardware), attaches his public key certificate, encrypts it using his private key and sends it to the vendor.

Step 2: The vendor decrypts the information using his private key, checks the purchaser's certificates, signature and cheque, attaches his deposit slip, and endorses the deposit attaching his public key certificates. This is encrypted and sent to his bank.

Step 3: The vendor's bank checks the signatures and certificates and sends the cheque for clearance. The banks and clearing houses normally have a private secure data network.

Step 4: When the cheque is cleared, the amount is credited to the vendor?s account and a credit advice is sent to him.

Step 5: The purchaser gets a consolidated debit advice periodically.

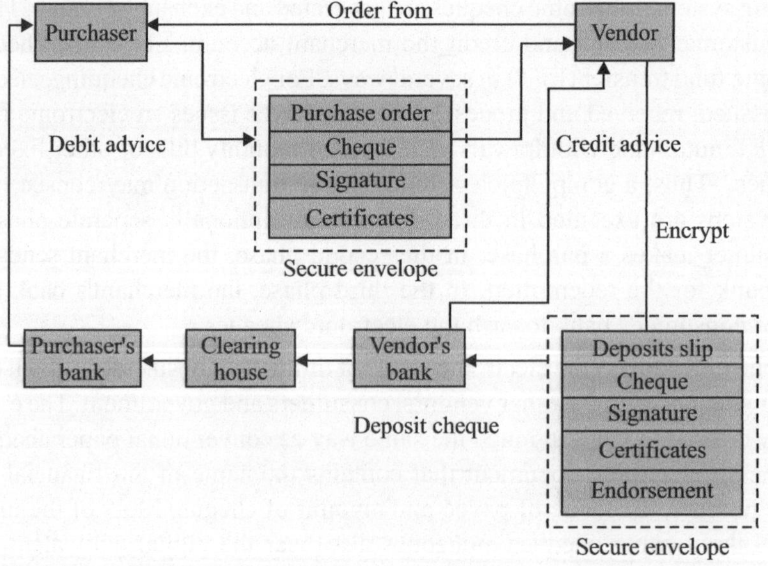

Fig. 8.7: Clearing Cheque Payment Electronically

E-cheque provide a security rich Internet payment option for businesses and offer an easy entry into electronic commerce without a significant investment in new technologies or legal systems.

8.7 ELECTRONIC CASH PAYMENT SYSTEM

E-cash portability means that it must be freely transferable between any two parties in all forms of E-Commerce transactions. In contrast, credit cards do not possess this property of portability or transferability between every combination of two parties. In credit card transactions, the credit card payment recipient must already have a merchant account established with a bank- a condition that is not required with electronic cash.

Electronic cash (e-cash) is a new concept in online payment system because it combines computerized convenience with security and privacy that improve on paper cash. Its versatility opens up a host of new markets and applications. E-cash is an electronic or digital form of value storage and value exchange that have limited convertibility into other forms of value and require intermediaries to convert. E-cash presents some characteristics like monetary value, storability and irretrievability, interoperability and security. All these characteristics make it more attractive payment system over the Internet. Added to these, this payment system offers numerous advantages like authority, privacy, good acceptability, low transactions cost, convenience and good anonymity.

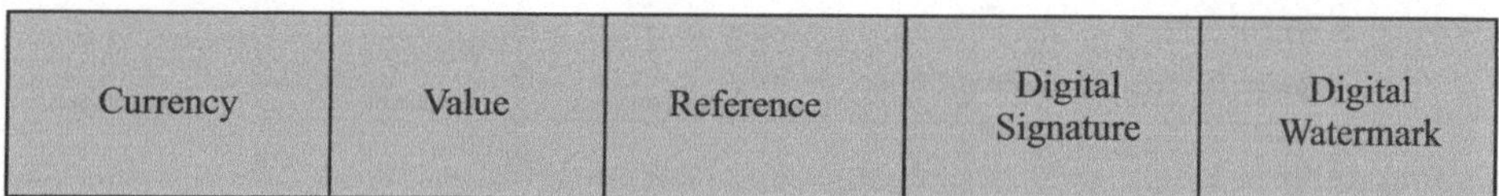

Fig. 8.8: E-cash Structure

8.8 SMART CARDS BASED ELECTRONIC PAYMENT SYSTEM

Smart cards are receiving renewed attention as a mode of online payment. They are essentially credit card sized plastic cards with the memory chips and in some cases, with microprocessors embedded in them so as to serve as storage devices for much greater information than credit cards with inbuilt transaction processing capability.

This card also contains some kinds of an encrypted key that is compared to a secret key contained on the user's processor. Some smart cards have provision to allow users to enter a personal identification number (PIN) code. Smart cards have been in use for well over the two decades now and have been widespread mostly in Europe and Asian Countries. Owing to their considerable flexibility, they have been used for a wide range of functions like highway toll payment, as prepaid telephone cards and as stored value debit cards. However, with the recent emergence of E-Commerce, these devices are increasingly being viewed as a particularly appropriate method to execute online payment system with considerably greater level of security than credit cards.

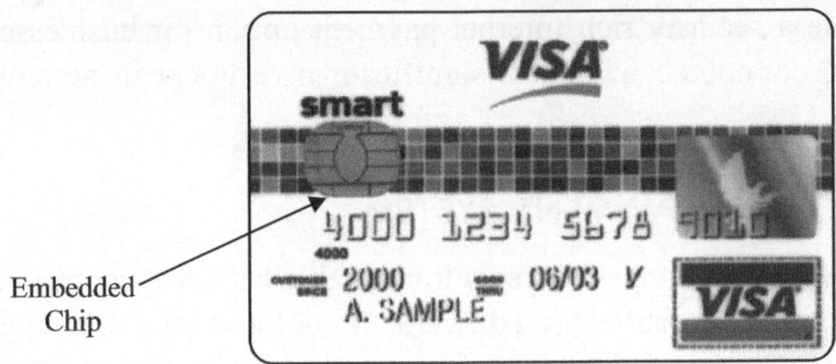

Fig. 8.9: Smart Card Image

Table 8.1: Electronic payment in India

E-Commerce Payment Systems	Percentage	Rank
Credit Card	35	1
Debit Card (Smart Card)	26.5	2
Cash on Delivery	23.5	3
Bank Transfer	9	4
Money Transfer	5	5
Postal Transfer	1	6
Prepaid Card	0	0
Payment Through Convenience Store	0	0
Total	**100**	**0**

8.9 MAGNETIC STRIP AND DIGITAL TOKEN

A consumer first had to establish an account at a bank that was using e-cash system. Once the account is established, the consumer then downloaded the e-wallet software onto his/her computer's hard drive. Then consumer could request a transfer of digital cash. Once the digital wallet had cash, the consumer could spend that cash at merchants who were willing to accept it. The software would deduct the cash from digital wallet and transfer it to the merchant. The merchant could then transfer the cash back to the bank to confirm that it had not been double spent. The bank would cancel the e-coins or credit the merchant account at bank. Credit cards store a single charge account number in the magnetic strip on the back, smart cards can hold 100 times more data, including multiple credit card numbers and information regarding health insurance, transportation, personal identification, bank accounts and loyalty programs, such as frequent flyer accounts. This capacity makes them attractive alternatives to carrying a dozen or so credit and ID cards in a physical wallet.

A Digital token (or sometimes a hardware token, authentication token or cryptographic token) may be a physical device that an authorized user of computer services is given to aid in authentication. The term may also refer to software tokens.

Hardware tokens are typically small enough to be carried in a pocket or purse and often are designed to attach to the user's keychain. Some may store cryptographic keys, such as a digital signature, or biometric data, such as a fingerprint. Some designs feature tamper resistant packaging, other may include small keypads to allow entry of a PIN.

8.10 SUCCESS FACTORS OF E-COMMERCE PAYMENT SYSTEM

The factors which are critical for the success of E-Commerce payment systems are multifaceted. These include integrity, non-repudiation, authentication, authorization, confidentiality and reliability, which are discussed below:

Integrity: transaction data are transmitted and received unchanged and as intended.

Non-repudiation: transactions have the quality of non deniable proof or receipts.

Authentication: identities and attributes of parties engaged in commerce are established at some tolerable level of risk.

Authorization: individuals are established and recognized as entitled to receive, send or view transactions.

Confidentiality: transactions can be protected from view except by those who are authorized.

Reliability: probability of failure in the transaction-send, receive, acknowledge-is low.

8.11 COMPARISON OF ELECTRONIC PAYMENT SYSTEMS

The electronic payment system- the ability to pay electronically for goods and services purchased online- are an integral part of E-Commerce and an essential infrastructure for E-Commerce models. One of the major reasons for the widespread of E-Commerce transactions is perhaps the rapid development and growth of various electronic payment systems. In the developed countries, credit cards have been used even before the advent of Internet. The present part of the study revealed many electronic payment systems and broadly these electronic payment system can be grouped or classified into four categories:

1. Online Credit Card Payment System
2. Online Electronic Cash System
3. Electronic Cheque System and
4. Smart Cards based Electronic Payment System.

These payment systems have numbers of requirements: e.g. security, acceptability, convenience, cost, anonymity, control, and traceability. Therefore, instead of focusing on the technological specifications of various electronic payment systems, the researcher have distinguished electronic payment systems based on what is being transmitted over the network; and analyze the difference of each electronic payment system by evaluating their requirements, characteristics and assess the applicability of each system.

Table 8.2: Comparison of electronic payment systems				
Features	**Online Credit Card Payment**	**Electronic Cash**	**Electronic Cheque**	**Smart Cards**
Actual payment time	**Paid later**	**Prepaid**	**Paid later**	**Prepaid**
Transaction information transfer	The store and bank checks the status of the credit card	Free transfer. No need to leave the name of involved	Electronic checks or payment indication must be endorsed	The smart card of both parties make the transfer
Online and offline transactions	Online transactions	Online transactions	Offline transfers are allowed	Offline transfers are allowed
Bank account involvement	Credit card account makes the payment	No involvement	The bank account makes the payment	The samrt card account makes the payment
Usres	Any legitimate credit card users	Anyone	Anyone with a bank account	Anyone with a bank or credit card account
Party to which payment is made out	Distributing Bank	Store	Store	Store
Consumer's transaction risk	Most of the risk is borne by the distributing bank, consumers only have to bear part of the risk	Consumer is at risk of the electronic cash getting stolen, lost, or misused	Consumer bearns most of the risk, but the consumer can stop check payments at any time	Consumer is at risk of the smart card getting stolen, lost or misused
Current degree of popularity	Credit card organizations check for certification then total the purchases. Therefore, it can be used internationally, and is the most popular payment type	Unable to meet financial internet standards in the areas of expansion potential and internationalis m.	Can not meet international standards, therefore its not very popular	Credit card organizations check for certification then total the purchases. Therefore, it can be used internationally, and is becoming more widely used.
Anonymity	Partially or entirely anonymous	Entirely anonymous	No anonymity	Entirely anonymous, but if needed, the central processing agency can ask stores to provide information about a consumer

(Contd...)

Table 8.2: Comparison of electronic payment systems (Contd...)				
Features	**Online Credit Card Payment**	**Electronic Cash**	**Electronic Cheque**	**Smart Cards**
Actual payment time	**Paid later**	**Prepaid**	**Paid later**	**Prepaid**
Small payments	Transaction costs are high. Not suitable for small payments	Transaction costs are low, suitable for small payments	Allows stores to accumulate debts unitl it reaches a limit before paying for it. Suitable for small payments	Transaction costs are low. Allows stores to accumulate debts unitl it reaches a limit before paying for it. Therefore, it is suitable for small payments.
Database safeguarding	Safeguards regular credit card account	Needs to safeguard a large database and maintain records of the serial numbers of used electronic cash.	Safeguards regular account information	Safeguards regular account information
Transaction information face value	Can be signed and issued freely in compliance with the limit	Face value is often set, and cannot be changed	Can be signed and issued freely in compliance with the limit	Can be deducted freely in compliance with the limit.
Real/Virutal world	Can be partially used in real world	Can only be used in the virtual world	Limited to virtual world, but can share a checking account in the real world.	Can be used in real or virtual worlds.
Limit on transfer	Depends on the limit of the credit card	Depends on how much is prepaid	No limit	Depends on how much money is saved.
Mobility	Yes	No	No	Yes

After analysis and comparison of various modes of electronic payment systems, it is revealed that it is quite difficult, if not impossible, to suggest that which payment system is best. Some systems are quite similar, and differ only in some minor details. Further, all these systems have ability or potential to displace cash. Added to this, widely different technical specifications makes it difficult to choose an appropriate payment system. On the basis of above analysis it is concluded that, smart cards based electronic payment system is best. It has numerous advantages over the other electronic payment systems. Therefore, establishing a standard smart card based system, or making different system interoperable with one another is critical success factor for the smart cards based payment system. Smart card organizations around the world must establish a smart card interface standard and a conformance testing organization to make all smart card system compatible; otherwise smart card related products will not develop fully.

Technology has inarguably made our lives easier. It has cut across distance, space and even time. One of the technological innovations in banking, finance and commerce is the Electronic Payments.

Electronic Payments (e-payments) refers to the technological breakthrough that enables us to perform financial transactions electronically, thus avoiding long lines and other hassles. Electronic Payments provides greater freedom to individuals in paying their taxes, licenses, fees, fines and purchases at unconventional locations and at whichever time of the day, 365 days of the year. On the basis of present study, first remark is that despite the existence of variety of E-Commerce payment systems, credit cards are the most dominant payment system. This is consequences of advantageous characteristics, most importantly the long established networks and very wide users? base. Second, alternative E-Commerce payment systems are some countries are debit cards. In fact, like many other studies, present study also reveals that the smart card based E-Commerce payment system is best and it is expected that in the future smart cards will eventually replace the other electronic payment systems. Third, given the limited users bases, e-cash is not a feasible payment option. Thus, there are number of factors which affect the usage of E-Commerce payment systems. Among all these user base is most important.

Added to this, success of E-Commerce payment systems also depends on consumer preferences, ease of use, cost, industry agreement, authorization, security, authentication, non-refutability, accessibility and reliability and anonymity and public policy.

SUMMARY

SET (Secure Electronic Transaction) is a protocol that was developed by Visa and MasterCard and that uses the SSL standard.

SET is based on the use of an electronic signature from the buyer and a transaction involving not only the buyer and the seller, but also their respective banks.

Internet has been one of the most dominant technologies in the field of computers in the last decade. The domain of internet usage ranges from sharing information, enabling communication between people, sharing resources, remote education, distributed computation, online shopping, etc. The advent of Internet led to the beginning of a whole new set of technologies. One such technology that redefined the manner in which business was conducted is Electronic Commerce (E-Commerce).

E-Commerce or E-Business is the method of conducting business and transactions through networks and computers. E-Commerce involves buying and selling of goods, business-to-business exchange of data and trading with the participating entities in remote locations. Indeed, this was a very convenient way of doing business and soon business through E-Commerce was a norm. But this convenience also brought along with it some serious security concerns.

All the transactions carried out through E-Commerce are monetary and it involves the flow of money in some form from one remote place to another through networks. The most common way in which money is transferred in E-Commerce is using a credit card. Since the networks are inherently insecure it is possible for the malicious intruder to break into a network and gain access to secure data (Ex. reading credit card number).

This requires securing communication channels by encrypting data, identifying and authorizing participating entities, limiting access to resources and by implementing security protocols to provide the needed security.

Transport Layer Security (TLS), Secure Sockets Layer (SSL) and Secure Electronic Transaction (SET) are some of the popular security protocols. Transport Layer Security (TLS) is a protocol that ensures privacy between communicating applications and their users on the Internet. Secure Socket Layer (SSL) is a protocol developed by Netscape for transmitting private documents or data via the Internet. SET (Secure Electronic Transaction) is a system for ensuring the security of financial transactions on the Internet.

The security protocols are a collection of algorithms that facilitate the secure communication of data. Immaterial of the environment these protocols are used, the users of these protocols depend highly on the correctness of these protocols. Any minor flaw in these protocols could compromise the security of the data which these security protocols are intended to protect.

Due to the critical nature of data, documents or applications these security protocols protect, it is doubly important to prove the correctness of these protocols. Formal methods have been used in a wide variety of environments to verify whether complex systems accomplish their intended functionality. One area where formal methods received wide attention is in the area of security protocol verification.

EXERCISE

1. What do you mean by Set protocol?
2. What is payment gateway?
3. What is electronic payment system?
4. What is smart card?
5. Explain credit card, magnetic strip card and E-check.
6. What do you mean by digital token?
7. Write down a comparison among all the payment system.

CHAPTER

9

E-Commerce Applications

9.1 ONLINE BANKING

A system allowing individuals to perform banking activities at home, via the internet. Some online banks are traditional banks which also offer online banking, while others are online only and have no physical presence. Online banking through traditional banks enable customers to perform all routine transactions, such as account transfers, balance inquiries, bill payments, and stop-payment requests, and some even offer online loan and credit card applications. Account information can be accessed anytime, day or night, and can be done from anywhere. A few online banks update information in real-time, while others do it daily. Once information has been entered, it doesn't need to be re-entered for similar subsequent checks, and future payments can be scheduled to occur automatically. Many banks allow for file transfer between their program and popular accounting software packages, to simplify record keeping. Despite the advantages, there are a few drawbacks. It does take some time to set up and get used to an online account. Also, some banks only offer online banking in a limited area. In addition, when an account holder pays online, he/she may have to put in a check request as much as two weeks before the payment is due, but the bank may withdraw the money from the account the day that request is received, meaning the person has lost up to two weeks of interest on that payment. Online-only banks have a few additional drawbacks: an account holder has to mail in deposits (other than direct deposits), and some services that traditional banks offer are difficult or impossible for online-only banks to offer, such as traveler's checks and cashier's checks.

Online banking (or **Internet banking**) allows customers to conduct financial transactions on a secure website operated by their retail or virtual bank, credit union or building society.

Online banking is the practice of making bank transactions or paying bills via the Internet. Thanks to technology, and the Internet in particular, we no longer have to leave the house. We can shop online, communicate online, and now, we can even do our banking online. Online banking allows us to make deposits, withdrawals and pay bills all with the click of a mouse. It doesn't get much more convenient than that.

Online banking solutions have many features and capabilities in common, but traditionally also have some that are application specific.

The common features fall broadly into several categories

- Transactional (e.g., performing a financial transaction such as an account to account transfer, paying a bill, wire transfer and applications apply for a loan, new account, etc.)
  1. Electronic bill presentment and payment - EBPP
  2. Funds transfer between a customer's own checking and savings accounts, or to another customer's account
  3. Investment purchase or sale
  4. Loan applications and transactions, such as repayments of enrollments
- Non-transactional (e.g., online statements, check links, co browsing, chat)
  – Bank statements
- Financial Institution Administration -
- Support of multiple users having varying levels of authority
- Transaction approval process
- Wire transfer

Features commonly unique to Internet banking include

- Personal financial management support, such as importing data into personal accounting software. Some online banking platforms support account aggregation to allow the customers to monitor all of their accounts in one place whether they are with their main bank or with other institutions.

9.1.1 Origin of Online Banking

The advent of the Internet and the popularity of personal computers presented both an opportunity and a challenge for the banking industry.

For years, financial institutions have used powerful computer networks to automate millions of daily transactions; today, often the only paper record is the customer's receipt at the point of sale. Now that its customers are connected to the Internet via personal computers, banks envision similar economic advantages by adapting those same internal electronic processes to home use.

Banks view online banking as a powerful "value added" tool to attract and retain new customers while helping to eliminate costly paper handling and teller interactions in an increasingly competitive banking environment.

9.1.2 Brick-to-click Banks

Today, most large national banks, many regional banks and even smaller banks and credit unions offer some form of online banking, variously known as PC banking, home banking, electronic banking or Internet banking. Those that do are sometimes referred to as "brick-to-click" banks, both to distinguish them from brick-and-mortar banks that have yet to offer online banking, as well as from online or "virtual" banks that have no physical branches or tellers whatsoever.

The challenge for the banking industry has been to design this new service channel in such a way that its customers will readily learn to use and trust it. After all, banks have spent generations earning our trust; they aren't about to risk that on a Web site that is frustrating, confusing or less than secure.

Most of the large banks now offer fully secure, fully functional online banking for free or for a small fee. Some smaller banks offer limited access or functionality; for instance, you may be able to view your account balance and history but not initiate transactions online. As more banks succeed online and more customers use their sites, fully functional online banking likely will become as commonplace as automated teller machines.

9.1.3 Virtual Banks

If you don't mind foregoing the teller window, lobby cookie and kindly bank president, a "virtual" or e-bank, such as Virtual Bank or Giant Bank, may save you very real money. Virtual banks are banks without bricks; from the customer's perspective, they exist entirely on the Internet, where they offer pretty much the same range of services and adhere to the same federal regulations as your corner bank.

Virtual banks pass the money they save on overhead like buildings and tellers along to you in the form of higher yields, lower fees and more generous account thresholds.

The major disadvantage of virtual banks revolves around ATMs. Because they have no ATM machines, virtual banks typically charge the same surcharge that your brick-and-mortar bank would if you used another bank's automated teller. Likewise, many virtual banks won't accept deposits via ATM; you'll have to either deposit the check by mail or transfer money from another account.

9.1.4 Advantages of Online Banking

- **Convenience:** Unlike your corner bank, online banking sites never close; they're available 24 hours a day, seven days a week, and they're only a mouse click away.
- **Ubiquity:** If you're out of state or even out of the country when a money problem arises, you can log on instantly to your online bank and take care of business, 24/7.
- **Transaction speed:** Online bank sites generally execute and confirm transactions at or quicker than ATM processing speeds.
- **Efficiency:** You can access and manage all of your bank accounts, including IRAs, CDs, even securities, from one secure site.
- **Effectiveness:** Many online banking sites now offer sophisticated tools, including account aggregation, stock quotes, rate alerts and portfolio managing programs to help you manage all of your assets more effectively. Most are also compatible with money managing programs such as Quicken and Microsoft Money.

9.1.5 Disadvantages of Online Banking

- **Start-up may take time:** In order to register for your bank's online program, you will probably have to provide ID and sign a form at a bank branch. If you and your spouse wish to view and manage your assets together online, one of you may have to sign a durable power of attorney before the bank will display all of your holdings together.
- **Learning curve:** Banking sites can be difficult to navigate at first. Plan to invest some time and/or read the tutorials in order to become comfortable in your virtual lobby.
- **Bank site changes:** Even the largest banks periodically upgrade their online programs, adding new features in unfamiliar places. In some cases, you may have to re-enter account information.
- **The trust thing:** For many people, the biggest hurdle to online banking is learning to trust it. Did my transaction go through? Did I push the transfer button once or twice? Best bet: always print the transaction receipt and keep it with your bank records until it shows up on your personal site and/or your bank statement.

9.2 E-GOVERNANCE AND EDI

e-Government (from electronic government, also known as e-gov, digital government, online government or in a certain context transformational government) refers to government's use of information technology to exchange information and services with citizens, businesses, and other arms of government. e-Government may be applied by the legislature, judiciary, or administration, in order to improve internal efficiency, the delivery of public services, or processes of democratic governance. It also refers to the citizen to government interaction including the feed back of policies. The primary delivery models are Government-to-Citizen or Government-to-Customer (G2C), Government-to-Business (G2B) and Government-to-Government (G2G) & Government-to-Employees (G2E). The most important anticipated benefits of e-government include improved efficiency, convenience, and better accessibility of public services.

9.2.1 What is E-Governance

It is the use of a range of modern Information and Communication Technologies such as Internet, Local Area Networks, mobiles etc. by Government to improve the effectiveness, efficiency, service delivery and to promote democracy

Governance : An Information perspective

- Representative democracy relies on supposition that best way to make a decision is wider participation for all its citizens having access to relevant information.
- Government is by nature an information intensive organization.
- Information is power and information management is political .

Governance : In IT framework

- Expansion of Internet and electronic commerce, is redefining relationships among various stake holders in the process of Governance.
- A new model of governance would be based upon the transactions in virtual space, digital economy and dealing with knowledge oriented societies.
- Electronic Governance is an emerging trend to re-invent the way the Government works.

E-Governance: Focus

- Greater attention to improve service delivery mechanism
- Enhancing the efficiency of production
- Emphasis upon the wider access of information

E-Governance vs. E-Government

- Government's foremost job is to focus society on achieving the public interest."
- Governance is a way of describing the links between government and its broader environment - political, social and administrative."

Table 9.1

Government	Governance
superstructure	functionality
decisions	processes
rules	goals
rules	performance
implementation	coordination
outputs	outcomes
e-Government	e-Governance
electronic service delivery	electronic consultation
electronic workflow	electronic controllership
electronic voting	electronic engagement
electronic productivity	networked societal guidance

9.2.2 Why introduced E-Governances

E-Government can transform citizen service, provide access to information to empower citizens, enable their participation in government and enhance citizen economic and social opportunities, so that they can make better lives, for themselves and for the next generation.

9.3 ELECTRONIC DATA INTERCHANGE (EDI)

Electronic Data Interchange is the computer-to-computer exchange of routine business data between trading partners in standard data formats. This definition contains 3 key concepts about EDI:

1. **Computer-to-computer:** EDI in its most efficient form flows directly out of a sender's computer system directly into a receiver's computer system without any human intervention; however, it is not always possible for EDI to flow in this most efficient manner.
2. **Routing business data:** EDI is used for routine business documents like Purchase Orders and Invoices. It is not used for non-routine business documents like complicated contracts or information meant for humans to read and analyze.
3. **Standard data formats:** A standard definition of the location and structure of the data is provided. Unstructured text is not EDI.

The diagram above illustrates how much slower the conventional paper process than the EDI process. Additionally, the conventional paper process includes substantially more human intervention to move business information from one company to another.

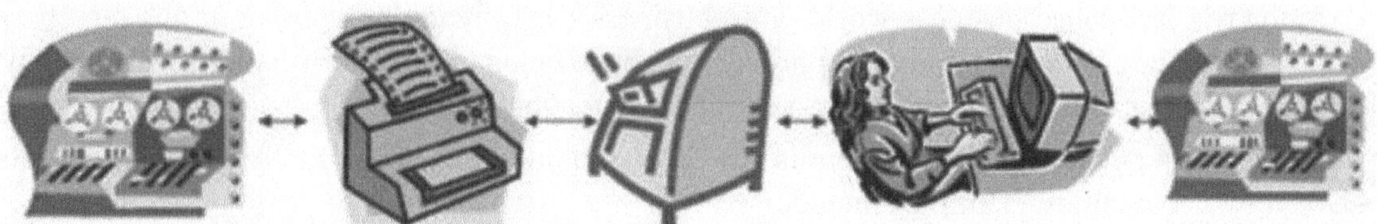

Conventional Paper Process

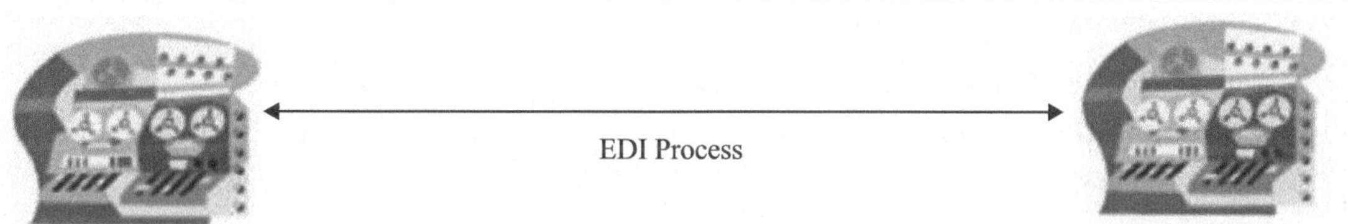

EDI Process

Fig. 9.1

The conventional process requires someone to handle a printed computer generated form and mail it. Then, the recipient re-keys the data back into another computer for their internal processing. (It is estimated that 80% of the data that is keyed into computers is output from other computers!) The EDI process is a computer transmitting the information directly to another computer, eliminating the paperwork and human intervention.

Electronic Data Interchange, or EDI, is not a new technology and in fact has been around since the late 1960s. While EDI has benefited enormously from advances in technology, eg the introduction of the internet, EDI is not technology dependant. There are preferred ways to implement EDI in a company, but there are many approaches to choose from. The approach chosen should be driven by a company's business needs, not a particular implementation or technology.

In its simplest form, EDI is the computer to computer exchange, between two companies, of standard business documents in electronic format. There are two key elements in basic EDI. First, electronic documents replace paper based ones. Second, the exchange of documents takes place in a standardized format. Using these two basic concepts, any business can enter the world of EDI and begin taking advantage of the speed and economy of electronic commerce, or E-Commerce.

Fig. 9.2

In today's fast-paced business world, your business may already be moving in this direction, customers or suppliers may already be approaching you to begin trading information electronically. For the newcomer to EDI, it may seem a very confusing subject area.

So what is a document? A document is any form of communication, usually paper based, sent between two companies, examples include:

- Purchase Orders
- Invoices
- Shipping Notices
- Export / Import Notices
- Carrier to carrier waybills
- Funds transfer
- Design specifications
- Health insurance claims

EDI is essentially a data processing concept which is independent of communication protocols or transmission media. EDI is a logical outgrowth of the standard computerization going on within companies over the last few decades. With EDI, the type of electronic communication between departments within a company can now easily be extended to reach out to other companies or trading partners.

EDI replaces human readable, paper or electronic based documents with machine readable, electronically coded documents. With EDI, the sending computer creates the message and the receiving computer interprets the message without any human involvement at all.

Before learning about what makes up an EDI system and how to implement one, it is important to look at an example that highlights some of the key differences between traditional paper document transactions and EDI. One of the first places where many companies implement EDI is in the exchange of a purchase order, (PO). In the traditional method of processing a purchase order, a buyer or purchasing agent will go through a fairly standard procedure to create a purchase order, consisting of the following steps:

- A buyer reviews data from an inventory or planning system
- The buyer enters data into a screen in the purchasing system to create a PO
- The buyer waits for the PO to be printed, usually on a special form
- After the PO is printed, the buyer mails it to the vendor
- The vendor receives the PO and posts it in their order entry system
- The buyer calls the vendor periodically to determine if the PO has been received and processed

When you add up the internal processing time required by the sender and receiver, and then add a couple of days in the mail, this process normally takes between three and five days. This assumes first that both the sender and receiver handled the PO quickly and that at every point along the way there were no errors in transcribing data from a form to a system.

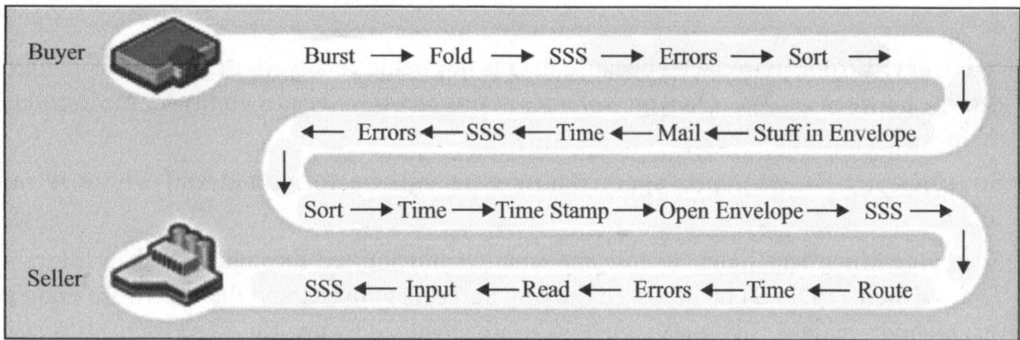

Fig. 9.3

Now consider the same document exchange when a company places its purchase orders electronically using EDI:

- The buyer reviews the data and creates the PO, but does not print it
- EDI software creates an electronic version of the PO and transmits it automatically to the sender within minutes
- The vendor's order entry system receives the PO and updates the system immediately upon receipt

What took up to five days with paper and the postal system has just taken less than one hour. By eliminating the paper handling from most of the stages of the process, EDI has the potential to transform a traditional paper based process to look like this:

The major benefits of implementing EDI within your business are discussed in more detail in the 'Benefits of EDI' section of this Micro site but in summary EDI can help improve speed and accuracy of transactions, reduce costs and it provides improved flexibility when interacting on a daily basis with your trading partners or customers.

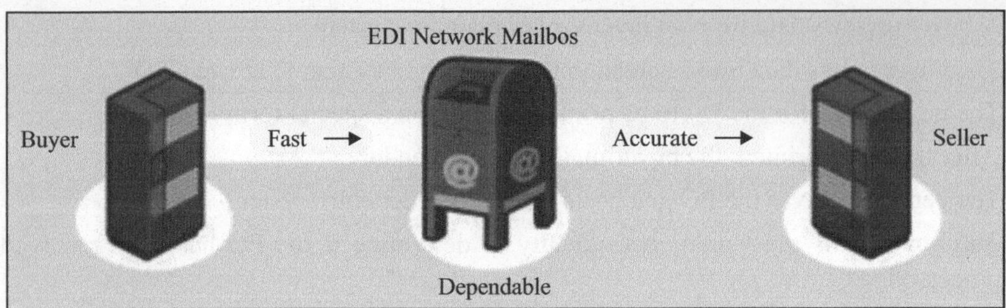

Fig. 9.4

9.3.1 Benefits of EDI

- **Speed:** Data can move directly out of one computer system and into another with little to no delay.
- **Accuracy:** Errors are reduced because data is not being re-keyed. Error rates from entering data are between .5 - 3%. On large volumes of transactions, the possibility for the introduction of errors is enormous.
- **Simplicity:** EDI standards specify how data will be formatted and where it can be found.
- **Security:** Much less likely to lose information transmitted through EDI than information sent via mail. EDI can be accessed only by authorized users, and then there are audit trails and archives of data. EDI data cannot be easily changed by unauthorized users. It is also not subject to viruses.

These 4 benefits produce the following results:

- Faster buy-sell cycle time
- Faster cash flow
- Reduced order lead time
- Reduced inventories
- Ability to conduct just-in-time manufacturing
- Improved trading partner relationships

9.3.2 How does the EDI Process Work in the Retail Environment?

The retailer will initiate the process with an electronic transmission of an electronic Purchase Order (850). The supplier will receive the order, case it and print UCC-128 labels. Then, the order is packed and the UCC-128 labels are placed on the cartons. The cartons are then shipped to the retailer and the supplier electronically transmits an Advanced Ship Notice (856). After the shipment has been sent, the supplier transmits an electronic Invoice (810) for the goods. These electronic documents are sent in a standard Electronic Data Interchange (EDI) format.

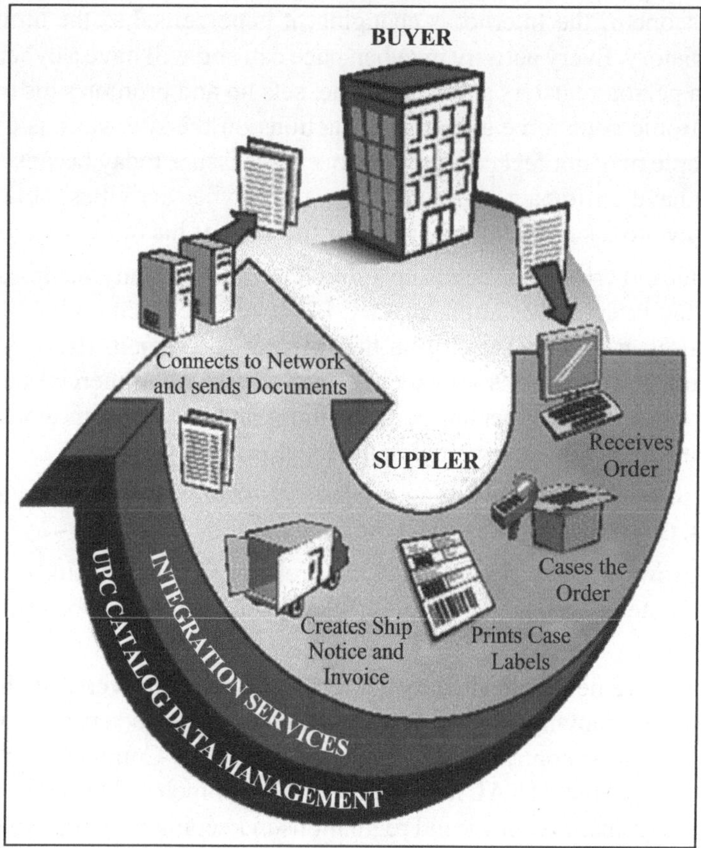

Fig. 9.5

9.4 LAW OF E-COMMERCE

Many believe the Internet to be full of natural anarchy, so that a system of law and regulation for the Internet seems contradictory. However, cyberspace is, in fact, governed by a system of law and regulation called cyberlaw. There is no single exhaustive definition of the term cyberlaw. One broadly accepted definition of cyberlaw is a generic term that refers to all the legal and regulatory aspects of Internet and the World Wide Web. Anything concerned with or related to or emanating from any legal aspects or issues concerning any activity of people in cyberspace comes within the domain of cyberlaw.

The growth of electronic commerce has created the need for vibrant and effective regulatory mechanisms, which would further strengthen the legal infrastructure that is crucial to the success of electronic commerce. All of these regulatory mechanisms and the legal infrastructure come within the domain of cyberlaw.

Cyberlaw is important because it touches almost all aspects of transactions and activities concerning the Internet, the World Wide Web and cyberspace. Cyberlaw also concerns everyone.

As the nature and scope of the Internet is changing, it is perceived as the ultimate medium ever evolved in human history. Every activity in cyberspace can and will have a cyber legal perspective. From the moment a person registers a domain name, sets up and promotes his or her web site, and then conducts electronic commerce and has transactions on the site, various cyberlaw issues are involved. Some people may not feel concerned about these issues today because they may feel that such issues do not have an impact or relevance to their cyber activities. However, each person would eventually have to take note of cyberlaw for the sake of his or her own benefit.

Awareness about cyberlaw has begun to grow. Previously, many technical experts felt that legal regulation of the Internet was not necessary. However, the rapid growth of technologies and the Internet made it clear that no activity on the Internet can remain free from the influence of Cyberlaw. Publishing a web page is an excellent way for any commercial business or entity to increase its exposure to millions of persons, organizations and governments worldwide. This feature of the Internet is causing much controversy in the legal fraternity.

Cyberlaw is also a constantly evolving process. As newer opportunities and challenges are surfacing, cyberlaw is being modifying to fit the needs of the time.

As the Internet grows, numerous legal issues arise relating to domain names, intellectual property rights, electronic commerce, privacy, encryption, electronic contracts, cybercrime, online banking, spamming and so on.

The arrival of the Internet and related technologies has made irreversible changes to the world today. In a world, which is moving steadily towards the information society and knowledge economy, it is essential that law must contribute its inputs to promote E-Commerce. In 1996, the United Nations came up with the UNCITRAL Model Law on E-Commerce. This law encouraged member states to legislate various national laws and regulations in keeping with principles contained in the Model Law. In 2001, the United Nations drew up the UNCITRAL Model Law on Electronic Signatures.

As cyberlaw develops around the world, there is a growing realization among different nation states that their laws must be harmonized and international best practices and principles must guide implementation. Many countries are trying to establish harmonized legal regimes in order to promote online commerce.

However, in the subregion of South Asia, especially among members of the South Asian Association for Regional Cooperation (SAARC), India and Pakistan are the two predominant players who have enacted E-Commerce laws. India enacted the Information Technology Act, 2000 while Pakistan promulgated the Electronic Transactions Ordinance, 2002. All of the countries in the SAARC region have not yet enacted E-Commerce laws at the time of this paper, the other SAARC members had not yet enacted E-Commerce laws.

India is an excellent example of how legal systems mature with the passage of time in order to provide the required boost to E-Commerce. This paper examines the example of India in slightly more detail. E-Commerce law in India is the Indian Information Technology Act, 2000 and it demonstrates the need for other countries to harmonize their legal systems to stay in tune with the rapidly growing requirements of E-Commerce.

The Parliament of India passed its cyberlaw in the form of the Information Technology Act, 2000, which provides the legal infrastructure for E-Commerce. The Act received the assent of the President of India and became the law of the land on 17 October 2000.

The objective of the Information Technology Act, 2000 would be to provide legal recognition for transactions carried out by means of electronic data interchange and other means of electronic communication, commonly referred to as electronic methods of communication and storage of information. The act would also facilitate electronic filing of documents with various government agencies and further to amend the Indian Penal Code, the Indian Evidence Act, 1872, the Banker's Book Evidence Act, 1891 and the Reserve Bank of India Act, 1934 for related matters.

The Act thereafter stipulates numerous provisions in order to provide for the legal framework so that legal sanctity is accorded to all electronic records and other activities carried out by electronic means. The Act further states that unless otherwise agreed to, the acceptance of a contract expressed by electronic means of communication shall have legal validity and enforceability. The Act would facilitate electronic intercourse in trade and commerce, eliminate barriers and obstacles to electronic commerce that result from the celebrated uncertainties relating to writing and signature requirements over the Internet. The objectives of the Act also aim to promote and develop the legal and business infrastructure necessary for implementing electronic commerce.

9.5 ANALYSIS OF OTHER ICT AND E-COMMERCE ELEMENTS

Analysis of other elements related to ICT and E-Commerce shows the diversity of approaches and a wide range in the scope and breadth of policy, laws and regulations.

Much of the work concerning the legal and regulatory frameworks for E-Commerce in South Asia has been done in India and Pakistan. Both countries have sought to legalize the electronic format and granted legality to electronic commerce transactions.

India and Pakistan have provided for authentication of the electronic documents and records. However, the approaches have differed. India has enacted a technology specific law by stating that the authentication of electronic information can only be done by use of an asymmetric crypto-system and hash function or public key cryptography. Pakistan has taken the more pragmatic approach by not committing the mistake of making a technology specific electronic law. Instead, the law is technologically neutral and talks about the authentication of electronic records by electronic signatures as compared to digital signatures.

9.6 CYBER LAW ISSUES IN E-BUSINESS MANAGEMENT

Consumer protection laws for cyberspace differ from country to country and court judgments passed in one country are often unenforceable in another country. This makes it difficult for online consumers to protect their rights. The increasing rate of cyber crime all over the world has made governments realize the need for cyber laws. In 1986, the CFAA were passed in the US to prosecute hackers.

The Act can be applied to any individual if he tries to access a system without having the required authorization. Another serious crime in cyberspace is credit card fraud. Credit card abuse laws have declared that disclosing, using and distributing credit card information of one individual to another with the intention to defraud, is a crime.

The US law declares that the possession of software to generate codes (that can help obtain the code of a stolen credit card) is a crime. The trading of pirated software is a billion dollar business. The web facilitates free trafficking of illegal copies of copyrighted software.

Many countries have framed laws to deal with software piracy. It is illegal to advertise or transfer or download copies of pirated software on the web. Hackers send harmful viruses over the Internet which can destroy data and cause huge losses to organizations. The cyber laws of many countries impose heavy penalties and imprisonment on people responsible for spreading viruses.

The ECP Act seeks to protect the privacy of users and businesses by declaring it illegal to intercept the communication on the Internet without any authorization. Some of the problems faced by companies marketing their products and services on the web are volatility, trust, and locus.

Online players operate in a highly volatile environment because of precarious consumer demands. The revenues, share prices, and customer response to a website may rise to peak at some points of time and may dwindle later. Customer confidence is vital for E-Commerce players.

They have to sustain and enhance customer confidence by offering user-friendly features and deploying advanced technology and security systems. The locus of an online customer is not restricted to a desktop computer. He may access the same website from different devices such as a mobile phone, PDA, or laptop at different times. An online player needs to provide the best quality of services to the customer irrespective of the medium he uses to access the company.

The major technical problems faced by online players are differences in application platforms, problems in communication and scarcity of skills. Online players also need to deal with legal issues regarding similarity in domain names, website content, and features. In the absence of a uniform regulatory framework for E-Commerce, businesses are finding it difficult to combat cyber crime. Public and private agencies, and businesses across the world have to work together to form comprehensive and uniform laws that are universally enforceable

9.7 OVERVIEW OF INDIAN IT ACT

The set of laws that are enforceable in India are known as Indian laws. The provisions of modern Indian laws are based on the stipulations of the English common law. Several legislations passed by the British Government in India, during the British rules, are still applicable. However, they have been amended to suit the modern times. Also, the Indian laws are influenced by the legislations of Western nations.

The primary sources of laws in India are the Constitution of India and the laws passed by authorized government bodies. Also, the President and the State Governors are empowered to issue ordinance. Another important source of Indian laws is the verdicts or judgments passed by the Supreme Courts, High Courts and Tribunals. Only a few Indian laws are in compliance with the guidelines provided by the United Nations on critical issues; this includes environmental pollution and human rights laws.

9.7.1 Key Branches of Indian laws

Indian labor laws

Indian labor laws are laws that govern the employment conditions, labor issues and industrial disputes in India. The primary objective of labor laws is to protect the interest of employers and workers. Important labor laws in India include:

- The Payment of Bonus Act, 1965.
- The Industrial Dispute Act, 1947
- The Wages Act, 1948
- The Employees State Insurance Act, 1948
- The Equal Remuneration Act, 1976
- The Factories Act, 1948
- The Child Labour Act, 1986

Personal Laws

Personal laws in India are applicable to individuals by virtue of their religion. The three fundamental branches of personal laws are Muslim laws, Hindu law, and Christian laws. Personal laws primarily govern the litigations related to personal matters, such as marriage, divorce, succession, adoption and guardianship.

Civil Laws

The working of Civil Courts in India is governed by the Civil Procedure Code (CPC). The CPC lays down guidelines to file civil court cases, requisite court fees, legal rights of the complainant and the defendant and power of the Civil Courts exercised to issue orders.

Criminal Laws

The Indian Penal Code (IPC) that came into effect in 1862 is applicable to the whole of India. It is known as Ranbir Penal Code (RPC) in the State of Jammu and Kashmir. It is applicable on all Indian citizens who commit any criminal offence.

Many countries other than India have their data protection laws as a separate discipline. They have well framed and established laws, exclusively for the data protection.

9.8 GOVERNMENT POLICIES AND AGENDA

Our constitution has provided the law relating to privacy. Its interpretation is found insufficient to provide adequate protection to the data. In the year 2000, effort has been made by our legislature to embrace privacy issues relating to computer system under the purview of IT Act, 2000. This Act contains certain provisions which provide protection of stored data. In the year 2006, our legislature has also introduced a bill known as 'The Personal Data Protection Bill' so as to provide protection to the personal information of the person.

9.8.1 Under IT Act, 2000

Section 43: This section provides protection against unauthorized access of the computer system by imposing heavy penalty up to one crore. The unauthorized downloading, extraction and copying of data are also covered under the same penalty. Clause 'c' of this section imposes penalty for unauthorized introduction of computer viruses of contaminants. Clause 'g' provides penalties for assisting the unauthorized access.

Section 65: This section provides for computer source code. If anyone knowingly of intentionally conceals, destroys, alters or causes another to do as such shall have to suffer a penalty of imprisonment or fine up to 2 lakh rupees. Thus protection has been provided against tampering of computer source documents.

Section 66: Protection against hacking has been provided under this section. As per this section hacking is defined as any act with an intention to cause wrongful loss or damage to any person or with the knowledge that wrongful loss of damage will be caused to any person and information residing in a computer resource must be either destroyed, deleted, altered or its value and utility get diminished. This section imposes the penalty of imprisonment of three years or fine up to two lakh rupees or both on the hacker.

Section 70: This section provides protection to the data stored in the protected system. Protected systems are those computers, computer system or computer network to which the appropriate government, by issuing gazette information in the official gazette, declared it as a protected system. Any access or attempt to secure access of that system in contravention of the provision of this section will make the person accessed liable for punishment of imprisonment which may extend to ten years and shall also be liable to fine.

Section 72: This section provides protection against breach of confidentiality and privacy of the data. As per this, any person upon whom powers have been conferred under IT Act and allied rules to secure access to any electronic record, book, register, correspondence, information document of other material discloses it to any other person, shall be punished with imprisonment which may extend to two years or with fine which may extend to one lakh rupees or both.

9.8.2 Law of Contract

These days' companies are relying on the contract law as a useful means to protect their information. The corporate houses enters into several agreements with other companies, clients, agencies or partners to keep their information secured to the extent they want to secure it. Agreements such as 'non circumvention and non-disclosure' agreements, 'user license' agreements, 'referral partner' agreements etc. are entered into by them which contains confidentiality and privacy clauses and also arbitration clauses for the purpose of resolving the dispute if arises. These agreements help them in smooth running of business. BPO companies have implemented processes like BS 7799 and the ISO 17799 standards of information security management, which restrict the quantity of data that can be made available to employees of BPO and call centers.

9.8.3 Indian Penal code

It imposes punishment for the wrongs which were expected to occur till the last decade. But it failed to incorporate within itself the punishment for crimes related to data which has become the order of the day.

The Personal Data Protection Bill, 2006

Upon the footprints of the foreign laws, this bill has been introduced in the Rajya Sabha on December 8th 2006. The purpose of this bill is to provide protection of personal data and information of an individual collected for a particular purpose by one organization, and to prevent its usage by other organization for commercial or other purposes and entitle the individual to claim compensation or damages due to disclosure of personal data or information of any individual without his consent and for matters connected with the Act or incidental to the Act. Provisions contained in this Act are relating to nature of data to be obtained for the specific purpose and the quantum of data to be obtained for that purpose. Data controllers have been proposed to be appointed to look upon the matters relating to violation of the proposed Act.

9.8.4 U.K Law

U.K. parliament framed its Data Protection Act (DPA) in the year 1984 which thereafter repealed by the DPA of 1998. This Act is basically instituted for the purpose of providing protection and privacy of the personal data of the individuals in UK. The Act covers data which can be used to identify a living person. This includes names, birthday, anniversary dates, addresses, telephone numbers, fax numbers, e-mail addresses etc. It applies only to the data which is held or intended to be held, on computers or other equipments operating automatically in response to instructions given for that purpose or held in a relevant filing system.

As per the Act, the persons and organizations which store personal data must register with the information commissioner, which has been appointed as the government official to oversee the Act. The Act put restrictions on collection of data. Personal data can be obtained only for one or more specified and lawful purposes, and shall not be further processed in any manner incompatible with that purpose or purposes. The personal data shall be adequate, relevant, and not excessive in relation to the purpose or purposes for which they are processed.

9.8.5 U.S Law

Though both U.S and the European Union focus on enhancing privacy protection of their citizens, U.S takes a different approach to privacy from that of the European Union. US adopted the sectoral approach that relies of mix of legislation, regulation, and self regulation. In U.S, data are grouped into several classes on the basis of their utility and importance. Thereafter, accordingly a different degree of protection is awarded to the different classes of data.

Several Acts were also passed in order to stabilize the data protection laws in the United States. The privacy Act was passed in the year 1974 which provided for establishing standards for when it is reasonable, ethical and justifiable for government agencies to compare data in different databases. Another Electronic Communications Privacy Act was passed for restricting the interception of electronic communications and prohibiting the access to stored data without the consent of the user or the communication service.

Further the Children's Online Privacy Protection Act was passed by the US Congress in October 1998 requiring website operators to obtain parental consent before obtaining personal information from children, and a Consumer Internet Privacy Protection Act required an ISP to get permission of the subscriber before disclosing his personal information to third parties.

However, the existing federal laws is not suffice to cover the broad range of issues and circumstances that make the new digital environment a threat to personal privacy. Furthermore, the US Government has been reluctant to impose a regulatory burden on Electronic Commerce activities that could hamper its development and has looked for an answer in self regulation.

9.9 BUSINESS TRANSACTION ON WEB

A Business Transaction is a consistent change in the state of the business that is driven by a well-defined business function.

A business transaction is driven by well-defined business tasks and events that directly or indirectly contribute to generating economic value, such as processing and paying an insurance claim, and has also an associated number of parameters that represent security and timing requirements. Business transactions always either succeed or fail with respect to the business tasks (functions) that initiated them and govern them throughout their execution. If a business transaction completes successfully then each participant will have made consistent state changes, which, in aggregate, reflect the desired outcome of the multi-party business interaction.

At structural level, a business transaction is made up of a requesting (initiating) business activity performed by an initiating partner (party) and a responding business activity performed by the responding business partner. The initiating business activity sends a business document to a responding business activity that may return a business signal (signifying the completion of an activity) and possibly a business document as the last responding message. A transaction is associated with an SLA that describes the agreed upon QoS requirements and usually outlines what each party can do in the event the intended actions are not carried out (e.g., promised services not rendered, services rendered but payment not issued). A series of collaborative activities that explicitly enforces the achievement of an agreed-upon business objective in end-to-end processes. This objective is subject to service-level agreements that govern the choreographed/orchestrated behavior, non-functional and timing requirements, correlated exchange of information, and control flow of composed services.

It also consists of the exchange of data to facilitate the financing and payment aspect of the business transaction. It is similar to buying and selling of products and services on the web.

Some of the advantages of doing business transaction on the web are:

1. **Global reach:** Goods and service can be sold to customers world wide.

2. **Personalization:** Companies can customize products and reduce inventory.
3. **Interactivity:** Customers and suppliers can negotiate prices online.
4. **Right time and integrated marketing:** Online retailers provide products when and where customers want them and promotions can be direct to individual customers.
5. **Cast reducing:** E-business can reduce cost.

9.9.1 Examples of Business Transactions

Choose your favorite five:

- A sale of merchandise or services.
- A purchase of supplies or raw material.
- Receipt of a payment for an Accounts Receivable.
- Payment of a bill in Accounts Payable.
- Receipt of loan proceeds.
- Repayment of a loan.
- Issuance of a paycheck.
- Payment of employer taxes.
- Payment of income taxes.
- Purchase of a Fixed Asset.

A business transaction may be as short as a phone call to the bank for an account balance or as long as a mortgage (from the initial mortgage application to final satisfaction being sent after the last payment) and perhaps even as long as the lifelong relationship with a bank (covering multiple accounts used for different purposes). Business transactions may have hierarchical relationships (such as the relationships between the business transaction represented by a check to the business transaction represented by a bank account).

Each type of business transaction may have multiple states before it is completed. At each stage in its lifecycle it may generate various measurements (financial or otherwise) that may be used by management/stockholders/regulators to monitor and/or control the business.

9.9.2 General Requirements

Long Running Transactions

The business transactions that I described above are not the traditional transactions that are handled by TP monitors such as CICS. They have a long lifetime (may even be days or years) and multiple interactions with users over their lifetime. The traditional transactions only cover a small part of the life of these transactions and multiple traditional transactions are often required in order to complete a single business transaction. Often, the traditional transactions execute in different environments and it becomes difficult to connect all of the pieces back to the original customer need that started the whole process.

I believe that a traditional transaction has approximately the same relationship to a business transaction that a method has to an object. Just as a method may transition an object from one valid state to another, a traditional transaction may transition a business transaction from one valid state to another.

Work Flow

A BTPS should have the ability to process work flows. Each state of the business transaction can be represented by a step in the work flow. Each step in the work flow may be composed of the following phases:

1. **Work Planning:** The periodic process of planning for future work. This often involves review of historical work levels and/or the results of Work Plans from "upstream" processing areas that generate work for this processing area.
2. **Work Receiving and Arrival Reporting:** The process of receiving and getting control over newly arrived work. This often includes notifications to processors of work awaiting processing.
3. **Work Monitoring:** Review all available work, prioritization and scheduling the work to be done.
4. **Work Processing and Recording:** Doing the work and recording the results of the work.
5. **Work Routing:** Based on the change in state to the work, pass the work along to the next stage in the processing.
6. **Work Evaluation:** On a periodic basis, analyze the work. The information from this step is often the input to the Work Planning phase (step 1 above).

The work flow component of the system should allow the rules that define sequence of steps (dependencies) and the rules that define the processing to be performed at each step to be easily modified by the users. (This process should also be a work flow.)

Accounting

Accounting information is only one type of information to be collected by the work flow processing. Since internal and external financial reporting is often used to monitor and control a business, collecting this information is important. However, there are many business transactions that are not directly recorded in the financial reporting systems (i.e. the number of calls to the "banking by phone" unit that did not get through to a bank employee) that may generate useful information for internal reporting purposes.

Authorization

Just as accounting records what happened after the transaction is processed, a large part of business transactions involves authorizing each transaction before the real processing is done. In my experience, these rules are changed on a fairly frequent basis as the business changes it policies. However, once the authorization step(s) is (are) completed the underlying work often does not change.

Queue Management

In order to decouple the work flow steps from one another it is usually necessary to add queues between steps. A good work flow engine should allow the users (and managers) to monitor queues in order to shift processing resources as necessary. (Mostly in Work Receiving and Arrival Reporting or Work Monitoring phases defined above.)

Difficult Problems

The work flow engine should be responsible for doing all of steps defined above except for Work Processing and Recording (phase 4 above) which is unique to each step in each business transaction. It is even possible to reuse Work Processing programs associated with authorization in multiple business transactions. However, there are three functions that look like responsibilities of the work flow engine that often require detailed knowledge of the business transactions. This breaks the encapsulation of the business transactions.

Authorization Rule Dependence on Business Transaction Data

The authorization rules often vary based on the current state (the values of some fields) of the business transaction. It is difficult to write a generic authorization processor without detailed knowledge of each business transaction.

Routing

It is often possible to route a business transaction to one of many steps depending on the results of the Work Processing in this step. The routing rules often vary based on the current state of the business transaction. It is difficult to write a generic routing engine without detailed knowledge of each business transaction.

Work Monitoring

When human beings are the business transaction processors at some point in the Work Processing they often need the ability to select work based on varying criteria (i.e. I normally want to process work in the order it was received except when I am near the end of day - when I want the "big" transactions first).

9.10 ETHICS

Ethics is a general term for what is often described as the “science (study) of morality”.

In philosophy, ethical behavior is that which is “good” or “right.” The Western tradition of ethics is sometimes called moral philosophy. This is one part of value theory (axiology) the other part is aesthetics of the four major branches of philosophy, alongside metaphysics, epistemology, and logic. Ethics (also known as moral philosophy) is a branch of philosophy which seeks to address questions about morality; that is, about concepts such as good and bad, right and wrong, justice, and virtue.

Ethics (also known as moral philosophy) is a branch of philosophy that addresses questions about morality that is, concepts such as good and evil, right and wrong, virtue and vice, justice, etc.

Major branches of ethics include:

- Meta-ethics, about the theoretical meaning and reference of moral propositions and how their truth-values (if any) may be determined;
- Normative ethics, about the practical means of determining a moral course of action;
- Applied ethics, about how moral outcomes can be achieved in specific situations;
- Moral psychology, about how moral capacity or moral agency develops and what its nature is; and
- Descriptive ethics, about what moral values people actually abide by.

9.11 ISSUE

Issues are about what is right and what is wrong. An example would be whether or not it is right to use genetic engineering, to have an abortion, legalize euthanasia etc. These are ethical ISSUES because there is disagreement about what is right and what is wrong.

9.12 ETHICAL ISSUES

The foundations of all secure systems are the moral principles and practices and the professional standards of all employ-ees of the organization, i.e., while people are part of the solution, they are also most of the problem. The following issues are examples of security problems which an organization may have to deal with:

9.12.1 Ethics and Responsible Decision-Making

The foundation of all security systems is formed by moral principles and practices of those people involved and the standards of the profession. That is, while people are part of the solution, they are also most the problem. Security problems with which an organization may have to deal include: responsible decision-making, confidentiality, pri-vacy, piracy, fraud & misuse, liability, copyright, trade secrets, and sabotage. It is easy to sensationalize these topics with real horror stories; it is more difficult to deal with the underlying ethical issues involved.

The student should be made aware of his individual responsibility in making ethical decisions associated with infor-mation security.

9.12.2 Confidentiality and Privacy

Computers can be used symbolically to intimidate, deceive or defraud victims. Attorneys, government agencies and businesses increasingly use mounds of computer generated data quite legally to confound their audiences. Criminals also find useful phony invoices, bills and checks generated by the computer. The computer lends an ideal cloak for carrying out criminal acts by imparting a clean quality to the crime.

The computer has made the invasion of our privacy a great deal easier and potentially more dangerous than before the advent of the computer. A wide range of data are collected and stored in computerized files related to individu-als. These files hold banking information, credit information, organizational fund raising, opinion polls, shop at home services, driver license data, arrest records and medical records. The potential threats to privacy include the improper commercial use of computerized data, breaches of confidentiality by releasing confidential data to third parties, and the release of records to governmental agencies for investigative purposes.

The basic law that protects our privacy is the Fourth Amendment to the United States Constitution, which mandates that people have a right to be secure in homes and against unreasonable search and seizure. In addition, many laws have been enacted to protect the individual from having damaging information stored in computerized databases.

9.12.3 Piracy

Software piracy is the unauthorized reproduction of copyrighted software. The unauthorized copying may be done for personal use, business use, or it may be done to sell copies of the pirated software. The problem can be found wherever computers are used: in businesses, schools, libraries, and homes. The Business Software Alliance puts it bluntly when they point out that making unauthorized copies of software or downloading unauthorized copies of software via the Internet is against the law (Anonymous 2001 a). The problem of making illegal software copies has been recognized in the computer industry for decades and has increased to match the growing use of computers (Wood 1998).

Microcomputer software presents a particular problem since many individuals are involved in the use of this soft-ware. Section 117 of the copyright laws, specifically the 1980 amendment, deals with a law that addresses the prob-lem of backup copies of software. This section states that users have the right to create backup copies of their soft-ware. That is, users may legally create a backup copy of software if it is to be held in archive. Many software com-panies provide a free backup copy to users that precludes the need for to users purchase software intended to defeat copy protection systems and subsequently create copies of their software. If the software purchased is actually leased, you may in fact not even be able to make backup copies of the software. The distinction between leasing and buying is contained within the software documentation. The copyright statement is also contained in the software documentation. The copyright laws regarding leased material state that the leasor may say what the leaseholder can and cannot do with the software. So it is entirely up to the owner of the software as to whether or not users may make backup copies of the software. At a time when federal laws relating to copyright protection are evolving, sev-eral states are considering legislation that would bar unauthorized duplication of software.

The software industry is prepared to do battle against software piracy. The courts are dealing with an increasing number of lawsuits concerning the protection of software. Large software publishers have established the Software Protection Fund to raise between $500,000 and $1 million to promote anti-piracy sentiment and to develop addi-tional protection devices.

9.12.4 Fraud and Misuse

The computer can create a unique environment in which unauthorized activities can occur. Crimes in this category have many traditional names including theft, fraud, embezzlement, extortion, etc.

Computer related fraud includes the introduction of fraudulent records into a computer system, theft of money by electronic means, theft of financial instruments, theft of services, and theft of valuable data.

9.12.5 Liability

Under the UCC, an express warranty is an affirmation or promise of product quality to the buyer and becomes a part of the basis of the bargain. Promises and affirmations made by the software developer to the user about the nature and quality of the program can also be classified as an express warranty. Programmers or retailers possess the right to define express warranties. Thus, they have to be realistic when they state any claims and predictions about the ca-pabilities, quality and nature of their software or hardware. They should consider the legal aspects of their affirma-tive promises, their product demonstrations, and their product description. Every word they say may be as legally effective as though stated in writing. Thus, to protect against liability, all agreements should be in writing. A dis-claimer of express warranties can free a supplier from being held responsible for any informal, hypothetical state-ments or predictions made during the negotiation stages.

Implied warranties are also defined in the United States by the UCC. These are warranties that are provided automatically in every sale. These warranties need not be in writing nor do they need to be verbally stated. They insure that good title will pass to the buyer, that the product is fit for the purpose sold, and that it is fit for the ordinary purposes for which similar goods are used (merchantability)..

9.12.6 Patent and Copyright Law

A patent can protect the unique and secret aspect of an idea. It is very difficult to obtain a patent compared to a copyright (please see discussion below). With computer software, complete disclosure is required; the patent holder must disclose the complete details of a program to allow a skilled programmer to build the program. Moreover, a United States software patent will be unenforceable in most other countries.

Copyright law provides a very significant legal tool for use in protecting computer software, both before a security breach and certainly after a security breach. This type of breach could deal with misappropriation of data, computer programs, documentation, or similar material. For this reason the information security specialist will want to be fa-miliar with basic concepts of to copyright law.

The United States, United Kingdom, Australia, and other countries have now amended or revised their copy-right legislation to provide explicit laws to protect computer program. Copyright law in the United States is governed by the Copyright Act of 1976 that preempted the field from the states. Formerly, the United States had a dual state and federal system. In other countries, such as Canada, the courts have held that the un-revised Copyright Act is broad enough to protect computer programs. In many of these countries the reform of copyright law is actively underway.

9.12.7 Trade Secrets

A trade secret protects something of value and usefulness. This law protects the unique and secret aspects of ideas, known only to the discoverer or his confidants. Once disclosed the trade secret is lost as such and can only be pro-tected under one of the following laws. The application of trade secret law is very important in the computer field, where even a slight head start in the development of software or hardware can provide a significant competitive ad-vantage.

9.12.8 Sabotage

The computer can be the object of attack in computer crimes such as the unauthorized use of computer facilities, al-ternation or destruction of information, data file sabotage and vandalism against a computer system. Computers have been shot, stabbed, short-circuited and bombed.

It is easy to sensationalize these topics with real horror stories; it is more difficult to deal with the underlying ethical issues involved.

Data Theft in Cyber Space – Issues and Laws

The rapid development of Information technology poses new challenges before the law. These challenges are not confined to any single traditional legal category but arise in, for example, Criminal Law, Intellectual Property Law, Contract and Tort. One such challenge is the growing menace of "Data Theft". It is the term used when any information in the form of data is illegally copied or taken from a business or other individual without his knowledge or consent.

Data as a Valuable Asset

Data is a valuable asset in this modern era of Information Technology (IT). Data is an important raw-material for Call Centers and I.T. Companies. Data has also become an important tool and weapon for Corporate to capture larger market shares. Due to the importance of Data in this new era, its security has become a major issue with the I.T. industry. The piracy of data is a threat, faced by the I.T. players, who spend millions to compile or buy data from the market. Their profits depend upon the security of their Data.

9.13 ISSUES IN DATA AND SOFTWARE PRIVACY

The major issue regarding Data Theft is its International character, for example Systems may be accessed in USA, the data manipulated in China and the consequences felt in India. The result of this ability is that different sovereignties, jurisdictions, laws and rules will come into play which again is an issue in itself. Further, collection of evidence in such circumstances become another issue as investigation in three different countries, all of whom may not be in talking terms, is almost impossible and poor technical know-how of our cops adds to the woes. Also, the lack of coordination between different investigating agencies and a not-so-sure extradition process is another head ache. However the biggest of all these issues is the lack of specific laws in the country dealing with this crime, so even if the culprit is caught he can easily get away by picking and choosing any of the of various loopholes in our law.

9.13.1 Does India have Sufficient Laws

The problem of data theft which has emerged as one of the major cyber crimes worldwide has attracted little attention of law makers in India. Unlike U.K which has The Data Protection Act, 1984 there is no specific legislation in India to tackle this problem, though India boasts of its Information Technology Act, 2000 to address the ever growing menace of cyber crimes, including data theft. The truth is that our IT Act, 2000 is not well equipped to tackle such crimes. The various provisions of the IT Act, 2000 which deal with the problem to some extent are briefly discussed below.

Section 43:- This section provides protection against destruction and unauthorized access of the computer system by imposing heavy penalty up to one crore. The unauthorized downloading, extraction and copying of data are also covered under this section. Clause 'C' of this section imposes penalty for unauthorized introduction of computer viruses of contaminants. Clause 'G' provides penalties for assisting the unauthorized access.

Section 65:- This section provides for computer source code. If anyone knowingly or intentionally conceals, destroys, alters or causes another to do as such shall have to suffer imprisonment of up to 3 years or fine up to 2 lakh rupees. Thus protection has been provided against tampering of computer source documents.

Section 66:- Protection against hacking has been provided under this section. As per this section, hacking is defined as any act with an intention to cause wrongful loss or damage to any person or with the knowledge that wrongful loss or damage will be caused to any person and information residing in a computer resource must be either destroyed, deleted, altered or its value and utility get diminished. This section imposes the penalty of imprisonment of up to three years or fine up to two lakh rupees or both on the hacker.

Section 70:- This section provides protection to the data stored in the protected system. Protected systems are those computers, computer system or computer network to which the appropriate government, by issuing gazette information in the official gazette, declared it as a protected system. Any access or attempt to secure access of that system in contravention of the provision of this section will make the person accessed liable for punishment of imprisonment which may extend to ten years and shall also be liable to fine.

Section 72:- This section provides protection against breach of confidentiality and privacy of the data. As per this, any person upon whom powers have been conferred under IT Act and allied rules to secure access to any electronic record, book, register, correspondence, information document of other material discloses it to any other person, shall be punished with imprisonment which may extend to two years or with fine which may extend to one lakh rupees or both.

9.14 LEGAL ISSUES FOR E-COMMERCE BUSINESS

If you're starting a business on the Web, there are important legal issues to consider.

Making decisions about legal matters is about how comfortable you are with risk. If you make huge revenue with a high risk business, you could decide that the money is worth the risk. Or you might choose to do it for a short period of time, collect your money, and get out. Just because there is risk does not mean that it isn't a good business for you. Everything in life has risks -- and your business is no exception.

9.14.1 Incorporation

Why Incorporate, Incorporation means that your company is a separate legal and financial entity from yourself. It even has its own social security number for tax purposes, called a Federal Tax ID. Most people incorporate to limit their personal liability so that their personal assets are not at risk for debts of the corporation. For example, if your incorporated company was sued and lost the suit, the winner could not take your personal car or home.

Plus, of course, incorporating makes you look more professional, and often helps with your taxes. Also, if you plan to receive investment in your company, have employees, and grow to be more than a one-person show, incorporation is an important step that helps promote these future goals. While incorporation protects you in many regards, it does not protect you from any criminal charges by you or the corporation, which can come into play if, for instance, you run an adult or gambling business on the Internet.

9.14.2 Trademark

The trademark act, or "Lanham Act", 18 USC Sec. 1051 etc. is meant to ensure that consumers can correctly identify the sources of goods or services. A trademark is a word, phrase, symbol or design, or combination of words, phrases, symbols or designs, which identifies and distinguishes the source of particular goods. A service mark is the same as a trademark, except that it identifies and distinguishes the source of a service rather than a product.

Normally, a mark for goods appears on the product or its packaging, while a service mark appears in advertising for the services. A "tm" on a product indicates unregistered (common law) trademark rights, and an "®" indicates a registered mark. It is illegal to place an "®" on a mark that does not have national registration.

As your domain name and your branding is valuable, you should think in terms of trademark registration. This can be done later in the business process once you have more revenue available, but it is important to consider it upfront in choosing your domain name, company name, product and/or service name.

You don't want to use a name which is someone else's trademark, as they could sue you to stop your use, including taking the domain name. At the minimum, go to www.uspto.gov and run a trademark search for the names you're considering -- at least to get an idea of how many other folks there are who could possibly have a claim to the mark you intend to use. Be aware that getting few or no results does not mean that you're in the clear, due to the complexities of trademark law, and the fact that the USPTO database runs a year behind. However, taking these steps will still lower your risk.

When trying to determine whether you've picked a good name in relation to others' marks, remember that the point of trademark law is to prevent consumer confusion about the source of goods or services. Ask yourself whether a consumer would confuse your name with that of another product, service or company.

9.14.3 Copyright

Copyright can be important when you obtain content for your site, and in the protection of your site's content.

The owner of a copyright has the exclusive right:

- to copy the work
- to modify the work (create "derivative works")
- to distribute the work
- to perform the work publicly
- to display the work publicly

Copyright arises upon the creation of a copyrightable works (typically substantial text, images, music, etc.). Facts, titles, recipes, form designs, alphabetical lists and other items do not have the required "originality" to merit copyright protection. Your are not required to register works to have copyright protection, however if you do register your materials, you preserve the fact that they are yours as of the date of registration, and you gain more rights under Copyright law, such as being able to win attorneys' fees and, sometimes, higher damages.

The term "Public Domain" does not mean that everything in public or on the Internet is freely usable. It refers to items that either do not qualify for copyright protection under the law, or for which the protection has expired.

When you buy content for your Website or business, the best approach is to obtain a warranty from the seller or licensor stating that the seller owns all the rights in it and agrees to indemnify you (i.e. pay you for the costs) if someone else sues you for using the content. Large content providers should be willing to do this, and many small ones will be also. If not, you'll have to hope for the best and take the risk.

If you create content, be sure to have your creator sign a contractor agreement with the language required under the Copyright Act so that you own the work product. If you don't, the creator will own the copyrights to the works.

9.15 FORM OF AGREEMENT

Global electronic commerce will be an engine of economic growth in the 21st century, with the potential to invigorate economies by enhancing productivity, streamlining distribution, and revamping corporate structures.

Electronic commerce will improve the standard of living of citizens in the United States and Ireland, as well as the rest of the globe, by creating new, high-paying jobs and opportunities. Small and medium-sized enterprises, in particular, will benefit from new opportunities to sell their products to a world-wide market.

It is recognised that the liberalisation of the telecommunications markets plays a key role in the development of electronic commerce.

The Governments of the United States and Ireland recognise the importance of global co-operation in the promotion of electronic commerce and the need to read coherent and effective global solutions in the construction of a seamless environment for electronic commerce and, in this respect, welcome the opportunity of building on the principles and guidelines agreed in the US-EU Joint Statement on Electronic Commerce and, in particular, would emphasise:

- the key role of industry in developing electronic commerce through the development of new services and by helping to set rules for the functioning of this market-place;
- that the role of government is to provide a clear, consistent and predictable legal framework, to promote a pro-competitive environment in which electronic commerce can flourish and to ensure adequate protection of public interest objectives such as privacy, intellectual property rights, prevention of fraud, consumer protection, and public safety.
- that unnecessary legal and regulatory barriers should be eliminated and the emergence of new ones should be prevented. Where legislative action is deemed necessary, it should not be to the advantage or disadvantage of electronic commerce compared with other forms of commerce;
- that taxes on electronic commerce should be clear, consistent, neutral and non-discriminatory; that there should be close co-operation and mutual assistance to ensure effective tax administration and to combat and prevent illegal activities on the Internet;
- the strong desirability of continuing the current practice of not imposing customs duties on electronic transaction; and
- the it is important to enhance the awareness and confidence of citizens and 5ME's in electronic commerce and to support the development of relevant skills and network literacy.

The united states and Ireland support and endorse the following fundamental which should quide the development of electronic commerce which should be essentially market-lod and driven by private initative:

1. **Authentication/Electronic Signatures:** Governments should support a global uniform commercial legal framework that recognises, facililates, and enforces electronic transactions world-wide. A wide variety of authentication methods and technologies are developing rapidly. With respect to authentication and electronic signatures, efforts of the private sector in constructing rules and guidelines should be encouraged.

   The commercial legal framework should conform with the following principles:

   — the acceptability of electronic signatures for legal and commercial purpcses;

   — the propriety and desirability of allowing parties to a transaction to determine the appropriate technological and business methods of authentication for their transaction; and

— the tostening of mutual cross-border recognition of electronic authentication methods and a non-discriminatory approach to electronic signatures from other countries as a necessary step in the removal of artificial barriers to cross-border commercial transactions.

2. **Privacy:** Ensuring effective protection of privacy with regard to the processing of personal data on global information networks is necessary.

3. **Combating Illegal Use and Content:** We encourage international co-operation between law enforcement authorities as a means of combating and preventing illegal activities of the Internet and the exploitation and illegal use of electronic commerce by criminal and terrorist organisations.

   Industry, through self-regulation, should establish effective measures to counter the proliferation of illegal content on the Internet.

4. **Access Issues:** In instances, where users, such as parents, do not wish to receive certain types of content, industry should be encouraged to make available filtering or blocking systems or other tools, as appropriate. Industry should also be encouraged to develop content-rating systems to improve the effectiveness of filtering tools.

   Governments should not prvent their citizens from accessing information simply because it is posted in another country or in a foreign language. Furthermore, govenments can use information technology to become more open, responsive, efficient and accessible to the public.

5. **Electronic Payments:** Market-driven developments in this area should be ecouraged.

6. **Intellectual Propery Rights:** Growth of electronic commerce depends on the adequate protection of intellectual property rights, which will be assisted by ratification and implementation, as soon as possible, of the W.I.P.O. Copyright Treaty and the W.P.O. Performances and Phonograms Treaty.

7. **Domain Name System:** In order to reach its full potential, the system for registering, allocating and governing Internet domain names should be global and market-based and reflect the geographically and functionally diverse nature of the Internet.

8. **Consumer Protection:** Electronic commerce should provide at least the same level of protection as in other forms of commerce.

9. **Taxes:** We will actively participate in the Organisation for Economic Co-operation and Development work toward developing framework conditions for the taxation of Electronic commerce. Close co-operation and mutual assistance are necessary to ensure effective tax administration and to prevent tax evasion on the Internet.

In the furtheance of the principles set out in this statement, the United States and Ireland shall seek to encourage:

- closer co-operation between the two countries for promoting electronic commerce and to build on the strong US-industry presence in Ireland and the growing base of Irish companies in the United States as a means of developing our mutual interests in this area;

- further bilateral discussions at expert level, where appropriate, regarding the development of global electronic commerce;
- dialogue and co-operation among the market participants in both countries, since the market should lead in the development of electronic commerce;
- close co-operation with a view to encouraging the development of statistical data on electronic commerce; and,
- enhanced co-operation within relevant international fora to achieve global consensus on an international framework for electronic commerce.

SUMMARY

A system allowing individuals to perform banking activities at home, via the internet. Some online banks are traditional banks which also offer online banking, while others are online only and have no physical presence. Online banking through traditional banks enable customers to perform all routine transactions, such as account transfers, balance inquiries, bill payments, and stop-payment requests, and some even offer online loan and credit card applications. Account information can be accessed anytime, day or night, and can be done from anywhere. A few online banks update information in real-time, while others do it daily. Once information has been entered, it doesn't need to be re-entered for similar subsequent checks, and future payments can be scheduled to occur automatically. Many banks allow for file transfer between their program and popular accounting software packages, to simplify record keeping. Despite the advantages, there are a few drawbacks. It does take some time to set up and get used to an online account. Also, some banks only offer online banking in a limited area. In addition, when an account holder pays online, he/she may have to put in a check request as much as two weeks before the payment is due, but the bank may withdraw the money from the account the day that request is received, meaning the person has lost up to two weeks of interest on that payment. Online-only banks have a few additional drawbacks: an account holder has to mail in deposits (other than direct deposits), and some services that traditional banks offer are difficult or impossible for online-only banks to offer, such as traveler's checks and cashier's checks.

EXERCISE

1. What do you mean by online gateway?
2. What is EDI explain it with its advantages?
3. What is the role of EDI application in business.
4. What do you mean by E-Commerce law?
5. What are different policies and agenda used in E-Commerce?
6. Write down all the forms of agreement.

CHAPTER

10

Implementation of E-Commerce

10.1 OVERVIEW OF E-COMMERCE TECHNOLOGY

10.1.1 Electronic Commerce

Any web site that offers products and/or services for sale is a commercial web site. There are thousands of commercial web sites on the Internet. Some of them have been successful, and some weren't so lucky. What elements make up a good commercial web site? Of course, web pages should look attractive to a customer. However, even the most attractive web pages will not make a person come back to a web site where it takes too long to find the right product or where order forms don't work. In this lecture we will discuss what functionality is needed for a successful commercial web site and what technology implements various web site elements.

10.1.2 Examples of Commercial Web Sites

Let's browse the following two web sites, which are fairly typical web sites for online shopping.

- **Online bakery.** A web site for a small business.
- **Trains.com** Online sore of model trains and related products. An example of a larger commercial web site.

10.1.3 Components of a Well-functioning Commercial Web Site

A well-organized web site should be easy for a customer to use and easy for the owner to maintain. It takes a lot to build a well-organized web site. Below is a list of the most important elements that a good web site should have:

1. A well-organized collection of products and/or services. Smaller web sites can just list all their products on one or several web pages. Larger sites provide indices of products and search engines so that customers can find what they need. There should be a way for customers to get all necessary information about products, compare several products, get an advice on related products that they might want to get, etc.

To maintain a web site, the owner should be able to change product information easily. A web site where a price change of a single product requires changing 3 web pages is just bound to have inconsistencies. The owner should be able to add or remove products based on every day's availability, change prices, add product cross-references, etc. without making the web site inconsistent even for a minute.

2. A convenient way for a customer to select products. Usually implemented as a shopping cart or a shopping basket. The customer should be able to select and delete products while browsing the web site.
3. Convenient order forms. The form should be flexible enough to allow to specify a different address for the product delivery, a gift message, etc. It should have as few required fields as possible. A returning customer should be provided default information so that not to type it every time. For both the customer and the owner it is essential that the form catches simple typos (s.a. 4 digits in a zip code).
4. Convenient ways of payment. There should be options of paying by a credit card, by a check (not everyone has credit cards!), and by a credit card over the phone if the customer is not comfortable sending his/her credit card number. The options may include some electronic payment systems.

   For the owner, there should be a quick way to verify the credit card information or in some other way to check that the payment is valid.
5. Secure communication system not only to protect transmission of a credit card number, but also to guarantee privacy of the customer (including details of the purchase). A web site might have a user registration system with a password, in which case all transactions by the user should be private. It is also important to prevent unauthorized access to the web site (by a hacker or accidental).
6. Some way of storing information about customers. This is convenient for customers so that they don't need to reenter their information every time they access the site. It also allows to "customize" the web site for someone's interests. This can be done via customer registration or by means of "cookies", which we will discuss later.

   The owner can benefit a lot from storing information about a customer: he/she can customize ads based on the customer's profile or send an e-mail advertising a new product (but keep in mind that many people don't like this!) However, the greatest benefit is the owner's ability to monitor customer's behaviour: which pages have the customer visited and which purchases (if any) he/she have made afterwards.
7. A way of keeping information about orders. This allows customers to track their orders, and for owners to get all kinds of financial and statistical information. It is also important to keep order information in case of later disputes.
8. The last, but not the least, customer support and feedback. There should be online documentation for all products ever sold on the web site, various FAQs, and, ideally, a way of customers to post their opinion about the product. Easy access to this information may make a difference between a frequently visited web site and a lonely online looser.

This aspect of a web site cannot be completely mechanized: a human being has to answer e-mail, judge the relevance of customer's comments (otherwise the web site may be flooded with nonsense), organize comments by topics, and so on. However, there is a lot that can be computer-aided in this process, for instance sorting incoming messages by their title and/or return address to forward them to an appropriate customer support person.

Note that we are only considering business-to-customer interactions here (so-called B2C), leaving out all the features related to business-to-business (B2B) interactions. While such interactions are basically similar to B2C, they can be optimized if a company has stable business partners which have more powerful computers than an average customer does. Even a customer oriented web site has a B2B part when dealing with vendors of products. We are not considering B2B connections in designing a web site.

Some technologies used to implement all this

1. Convenient storage and retrieval of information about products and customers require a database.

   Some terminology: A database is a collection of data organized in such a way that it can be easily accessed, managed, and updated. A query is a request to a database written in a form that's supported by the database. Every brand of databases has its own language of queries (a query language).

   A well-organized database allows you to store each piece of information only once, so if you need to change it, you change it in one place. Databases allow you to store information about orders, needed both for you and for customers. For instance, customers can track their orders by requesting information from the database, which will automatically reply whether the order has been shipped. You can use customer information to fill in forms for returning customers with their recorded information. You can store statistics about customers (how many times they have visited the web sites, which pages, what did they buy, and so on). Customer's feedback about products can be organized and displayed later when someone else is interested in the same product. It's hard to imagine an interesting web site that does not have a database behind it.

   There are various kinds of databases, from a simple one, which is a collection of "flat" files storing data, to very sophisticated commercial products, s.a. ORACLE. The most common kind is a relational database.

   A relational database is a database organized as a collection of tables. In this course we will use a simple relational database called McKoi database.

2. A convenient interface to the database from the web site. A customer does not need to know anything even about the existence of the database, not to mention details of its organization. He/she should be able to get all necessary information by typing in keywords and filling in electronic forms.

   Various programming languages (for instance, Java, JavaScript) provide libraries to implement a remote connection to a database server.

A server is a computer that provides a remote access to some service, for instance a web page server "serves" web pages, i.e. sends HTML files, graphics files, etc. in response to http requests, a databse server provides responses to database queries, and so on. One machine can provide several different services at the same time.

A client is a computer that makes a request for a service.

We will use a Java JDBC (Java Database Connectivity) package to facilitate a connection to a relational database. It does not depend on a particular kind of the database, as long as the database supports SQL (Structured Query Language).

SQL is a standard for a query language of a relational database. An interface has to provide way for customers to fill in forms, press buttons, etc. We will use javax.swing package to build an interactive graphical interface.

3. We need to be able to process user's forms, for instance order forms, and produce various web pages, depending on the request. Ways of processing electronic forms include various server-side scripts, s.a. CGI, PERL, asp (Active Server Pages, an extension of JavaScript) and others. We will use Java Servlets for this purpose.

4. A web site responds to requests for web pages. It doesn't "know" where the requests have come from, so it can't tell if two requests for web pages have been made by the same user. To keep track of a user during a session (and sometimes between sessions), a web server uses cookies.

   A cookie is a small text file placed by a web server on the client machine. The file gets sent back every time the client requests a web page from the server. A cookie has an expiration time, which may be just for the session or longer. Java Servlet package also implements cookies.

5. Encryption and security. A common way secure communications are implemented is via SSL (Secure Sockets Layer), which allows various forms of encryption, depending on the maximum level of encryption provided by the server and the client and on geographic location of the machines (a different level of encryption is allowed in the US for connections to domestic and foreign computers). We will study and compare several encryption algorithms. On the practical side, we will use Java packages which implement encryption and secure communications.

6. Electronic payment systems are based on customer's accounts with one of trusted vendors. A customer obtains certificates "signed" by the vendor which are analogous to checks ("personal money") and cash ("anonymous money"). The implementation should be such that mere copying of any piece of information transmitted in the transaction does not allow the thief to use the "money". We will study protocols for verifying validity of "checks" and "cash" in electronic transactions. We will also study ways of implementing "coins" on the Internet, i.e. certificates for small amounts of money (this allows some shortcuts in implementation, since the process of breaking even a simpler protocol may not be worth the money stolen).

10.2 THREE MOST IMPORTANT ELEMENTS OF GOOD WEBSITE

There are hundreds of articles and thousands of tips on how to make a website successful. True, websites vary greatly in content, style, focus and n-number of other aspects. Consequently, there can not be one great formula or key success factor. However, if we closely look into successful web-sites - a few features stand out, features that are common in almost all successful sites.

A successful web-site, evidently, is the one that is capable of attracting quality visitors and retain them. The core of this attractiveness is its content. However, only content is not enough - just as a good product needs good packaging a successful site needs elegant presentation and promotion.

We discuss 10 basic elements that can significantly contribute towards success of any website.

10.2.1 Content

No matter if you have a business site or a personal page, you have to give people a reason to stay on your site - the first question the visitor is going to ask - "what's in it for me?"

That doesn't mean you have to give away freebies - programs, books, tickets, holidays etc. etc. - it does mean that you have to offer something. That "something" could be:

- Information
- Utility (bulletin board, search engine, directory etc.)
- Entertainment
- Advice
- Help with a problem
- Opportunities to network with like minded people
- Links to useful sites

Remember, a successful site is a useful site. It should contain:

- information that is perceived to be 'useful' by its visitors (community)
- the information is unique (i.e. either not available elsewhere or is hard to find)
- the information is fresh (i.e. updated regularly)

10.2.2 Overall Look

Your home page is your billboard or store front-- it creates an immediate impression on visitors. Considering the importance of first impression, we all are aware of, it should look:

- Clean
- Uncluttered
- Professional
- Attractive

Do not be stingy with white space, spread them as much as required. Aim to "underwhelm" rather than overwhelm. Too many flashing lights, animations, colours, drop-down boxes, graphics etc. are distracting. It's a like those stores that play loud, frenetic music--your heart rate rises, your stress levels go up and you just want to get out - fast!

10.2.3 Speed

In this age of impatience - an average visitor will spend no more than 20 seconds to decide the worth of your site. You can well imagine what happens if the visitor spends that precious 20 seconds looking at a blank screen slowly loading tons of images..

So you must ensure that your home page at least, loads as quickly as possible. That means no big, flashy graphics.

Keep reminding yourself that your first page is like a billboard. When driving your car, you don't have time to read detailed descriptions, or admire intricate pictures on billboards. The signs flash past you and have to make an immediate impression.

Your web visitors are 'flashing past' as well, so keep your front page simple and fast.

10.2.4 Graphics and Lay-out

The graphics and lay-out of your home page contribute to that first impression--think about what image your site is trying to convey and make sure everything on your site contributes something towards that overall image.

If you have a serious business site, you don't want garish cartoons on your front page - but if you have a games site, then cartoons can be an integral part of the image.

Graphics are what eat up the loading time of your site. A rough rule of thumb to determine good loading time for a page is to keep the entire page around 50 Kb. Images should be between 6 and 8K. Each additional 5K may add one second to loading time.

If in doubt, right click the image and then click on "Properties" to get the size of the image.Colour is also an important part of your site; colours have different effects on our emotions:

Red and orange excite the senses and increase heartbeat, blues and greens are more restful. Yellow reminds us of sunshine and is a happy colour

Consider the effect you want to create and choose a colour that is appropriate. When reading Western texts, the eye travels from the top left of the page, across and then down to the bottom right. Remember this when you're placing graphics on your page.

Any graphic image which has a directional aspect should be placed to point towards the most important section of the page. If you have a picture of a bird on the top left corner of your page, make sure it is facing inward and that its beak is leading the eye to the centre of the page, not away from it.

The same applies to all graphics:

Faces should 'look' to the centre of the page. Cars should be 'parked' facing towards the centre of the page. Roads, neck ties etc should all be placed to lead the eye across from left to right, or down from top to bottom

This is also why you should place your navigation bars down the left side of your page - it keeps them constantly in the visitor's field of vision.

10.2.5 Text Readability

This doesn't refer to the words you use (we'll look at them in detail later) --but to the way the words look on the page. Going back to the concept of the billboard, your words need to stand out on your page - you need to surround them with plenty of white space.

Dark backgrounds make you feel as if you're in a small space and also have a depressing effect on your mood. Certain coloured backgrounds make it very difficult to read text; purples, orange tonings and reds dazzle the eyes.

The colour of your text is just as important--bear in mind that different browsers read colours differently--what looks great on your browser could well be invisible on another !

Take a lesson from the newspapers and divide your text into columns for easier (and quicker) reading--even two columns are better than one slab of text that covers the entire width of the page.

Another element that contributes to text readability is the font you choose. Plain fonts (Arial, Times New Roman, Garamond and Courier) are the easiest to read. Fancy fonts are fine for headings, but not for full pages (imagine trying to read a whole page in Gothic, Script, Westminster, or Cloister). Your eyes would soon tire of the effort involved and you'd be reaching for the back button!

10.2.6 Structure Each page

You have to make your page as easy for visitors to read as possible and this means breaking it up into little 'chunks'. We've already looked at the need for columns, (which divide the page vertically); you also need to divide your page horizontally, through the use of headings and sub-headings.

10.2.7 Fonts

Select a font for all your headings and sub-headings (and stick to it). It's not necessary to have a different font for headings (just go up one size for headings, and then use bold on all headings and sub-headings).

This way it's easy to recognise which is a heading (large and bold) and which is a sub-heading (same size but bold).

The purpose is to make it easy for your visitors to glance at your page and make out what the key points are. If what they see interests them, they'll stay and keep reading.

To draw attention to other important points, you can also highlight them by putting a whole sentence in bold or a different colour (or both). However, take care with the colours you select: some are quite difficult to read--even against a white background.

10.2.8 Navigation

Navigation is one of the most critical aspects of any web site - arguably the most important. No matter how good a site looks, and no matter how much useful information it offers, without sensible navigation scheme, it will only manage to confuse visitors and chase them away. A simple, logical, understandable navigation scheme can increase your number of page impressions, boost return visits, and improve your "conversion rate" (the number of visitors who are "converted" into customers). It's a critical aspect of site design that has a direct effect on the bottom line.

The core of any good navigational scheme is:

1. Tell people exactly what is available on your site
2. Help them get to the parts they want quickly
3. Make it easy to request additional information

Use a well-structured navigational bar. it should run down the left side of your page, for two reasons:

We're accustomed to reading from left to right and from top to bottom We're accustomed to finding navigation bars on the left of web pages -- why buck the system (especially when it works)?

On a long page it's also a good idea to have a brief nav bar along the bottom of the page (just home | top of page will suffice).

When you've found a system you're happy with, use it on every page so that your visitors know where to look for the information. Greater consistency leads to better readability and ease of use.

10.2.9 Privacy Statement and Testimonials

Credibility is an essential part of any business site, especially in the anonymous world of Internet. You must ensure that your potential customers feel confident dealing with you. Transparency and openness are the cornerstones of lasting trust - so tell people exactly what you're doing to safeguard their interests. In particular, how you're protecting their privacy. It's worth having a separate page which sets out, in detail, your policy towards their email addresses; how you accept orders; how you gather information; who has access to this information; how you use information gathered from children and so on.

Visitors also like to know that real people have used your products or services, so it's worth asking your satisfied customers if you can quote any positive comments they've made about you. Don't be afraid to ask for testimonials--we all like to know that our opinions are valued.

Set up a separate page for testimonials and offer to include links to your customers' pages in return for using their comments. This is one of those "win-win" situations

10.2.10 Words

Now we come to one of the most important elements. If this part is wrong, the rest of your efforts are largely wasted. How many times have you been impressed by a site's initial appearance, only to be disappointed by poor spelling, careless grammar and punctuation ?

It reflects badly on the site owner and indicates that whoever is responsible for this page is sloppy, careless, lazy, unprofessional or all of the above! Would you entrust any of your hard-earned money to someone who doesn't even care enough to check the expression of his/her own site?

- You can take steps to improve your own writing skills
- You can employ someone to proof read and edit your work
- You can employ someone to write your pages for you

When it comes to website design, there are three very important elements that must influence the process of developing a site which can be viewed on the Internet.

1. **Customer Satisfaction:** Although this should be common sense customer satisfaction does not always take a front row seat in the priority department for many agencies. It seems that in the era of our fast paced society a lack of customer satisfaction is the status quo. Companies often rush from completing one job to the next and in the process they somehow skip steps, miss promised timelines, or fail to meet agreed upon priorities. Which comes to my next point.
2. **Listening to the Customer's Needs:** The old adage that the customer is always right has been somewhat lost. Clients generally have an idea of what they want to achieve with their websites. Usually, for businesses, it is to bring in new business or increased revenue. What they often do not know; however, is how to accomplish this online in the form of their website. This should not really be a surprise, because often this is not an area of expertise for many entrepreneurs or company executives. This also does not mean that the web development firm hired to complete the website should just run ahead without consulting the client on their needs.

   It takes a practiced skill to help the client identify what they want to accomplish online and what the look and feel of the website should be. This initial groundwork will certainly go a long way in understanding the overall goal of the site, and how to best achieve this within best design and development practice.
3. **The Ability to Communicate with the Client:** This skill of helping the client identify what they want to accomplish online can be best identified as communication. It is the process of exchanging information through various means to accomplish an understanding or shared meaning of ideas. The ability to do this well only comes with skill and practice.

A good analogy of this process would be the traveller looking for directions in a foreign place using a different language. The traveller is like the website design firm looking for directions from the local: the client. Like the local who may or may not know the directions, the client may or may not know what they are looking for in their website. A good project manager in the web design firm will use all their skills to gather the information, and help the client along in their journey of conveying what they want in their website.

These skills may include interpersonal projection, asking for clarification, using probing questions to seek further details, and evaluating and explaining the process thoroughly. The client needs to know sooner than later what is possible with the budget specified, and how modifications during the website design process can increase the cost to develop the website.

Although there are many other elements that contribute to excellent website design, web designers or their project managers must be able to provide these three main aspects for the web design project to be on a successful track.

10.3 E-COMMERCE SHOULD HAVE A GOOD WEBSITE

Online publicity is an important element of your marketing plan if you're to rise above the noise level on the Net. But getting that publicity is not easy it takes a lot of work, and can be froth with dangers. It takes a lot of planning and preparation and is definitely not a one-shot effort. A well-thought-out publicity plan gives your eBusiness the kind of portrayal you want in the media and your community. Over the long haul, good portrayal generates good credibility for your eBusiness.

The goal is to generate important coverage of your eBusiness at exactly the right time and in exactly the right place.

Although Public Relations (PR) is a part of marketing, it's really not marketing. Marketing manages demand whereas PR manages your company's image and its awareness on the Net. Online PR is not the process of submitting your Web store to search engines. Good PR appeals to people, not machines. Good PR builds awareness and visibility with minimal cash.

10.3.1 Creating the Buzz

The Buzz is one of the most important and most elusive forces in all of marketing. If you've got something to sell and are either short on cash or rolling in dough to promote it, creating a Buzz about it will get you millions of dollars in free publicity. Buzz is extremely influential and after it spreads, can boost your Web store's awareness considerably.

10.3.2 Get a Free PR Consultation

When you create a Buzz, it means that people are talking about you. You're mentioned in news articles, compared in features, talked about in chat rooms, and mentioned in newsgroups. It's the Holy Grail of marketing and is the marketing goal of every business today.

So how do you create the Buzz. By putting out timely press releases, interviews, and stories that showcase your business. And that means getting the attention of journalists.

Now, journalists are a fussy bunch. They're harassed daily by companies and individuals asking them to write about their latest "can't-live-without" product or service. But much too often, the news releases they do get are dry, boring, and have no connection to what interests them. Journalists respond to clever writing and news releases that describe how a new product or service is a solution to a business or consumer trend or problem. They respond to releases that piggyback on late-breaking stories that show how a company's product or service relates to current news.

What do you need to know to create a Buzz? First, learn how to write a compelling and timely press release. Second, know where to send it and how.

The key elements of a good publicly plan include a number of elements.

State Your Key Message Advantages

In any release you send out, you need to make sure that the main advantages of your product or service are clearly defined and stated. It's your Unique Selling Position again! Your goal is to have these key messages reported or implied in any news story about your eBusiness.

Target Your Publicity

Make a list of all magazines, newspapers, radio stations, and TV stations that would most likely carry your company story. You want to target these news outlets and make sure that what you do and the news you release match their audience interests. And remember to not just target a new source target a particular department or individual within it.

Media Calendar

Good PR is not a one-shot deal. A good public relations plan is designed to map out a strategy for several months to a year. For PR to be effective, you need a steady stream of it. You need to craft your news releases not only for publication, but to get interviewed for a timely story as well. So look at your product or service, and then look at a calendar. Prepare to send out news releases that show how your product or service relates to holidays such as Christmas, Easter, Valentine's Day, or Halloween and seasonal times such as swim and vacation season in the Summer, back to school in the Fall, winter activities in the Winter, and fashions in the Spring. Design both your marketing campaign and your public relations campaign to coincide with these events. Alert the media at each one of these points with news releases. The object here is to get the press coverage or better yet get an interview.

Knowing what is considered news and what's not is key in getting your news releases read. Simply stating that your Web site is open for business, or if you have redesigned your site, or have added new staff is not in itself newsworthy. What is newsworthy is focusing on something that's already prominent in the news or is about to become so. Issue a report related to your site's main theme, or conduct a survey and issue a report on the findings, buck a trend in the marketplace, announce an award you've won, or announce that when you reach a company milestone, such as celebrating your one millionth customer.

10.4 SIGNIFICANCE OF GOOD E-COMMERCE WEBSITE

Doing online business always seems to be complex unless the mode (website) we are using is not user friendly. Selling and buying of product & services is long and lengthy process but good functionality and visualization makes it simple and healthy profitable for the business holder. There are two main things that should be kept in mind by offshore developers while developing E-Commerce site, proper functioning at front hand and admin control of website that help clients to get maximum benefits for online business. Developing the eCommerce website with implementation of latest technologies is complex and if development of website is customize in nature then developers use to work hard to fulfill the demands of client.

Very first step for development of eCommerce website is requirement analysis of the client. eCommerce website is presentation mode for composition of various complex attributes of the business. Understanding the nature of business is very important for well functioning of E-Commerce website.

While developing the E-Commerce website developer have to be conscious about full fledge knowledge global business environment and current technology for proper functionality of website. Consumer behaviors aspects are also have great significance while developing the E-Commerce websites in order to understand the requirements of the clients business to achieve customer satisfaction.

Developing commercial website a professional developer use to implement various management concepts and he or she should be well versed with the management concepts also to render quality work. There are Catalog management, Category management, Product management, Customer management, Order management, Stock management etc.

Most important challenge for E-Commerce developers is to implement error free functionality for Shipping method, Tax company code, Payment method and other customized commercial methods. An offshore web developer is required to be aware about commercial systems of outsourcing country.

There are other facilities are also like Cart facilities (add, edit, delete), Registration facility/ check out/check in, Newsletter facility (other marketing tools), Attributes of product, Short message service reminder, fax, etc.

Well functioned E-Commerce site is result of appropriate skills and knowledge of developing team that ultimately helps in achieving goal of the business organization.

10.5 A FIVE-STEP APPROACH TO DEVELOPING AN E-COMMERCE SYSTEM

Once it has been determined that a business can benefit from an online presence, the business type, the product line, the business's organization, and the budget dictate what functionality the Webstore should have and how the Web site should be developed. Companies can choose from a number of different types of Web sites, including B2C, B2B, exchanges, and the like.

Sites of a particular type (e.g., retailer, provider of business services, manufacturer, distributor/wholesaler, media, travel/entertainment) usually use the same underlying applications and provide similar sorts of functionality. Although this simplifies the task of creating the underlying application architecture, the site requirements must still be considered carefully. Before discussing the best approach to developing a site, it would be useful to review previous chapters to consider the major characteristics, functionalities, and requirements of the EC system being developed.

A well-developed Web site not only adds to the value of products or services being offered, but it also enhances the worth of the company. Therefore, once you have a clear understanding of the e-commerce system requirements and consider all of the elements of the e-commerce system, it is important that a firm choose the correct development strategy to obtain the greatest return on its investment. The diversity of e-business models and applications, which vary in size from small stores to global exchanges, requires a variety of development methodologies and approaches.

Table 10.1: Capabilities Needed by Webstore Users

Buyers need the ability to:	
• Discover, search for, evaluate, and compare products for purchase using e-catalogs.	• Provide access to a current catalog of product offerings, allowing prospective buyers to analyze and evaluate the offering.
• Select products to purchase and negotiate or determine their total price	• Provide an electronic shopping cart in which buyers can assemble their purchases.
• Place an order for desired products using a shopping cart.	• Verify a customer's credit and approve the customer's purchase.
• Pay for the ordered products, usually through some form of credit.	• Process orders (back-end services).
• Confirm an order, ensuring that the desired	• Arrange for product delivery.
• Track orders once they are shipped.	• Track shipments to ensure that they are delivered.
• Track orders once they are shipped.	• Provide the means for buyers and visitors to register at the site, to make comments, or to request additional information.
• Pay for the ordered products, usually through some form of credit.	
• Confirm an order, ensuring that the desired product is available.	
• Track orders once they are shipped.	

10.5.1 Auctions and Application Development

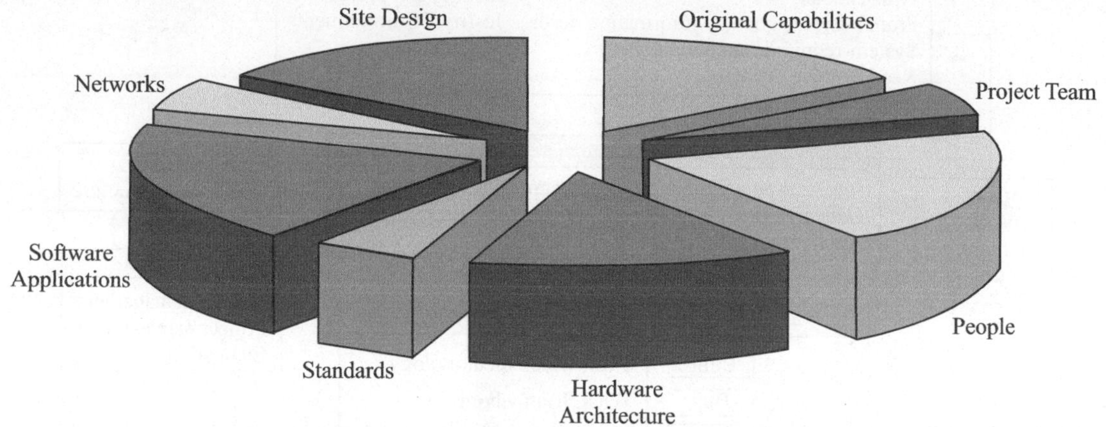

Figure 10.1: Elements of an E-Commerce System

10.6 ECOMMERCE SYSTEM LIFE CYCLE

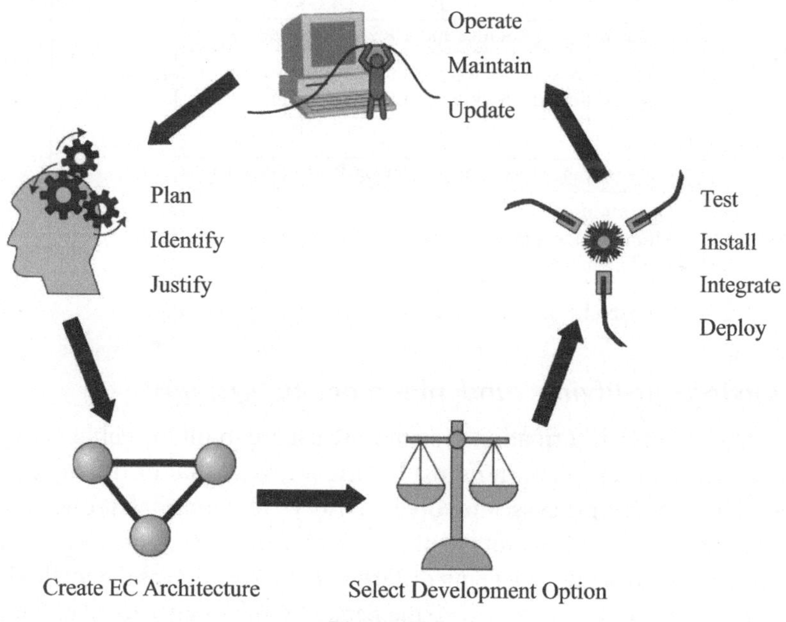

Figure 10.2

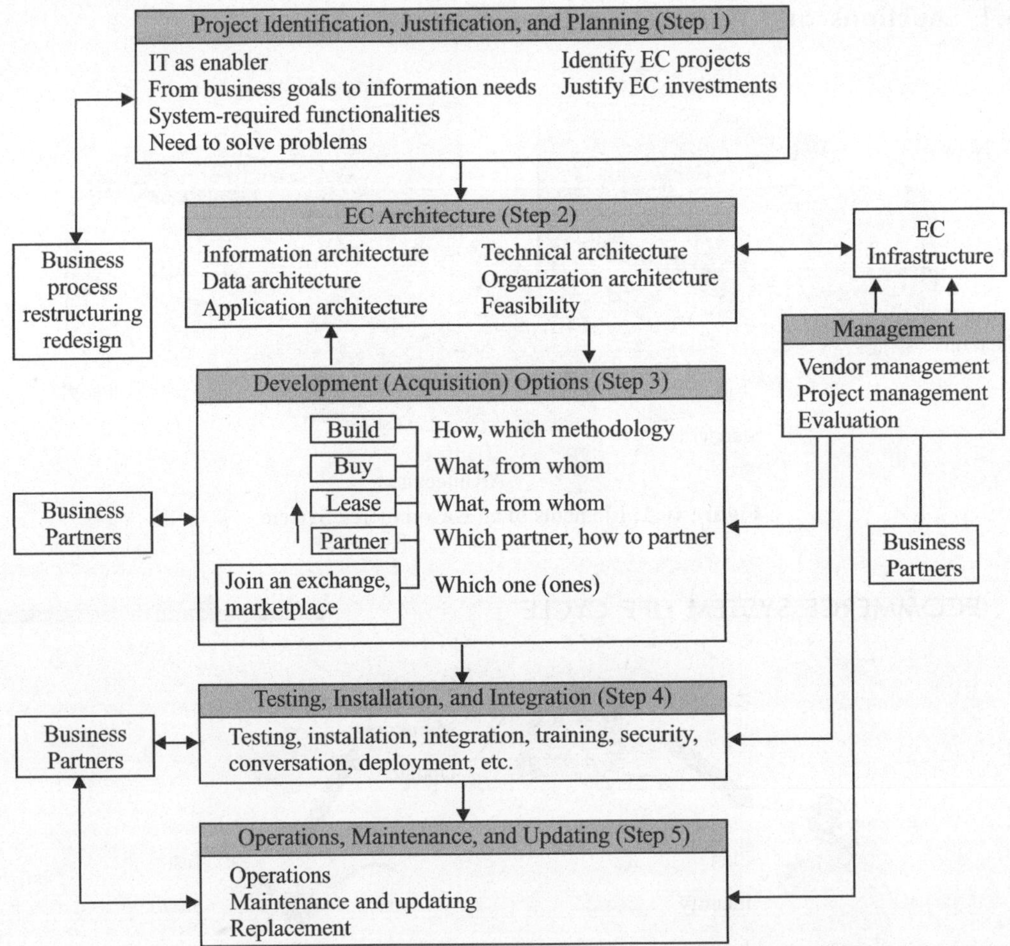

Figure 10.3: The EC Application Development Process

Step 1: Identifying, justifying, and planning EC systems

EC applications, like all other information systems, are usually built to enable one or more business processes. Consequently, their planning must be aligned with that of the organization's overall business plan and the specific processes involved. Always remember that existing processes may need to be restructured to take full advantage of the benefits of the supporting IT. Furthermore, each application must be carefully analyzed, using different methods, such as the methodology discussed in the opening case, to ensure that it will have the needed functionality to meet the requirements of the business processes and the users and that its benefits will justify its cost . Both of these activities may be complex, but they are necessary, especially for systems that require high investment to acquire, operate, and maintain. The output of this step is a decision to go with a specific application, with a timetable, budget, and assigned responsibility. This first step is typically performed in-house (with consultants if needed). All other steps can be completed either in-house or outsourced.

Step 2: Creating an Ec architecture

An EC architecture is a plan for organizing the underlying infrastructure and applications of a site. The plan specifies the following:

- Information and data required to fulfill the business goals and vision
- Application modules that will deliver and manage the information and data

Specific hardware and software on which the application modules will run

- Necessary security, scalability, and reliability required by the applications
- Human resources and procedures for implementing the architecture

Various IT tools and methodologies can be used to support the creation of an application architecture. Because the creation of an architecture is an iterative process, collaborative methodologies, such as joint application development (JAD), are especially useful in identifying and modifying system requirements.

For example, TD Banknorth, a leading banking and financial services company headquartered in Portland, Maine, wanted to upgrade its online customer services to provide information fast enough so that customers would not have to send e-mail or make phone calls. With the help of RightNow's on-demand solutions and professional services, TD Banknorth increased its 24-hour maximum response rate to customer e-mails from a mediocre 90 percent level to an impressive 97 percent and lowered e-mail volume by 55 percent, to about 35 messages a day.

The results obtained from step 2 are routed to a steering committee at the strategic planning level. Based on the results of step 2, the application portfolio may be changed. For example, the steering committee may discourage or scale down the specific project because it is too risky. Once the architecture is determined and the project gets final approval, a decision about how to develop the specific EC application must be made and a development option chosen.

Step 3: Selecting a development option

EC applications can be developed through several alternative approaches.

- Build the system in-house.
- Have a vendor build a customized system.
- Buy an existing application and install it, with or without modifications, by yourself or through a vendor.
- Lease standard software from an application service provider (ASP), lease as a service (SaaS), or lease via utility computing.
- Enter into a partnership or alliance that will enable the company to use someone else's application.
- Join a third-party e-marketplace, such as an auction site, a bidding (reverse auction) site, or an exchange, that provides needed capabilities to participants (e.g., Yahoo! Store).
- Use a combination of approaches.

Once an option is chosen, the system can be developed. At the end of this step, an application is ready to be installed and made available. No matter what option is chosen, it is important to keep in mind that all the different applications that support the various capabilities of the Web site must be coordinated and considerable collaboration between developers and users is necessary.

Step 4: Installing, testing, integrating, and deploying EC applications

Once a system has been developed, the next step involves getting the application up and running in the selected hardware and network environment. One of the steps in installing an application is connecting it to back-end databases, to other applications, and often to other Web sites. For example, if a prospective customer orders a product from a site, it would be helpful if the site could determine if the product is in stock. To do this, the ordering system would need to be connected to the inventory system.This step can be done in-house or outsourced.

At this point, the modules that have been installed need to be tested using a series of different tests:

- Unit testing.Test each module one at a time.
- Integration testing.Test the combination of modules acting in concert.
- *Usability testing.*Test the quality of the user's experience when interacting with the site.
- Acceptance testing. Determine whether the site meets the firm's original business objectives and vision.

Once all of the Web site applications pass all of the tests, they can be made available to the end users. At this stage, developers may need to address issues such as conversion strategies, training, and resistance to change.

Step 5: Operations, maintenance, and updates

It typically takes more time, effort, and money to operate and maintain a site than it does to build and install it in the first place. To enjoy continual usage, a site needs to be updated frequently. For example, at a B2C site new products need to be added to the catalog, prices need to be changed, and new promotions need to be run. These changes and updates need to undergo the same testing procedures used during the installation process. Additionally, usage patterns and performance need to be studied to determine which parts of the underlying applications should be modified or eliminated from the site.

10.7 MANAGING THE DEVELOPMENT PROCESS

The development process can be fairly complex and must be managed properly. For medium-to-large applications, a project team is usually created to manage the process and the vendors. Collaboration with business partners also is critical. some e-business failures are the result of a lack of cooperation by business partners. For example, a firm can install a superb e-procurement system, but if their vendors do not use it properly, the system will collapse. Projects can be managed with project management software. Best practice management also includes periodic evaluations of system performance. Standard project management techniques and tools are useful for this task.

Finally, do not rule out the possibility that implementing an EC project may require restructuring one or more business processes.

10.8 DEVELOPMENT STRATEGIES FOR E-COMMERCE MAJOR APPLICATIONS

If the desired Web site is relatively simple, a firm may decide to build the Web site itself. However, the firm must ask a few questions: Is the firm capable of developing the site? Does the firm have access to the proper tools to create the pages? If the firm does not have these capabilities, it is usually best to turn over the task to a professional developer.

10.9 IN-HOUSE DEVELOPMENT: INSOURCING

The first generation of EC development was accomplished largely through proprietary programming and in-house development that is widely referred to as insourcing. Using this approach, the Internet browser serves as the development platform. The programmers write EC systems using a combination of HTML and script languages such as HTX, CGI, IDC, and JavaScript. Databases developed on top of a database management system (DBMS) usually serve as the information repository to store EC data. Although this first generation of EC development has built up valuable experience and achieved industrial momentum, the lack of reusability (i.e., the likelihood a segment of source code can be used again to add new functionalities with slight or no modification) in current EC applications and the lack of interoperability (i.e., the ability to connect people, data and diverse systems, standards) created a great barrier to widespread application of EC.

Although in-house development in sourcing can be time-consuming and costly, it may lead to EC applications that better fit an organization's strategy and vision and differentiate it from the competition. Companies that have the resources to develop their e-business application in-house may follow this approach in order to differentiate themselves from the competition, which may be using standard applications that can be bought or leased. The in-house development of EC applications, however, is a challenging task, because most applications are novel, have users from outside the organization, and involve multiple organizations.

10.10 SELECTING A DEVELOPMENT METHOD

When choosing one or more development methods, a number of questions must be carefully answered. For example, will the chosen method(s) facilitate the completion and implementation of the e-commerce system within the time prescribed? Can the project be brought in on budget? Does the Web site adequately provide all the specified functionality? In doing so, it is important to also prioritize the different criteria in relation to current and future business needs.To help in selecting a development approach, software comparisons are available from several independent organizations and magazines. The majority of vendors offer software demos for limited testing times and many will offer proof of concept demonstrations.

10.11 SOFTWARE ON DEMAND

To accommodate the increasingly popular move to EC development by vendors, a less risky outsourcing option known as software on demand has emerged as a development method. Initially, this leasing option was provided through utility computing, then through ASPs, and more recently, through firms that provide software as a service (SaaS). Large and small firms alike will often choose the lease option to experiment with new software before making a large up-front investment or as an ongoing method of acquiring and supporting EC software. Another benefit is that it enables firms to protect their internal networks.

Through leasing, new entrants into e-business (usually smaller firms) are able to establish a market presence in a much shorter period of time. Each of these alternative sources of software acquisition is discussed in the following sections.

10.12 UTILITY COMPUTING

Utility (on-demand) computing is a business model whereby computer resources are provided on an on-demand and pay-per-use basis. This contrasts sharply with the traditional SDLC model of purchasing physical systems, configuring them, and devoting them to one application for their useful life.With utility computing, customers do not own the expensive computer resources but are billed only for their actual use of the resources. Because the utility computing provider can spread customers' variance in resource needs, resource utilization can be optimized. Because the utility computing service is based on usage, computing resources are metered and the user charged on that basis. This is comparable to the use of electricity, gas, and most other utilities; hence, the name utility computing. Utility computing is sometimes also called on-demand computing.

Utility computing has a long history. Utility computing was first described by John McCarthy in 1961 at the MIT Centennial as follows:

If computers of the kind I have advocated become the computers of the future, then computing may someday be organized as a public utility just as the telephone system is a public utility. . . . The computer utility could become the basis of a new and important industry.

HP was the original leader of the utility computing concept, recognizing that computing power and resources can be delivered as a service, flowing on demand as and where needed. Subsequently, IBM offered this type of flexible delivery of computing power and database storage to big banks from its worldwide data centers. In 2000, Sun offered utility computing to consumers through its Sun Grid service. HP introduced the Utility Data Center in 2001. Since 2000, many companies have entered the utility computing market.

Each tool must be seamlessly integrated to create a comprehensive solution but will usually be implemented separately.These three tools are:

1. **Policy-based service-level management tools,** which coordinate, monitor, and report on the ways in which multiple infrastructure components come together to deliver a business service.

2. **Policy-based resource management tools,** which coordinate, monitor, and report on the ways in which multiple infrastructure components come together to deliver a business service. They automate and standardize all types of IT management best practices, from initial configuration to ongoing fault management and asset tracking.
3. **Virtualization tools,** which enable server, storage, and network resources to be deployed and managed as giant pools and seamlessly changed as needs change. These tools share multisourcing delivery and financing services (left side of Exhibit 18.5) and provide for customer access and management services (right side of Exhibit 18.5).

10.13 APPLICATION SERVICE PROVIDERS (ASPS)

An application service provider (ASP) manages application servers in a centrally controlled location rather than on a customer's site. Applications are then accessed via the Internet or value-added networks through a standard Web browser interface. Such an arrangement provides a full range of services for the company using the ASP.

Applications can be scaled; upgrades and maintenance can be centralized; physical security over the applications and servers can be guaranteed; and the necessary critical mass of human resources can be efficiently utilized.

The end-user businesses pay a licensing fee. Monthly fees are separate and are paid to the maker of the software and to the ASP "host" of the software. In general, these fees include payment for the application software, hardware, service and support, maintenance, and upgrades. The fee can be fixed or may be based on utilization.

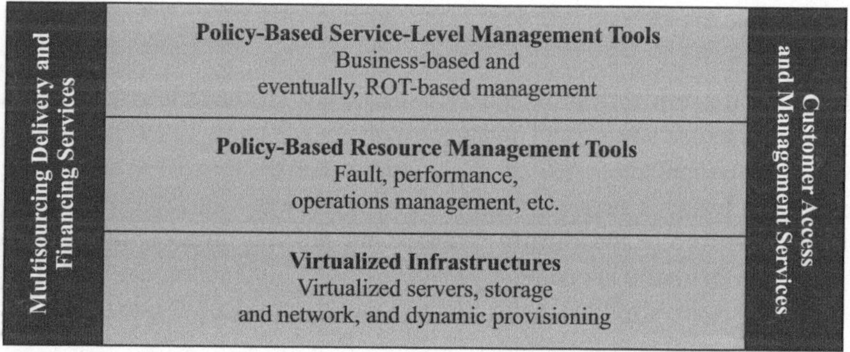

Figure 10.4: The five elements of a successful Utility-computing Value Proposition

Advantages and Disadvantages of ASPs

Leasing from an ASP is a particularly desirable option for SMEs, for which in-house development and operation of IT applications can be time-consuming and expensive. Leasing from ASPs saves various expenses (e.g., labor costs) in the initial development stage. It also helps reduce software maintenance, upgrading, and user training costs in the long run. A company can select other software products from the same ASP to meet its changing needs and does not have to invest further in upgrading the existing one. Thus, overall business competitiveness can be strengthened through reducing time-to-market and enhancing the firm's ability to adapt to changing market conditions. ASPs are particularly effective for IT applications for which timing, flexibility, and agility are crucial.

Leasing from ASPs does have its disadvantages. ASP applications are typically hosted by third parties, who ordinarily do not have application expertise but merely manage the servers; they serve up traditional client-server applications with front-ends added as an afterthought. ASPs generally do not build the application themselves but instead take an off-the-shelf application (such as a messaging platform, an enterprise requirement planning tool, or a sales force automation package) and run it for customers. For example, an ASP might make the latest version of Microsoft Office available across the Web to customers who pay a fee per month for access to the software.

In addition, many companies are concerned with the adequacy of protection offered by ASPs against hackers, theft of confidential information, and virus attacks. Leased software often does not provide the perfect fit for the desired application. It is also important to ensure that the speed of the Internet connection is compatible with that of the application to avoid distortions in its performance. For example, it is not advisable to run heavy-duty applications on a modem link below a T1 line or high-speed DSL.

From the ASP vendor's point of view, the benefits presented by the ASP model are many. For one, in the long-distance carrier and Internet service providers (ISP) markets, revenues are squeezed due to heavy competition. These companies are looking to generate revenues from sources other than connectivity and transport, and ASP services offer a new outlet. The ASP Industry Consortium has emerged to support the ASP concept; its founding members include AT&T, Cisco, Citrix Systems, Ernst & Young, Verizon, IBM, Marimba, Sharp Electronic, Sun Microsystems, UUNET, and Verio.

10.14 SOFTWARE AS A SERVICE (SAAS)

Because most applications typically provided by ASPs are not written as Internet native applications, performance can be poor and application updates are often no better than self managed applications. Consequently, a need to supplement ASP offerings emerged. in the form of an on-demand computing software known as software as a service (SaaS). Software as a service (SaaS) is a form of software delivery in which software is specifically designed for delivery in an online environment. It is essentially "leased" from a software company that provides maintenance, daily technical operation, and support for the software provided to the client. "Leading the charge" into this software delivery paradigm shift is Google.

To engage in SaaS, the user pays the software provider for the user's actual usage or a fixed monthly/quarterly/annual fee instead of the one-time large fee plus support, as with the traditional software licensing model. SaaS is particularly advantageous when a company wants to experiment with a package before making a heavy up-front investment. This solution also enables a firm to protect its internal networks and quickly establish a presence in the market. With SaaS, software can be delivered to any market segment, including home office users, small businesses, and medium and large businesses. It can result in substantial cost and time savings. Although SaaS is useful to any size company, it is particularly appealing for SMEs, who often have limited IT resources and tight budgets.

Table 10.2: Benefits and Risks of using an ASP

Type	Benefits	Potential Risks
Business	Reduces the need to attract and retain skilled IT professionals Enables companies to concentrate on lack of strategic use of IT Enables SMEs to use tier-1 applications (e.g., ERP, SCM and CRM) Application scalability enables rapid growth of companies	Loss of control and high level of dependence on ASP Inability of ASP to deliver quality of service; skills and experience
Technical	Fast and easy application deployment Higher degree of application standardization Access to wide range of applications Application maintenance simplified and performed by ASP Simplified user support and training	Level of customization and legacy application integration offered by ASP is insufficient Low reliability and speed of delivery due to bandwidth limitations Low capability of ASP to deal with security and confidentiality issues.
Economic	Low total cost of ownership Low up-front investments in hardware and software Improved cost control as a result of predictable susbscription costs	Pricing changes, by ASP uppredictable application updates and sevices

SaaS allows organizations to access business functionality from a central location over the Web at a cost typically less than that for licensed applications because SaaS pricing is based on a fee. Also, because the software is hosted remotely, users do not need to invest in additional hardware or software support. SaaS removes the need for organizations to handle installation, setup, and daily upkeep and maintenance. SaaS may also be referred to as hosted applications.

10.14.1 Service-Oriented Architecture (SOA)

Service-oriented architecture (SOA) is a term that has emerged to describe executable Components such as Web Services that can be invoked by other programs that act as clients or consumers of those services. The basic premise of SOA is to reuse and reconnect existing IT assets (also called services) rather than take the time and expense to invent new systems. A growing number of firms are addressing the constraints of their current IT architecture and infrastructure by moving to SOA.

The three basic SOA roles are the service provider, the service consumer, and the service broker. A service provider makes the service available and publishes the contract that describes its interface. It then registers the service with a service broker. A service consumer queries the service broker and finds a compatible service. The service broker gives the service consumer directions on where to find the service and its service contract. The service consumer uses the contract to bind the client to the service. For the three conceptual roles to accomplish the three conceptual operations, an SOA system must supply four core functional architecture components:

- Transport. The transport component represents the formats and protocols used to communicate with a service.
- Description. The description component represents the language used to describe a service. The description provides the information needed to tie it to a service.
- Discovery. The discovery component represents the mechanism used to register or advertise a service and to find a service and its description.
- Registration. The registration component registers the services of a service provider with a service broker.

With SOA and Web Services, functions within existing programs and suites, as well as functions within ERP (enterprise resource planning), CRM (customer relationship management), SCM (supply chain management), and other packages, can be invoked automatically and executed anywhere in the world based on business rules. A developer does not need to know how the programs work only the input that they require, the output they provide, and how to invoke them for execution. Developers can also swap out one service and replace it with another service that is designed to achieve the same or an enhanced result without having to worry about the inner workings of the services. SOA and Web Services are expected to totally transform the way EC systems are built, moving from slow, error-prone manual coding to automation.

The essence of an SOA is reusable services and the ability to link disparate applications. EC service components (such as credit card processing or bills payment) can be created once and then reused to drive better cost efficiency from EC and IT investments. What an SOA aims to achieve is to align IT with real business requirements. So, if a business user has a requirement, it can be translated into services in the SOA environment. A number of software vendors are currently competing in the SOA environment, including IBM, with its award-winning WebSphere Portal V6, which offers improved efficiency and productivity through a significantly enhanced user experience and additional personalization capabilities. An up-and-coming subset of SOA that provides business partners with a way to connect, integrate, and mash up is Web-oriented architecture. The term Web-oriented architecture (WOA) was coined by Nick Gall of the Gartner Group and is used to describe a set ofWeb protocols (e.g., HTTP and plain XML) as the most dynamic, scalable, and interoperable Web Services approach. The main difference between a traditional SOA and aWOA is that aWOA advocates REST, an increasingly popular, powerful, and simple method of leveraging HTTP as aWeb Service. Representational StateTransfer (REST) refers to a collection of architectural principles. The term also is used in a loose sense to describe any simple interface that transmits domain-specific data over HTTP without an additional messaging layer. It is important to note, however, that certain applications, particularly in the high end of the enterprise, require the more sophisticated component of SOA. However, for the vast majority of uses, it would appear that WOA is the most interoperable, easiest to implement, and most highly scalable technique for building openWeb Services that anyone can use.

An example of the growing trend of integrating Web 2.0 and SOA can be found at H&R Block, a large income tax preparation firm and the largest seasonal employer in the United States. To streamline staffing operations, H&R Block delivered SOA-connected Ajax portlets to more than 12,000 branch offices to support temporary work spaces. Moving away from PC-based software, their IT department was able to offer a faster, cheaper, and more flexible solution to the company's seasonal staffing needs.

10.15 SUPPORTING WEB 2.0 IN THE ENTERPRISE

Not surprisingly, new software tools, such as IBM's WebSphere Community Edition, Intel's SuiteTwo, Microsoft's Expression Web, and Oracle's WebCenter, have been introduced to support the Enterprise 2.0 environment as companies realize its potential to engage customers and generate content for their Web sites in a way not previously possible. The potential to add an additional dimension to a flat consumer Web site and to develop closer connections to a company's customer base is becoming very attractive to an increasing number of businesses.

The latest generation of the Web does not just link information; it links people. For example, a company can allow consumers who visit its Web site to create their own profiles and rate and comment on products. Consumers can also create their own topic areas within forums and build online communities around shared interests pertaining to the company's products.

Those sites with streaming video capabilities can also encourage consumers to provide user supplied videos of customers using their products and solicit consumer feedback on beta versions of product commercials before final release. Just imagine the immeasurable value to small firms that are unable to afford large market research and advertising campaigns; essentially, a Web 2.0 environment provides an ongoing 24/7 customer focus group, supplying firms with an unending stream of data to analyze and act upon.

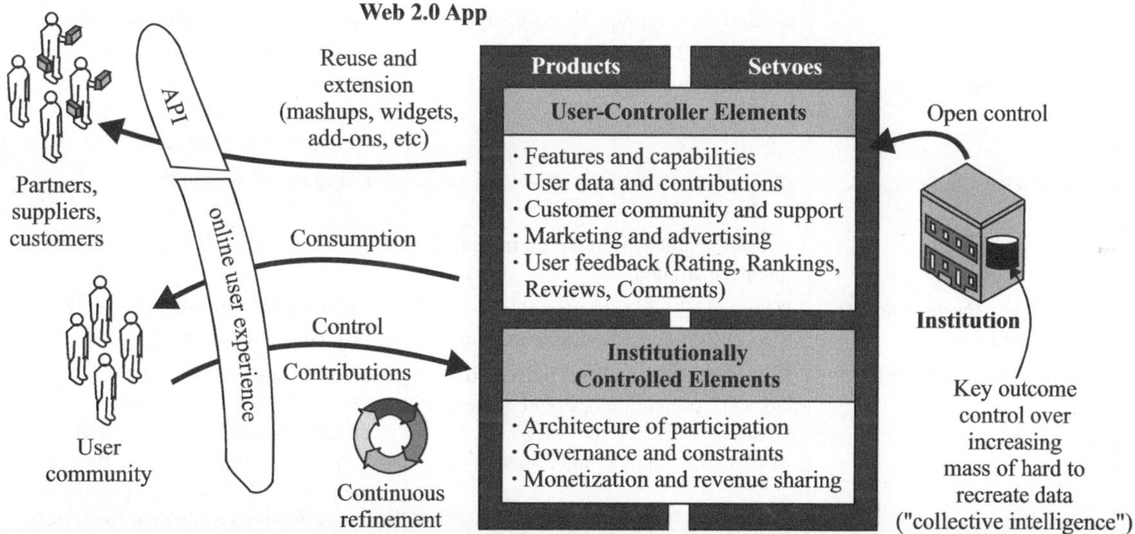

Figure 10.5: Product development 2.0: Using the Web to put Users in Control and Co-Create Better, Richer Products Faster

Table 10.3: The move to product development 2.0

	Product Development 1.0	**Product Development 2.0**
Primary customer interaction channel	Telephone, mail, face-to-face, one-way media (print, TV, radio, etc.), e-mail	World Wide Web, e-mail, IM
Source of innovation	Organizations	Customers
Innovation cycle	Months, years	Minutes, hours, days, weeks
Content creators	Internal producers	External producers
Feedback mechanisms	Market research, satisfaction surveys, complaints, focus groups	Analytics, online requests, user-contributed changes
Customer engagement style	Controlled, well-defined process	Spontaneous and chaotic
Product development process	Up-front design	Less up-front, much more emergent
Product architecture	Closed, not designed for easy extension or reuse by others; walled garden	Open, very easy to extend, regine, change and add on to, ecosystem friendly, designed (and legal) for widespread remixing and mashups
Product development culture	Hierarchical, centralized, not invented here, somewhat collaborative, expert driven	Egalitarian, decentralized, remix instead of reinvent, highly collaborative, wisdom of crowds
Product testing	Internal, dedicated test groups, handipicked select customers	Users as testers
Customer support	Customer service	User community
Product promotion	One-way marketign and advertising of network effects, word of mouth, user-generated and two- way advertising	Viral propagation, explicit leveraging
Business model	Product sales, customer service and support fees, service access charges, servicing high-demand products	Advertising, subscriptions, product sales, servicing all product niches (the long tail), unintended uses
Customer relationship	External buyer (consumer)	Partner and — increasingly remunerated — supplier (consumers as producers)
Product ownership	Institution, particularly executive management and shareholders	Entire user community
Partnering Process	Formal, explicit, infrequent, mediated disintermediated	Ad hoc, thousands of partners online,
Product development and integration tools	Heavyweight, formal, complex, time-consuming, enterprise oriented	Lightweight, informal, simple, free, fast, consumer oriented
Competitive advantage	Superior products, legal barriers to entry (IP protections), brand name advantage, price, popularity, distribution channel agreements	Number one or two leader, leveraging crowd sourcing effectively, mass customization, control over hard-to-create data, end user sense of ownership, popularity, cost-effective customer self-service, audience size, best of breed architectures of participation.

10.16 CONNECTING TO DATABASES AND OTHER ENTERPRISE SYSTEMS

The major integration areas discussed in this chapter are connecting to databases and to back-end systems.

10.16.1 Connecting to Databases

Nearly every EC application requires database access. For example, when a customer orders a product online, the product description, inventory count, and order information are likely to be retrieved from and stored in one or more databases. To check availability, the ordering system must be connected to the inventory system. An EC application can be connected to a back-end database in a variety of ways. Today, most of these connections are accomplished via a multitiered application architecture, which is an EC architecture that consists of four tiers: Web browsers,Web servers, application servers, and database. Customers with a Web browser can then access catalogs in the seller's database, request specific data, and receive an instance response. Here the application server manages the client request.The application server also acts as the front end to complex databases.

This architecture has four tiers:

1. A Web browser that presents data and information to and collects data from the end user
2. A Web server that delivers Web pages, collects the data sent by the end user, and passes data to and from the application server
3. An application server that executes business rules (e.g., user authorization), formulates database queries based on the data passed by the Web server, sends the queries to the back end database, manipulates and formats the data resulting from the database query, and sends the formatted response to the Web server
4. A database server in which the data are stored and managed and database requests are Processed

10.16.2 Connecting to Back-end Systems

Several technologies can be used to integrate an EC application with a back-end database. Many of the commercial electronic catalogs and EC suites have built-in integration capabilities. If a company wants to build its own database interface, a couple of options are available. First, all of the Web scripting languages (e.g., PHP, JSP, and Active Server Pages [ASP]) have commands that simplify the process. More specifically, these scripting languages enable a programmer to build Web pages that can issue queries to a back-end (relational) database and process the database's response to the query. Second, a number of specialized application servers are available that simplify the task of integrating an EC application with one or more back-end databases. Among these specialized servers, BEA's WebLogic Server 9.2 (bea.com) is a market leader.

In addition to connecting to back-end databases, most EC applications also require integration with a variety of other systems-ERP, CRM, SCM, EDI, data warehouses, and other important internal systems-both inside and outside the company. Again, electronic catalogs and EC suites usually have built-in modules for integration with these systems. The integration can also be handled with enterprise application integration (EAI) software.These products focus on the integration of large systems. TIBCO (tibco.com), WebMethods (www-01.ibm.com/ software/integration/wbiserver/ics), and IBM's WebSphere InterChange Server (ibm.com) are examples of companies that have offerings in the EAI arena.

10.16.3 Connecting to Business Partners

As discussed earlier, companies and organizations are now building enterprisewide EC systems by integrating previously independent applications together with new developments. EC applications also must be connected to items such as the partners' systems or to public exchanges.

Such connections are referred to as integration. EC users interact with Internet applications through a variety of devices whose characteristics and performance figures span an increasingly wide range. Applications use communication protocols and intermediate software that resides on top of the operating systems to perform the following functions:

- Hiding distribution (i.e., the fact that an application is usually made up of many interconnected parts running in distributed locations)
- Hiding the heterogeneity of the various hardware components, operating systems, and communication protocols Providing uniform, standard, high-level interfaces to the application developers and integrators so that applications can be easily composed, reused, ported, and made to interoperate
- Supplying a set of common services to perform various general-purpose functions to avoid duplicating efforts and to facilitate collaboration between applications.

The intermediate software layers have come to be known under the generic name of middleware. Middleware is essentially a separate program that provides an interface between diverse client and server systems. Its main function is to mediate interaction between the parts of an application or between applications. For more information, see middleware.objectweb.org. IBM is the leading provider of middleware. The company offers a number of on-demand solutions for communication, government, retail, banking, financial markets, and many other industries. IBM Middleware (ibm.com/middleware) helps automate systems, integrate operations, connect people, and develop software.

10.17 USAGE ANALYSIS AND SITE MANAGEMENT

To improve EC Web sites, it is advisable to monitor what customers are doing there (usage analysis). Both B2C and B2B Web sites require a thorough understanding of the usage and patterns the who, what, where, when, and how. This can be done by analyzing Web log files.

10.18 LOG FILES

Every time a user accesses a Web server, the server logs the transaction in a special access log file. Access logs are text files in which each line of the file details an individual access. Regardless of the type of Web server, access logs use a common log file format. This makes them easy to analyze and compare. Because log files can become quite voluminous, it is hard to analyze the accesses by hand. For this reason, most Web server EC software vendors provide free software for analyzing access log files. Commercial products that provide more sophisticated log analyses also are available (e.g., NetIQ's WebTrends).

Access logs provide a variety of statistics that can be used for analyzing and improving marketing and advertising strategies. Among the more valuable statistics are the following:

- **Pageviews by time slot.** Pageview statistics allow frequent review of the number of site accesses. Grouping pageviews by "time bucket" (time slot) also enables a company to ascertain the time slots, such as morning, afternoon, or evening, during which customers visit the site.
- **Pageviews by customers' log-in status.** This information helps determine whether requiring customers to log in is worthwhile. For instance, if the number of pageviews of customers who log in is substantially greater than those who do not, the company may find the log-in requirement effective and worthwhile.
- **Pageviews by referrers.** Some customers are drawn or referred to the site by clicking on banners or links on other Web sites. Knowing the source of such referrers is useful for assessing the effectiveness of the location of banners, and customers' interests can also be determined from the nature of the Web site with those banners.
- **Pageviews by visitor's hardware platform, operating system, browser, and/or browser version.** These types of pageviews enable a company to obtain information on the hardware platform (e.g., Mac or PC) and browser type (e.g., Internet Explorer or Netscape) used by the viewer.
- **Pageviews by visitor's host.** This type of pageview provides information on the customers' host sites. Knowing where customers are coming from can enable the company to target potential customers via popular hosts such as Yahoo!

10.19 E-COMMERCE MANAGEMENT TOOLS

Managing the performance of a Web site is a time-consuming and tedious administrative task. Several vendors offer suites of products or individual packages that can assist with the management process. One of the more prominent vendors of IT and Web management tools is BMC Software, Inc. (bmc.com). Some of the products offered by BMC include:

- Patrol for E-Business Management. This package includes Patrol for Internet Services, which measures Web response time; Patrol for Firewalls, which provides firewall administration; and Patrol for Microsoft or Netscape application servers.
- MainView for E-Business Management. This package includes MainView for WebSphere, which aids in the management of mainframe-based EC applications; MainView for Network Management, to monitor mainframe network connections; and MainView for Systems Management, to provide systems administration.

Other EC management tools include site version control tools, combined utilities/tools, server management and optimization tools, and authoring/publishing/deployment tools that include significant site management or testing capabilities. A detailed list of vendors is provided by Hower (2009). The following are some examples:

- COAST WebCentral. This site management tool from Coast Software, Inc. (e-tamed.co.uk/products/coast4.html) monitors compliance standards related to privacy, information assurance, accessibility, and Web governance. Capabilities include highlevel summary reports, site scores, and trend analyses using intuitive browser-based reports; roll-up of results from different business units or global Web sites for overall views of site compliance; complete inventory of Web sites; and comparison inventory reports to compare different versions of a Web site.
- Maxamine Knowledge Platform. This integrated site management tool from Maxamine Inc. (maxamine.com) combines site content, structure, and visitor traffic data into one searchable database, enabling detailed analysis of what is going on behind the scenes of Web operations.
- WebCEO. Companies can use this tool from Radiocom Ltd. (webceo.com) to maintain, promote, and analyze Web sites. It includes a link checker, a WYSIWYG editor, and FTP/publishing, traffic analysis, and site monitoring capabilities.
- ManageEngine Applications Manager. This site management tool from AdventNet (adventnet.com) works with a variety of Web servers, database servers, service types, and operating systems.

10.20 MERCHANT ACCOUNT

A merchant account is a type of bank account that allows businesses to accept payments by debit or credit cards. A merchant account also serves as an agreement between a retailer, a **merchant bank** and payment processor for the settlement of credit card and/or debit card transactions, An industry term for a business banking relationship whereby you and a bank have arranged to accept credit card payments (usually, a local bank can suffice for this kind of relationship). Setting up a merchant account usually involves the bank understanding your business and working with a third-party processor to arrange a mechanism for accepting payments. Merchant accounts are usually required for accepting customer credit card and electronic payments through an **electronic commerce Web site**.

Does your **business**, whether online or offline, accept credit cards? If it doesn't, you are losing a lot of money. In fact, taking credit cards could as much as triple your income. If you are online, your customers expect you to take credit cards. If you do not, then it is time to learn about merchant accounts

Function

A merchant account is a special type of bank account that allows a business to accept credit card payments. When a business takes a customer's credit card information, either through a paper form, online form or swiping it at a terminal, the information is sent to the major credit card company and the customer's bank through the merchant account. The bank or credit card company will verify that funds are present and approve the sale. The merchant then finishes the transaction. Later, the information is sent to the credit card company and funds are deposited into the merchant's account.

Types

There are three main types of merchant accounts. Retail stores that have a brick-and-mortar location will have retail accounts. These are connected to a credit card processing terminal that the merchant can use to scan the customer's credit card. A mail order-telephone order merchant account allows a merchant to take credit card orders through written forms or telephone orders. Internet based merchant accounts are used by online businesses that allow customers to pay by entering their credit card information into an online form.

Significance

Merchant accounts are not free. Many programs offer free incentives, such as a free credit card processing machine or setup on the merchant's website. However, you will pay for merchant account services. Typically you will pay a per-transaction fee. This can be a few cents per transaction or a small percent of the transaction amount. Merchant accounts that charge a percent per transaction often have a minimum charge for very small transactions. This minimum charge is usually a couple of cents.

Considerations

If you are looking to set up a merchant account, shop carefully as there are many differences between the different programs. Find a company that offers an incentive, such as free set up. Also, look at the per-transaction cost. What works best for you will depend on the types of sales you do. If you typically ring up large amounts, a fixed per-transaction charge is probably the most affordable option. If your totals are typically low dollar amounts, a percent based charge may be ideal.

Expert Insight

Some business owners do not like the idea of paying someone else to allow them to accept credit cards, and they do not set up merchant accounts as a result. This is sad, because these business owners are losing significant income. According to accounting firm PricewaterhouseCoopers, credit card purchases are typically three times as large as cash or check purchases. Not only that, but customers feel comfortable paying with credit cards, and you may lose some people's business if you do not accept them.

10.20.1 Methods of processing credit cards

Today a majority of credit card transactions are sent electronically to merchant processing banks for authorization, capture and deposit. Various methods exist for presenting a credit card sale to "the system." In all circumstances either the entire magnetic strip is read by a swipe through a credit card terminal/reader, a computer chip is read, or the credit card information is manually entered into a credit card terminal, a computer or website. The earliest methods, submitting credit card slips to a merchant processing bank by mail, or by accessing an Automated Response Unit (ARU) by telephone, are still in use today but have long been overshadowed by electronic devices. These early methods used two-part forms and a manual device for mechanically imprinting the embossed card number information onto the forms.

10.20.2 Credit Card Terminal

A credit card terminal is a stand-alone piece of electronic equipment that allows a merchant to swipe or key-enter a credit card's information as well as additional information required to process a credit card transaction. A credit card terminal is a dedicated piece of equipment that only processes credit cards although it is common for related transactions including gift cards and check verification to also be performed. A credit card terminal typically must be plugged in to a power supply and connected to a telephone line. However, some terminals may be powered by batteries and communicate over the Internet or through a cellular phone data network. When a credit card is processed (either swiped through the magnetic stripe reader or keyed-in to the keypad), it contacts the network to verify if the credit card can be authorized. The transaction is then stored on the machine until the polling window is opened. The machine will either upload the electronic funds directly to the merchant bank, or a polling service provider will dial in to collect, process then submit the data to the merchant bank. The most popular credit card terminals consist of a modem, keypad, printer, magnetic stripe reader, power supply and memory card. They have had the same basic design since the 1980s. As with computers, there is a wide range of memory capacities and other features like built-in printers and debit card pinpads that affect the manufacturing cost of a credit card terminal.

10.20.3 Automated Response Unit (ARU)

An ARU (also known as a voice authorization, capture and deposit) allows the manual keyed entry and subsequent authorization of a credit card over a cellular or land-line telephone. With this method a merchant typically imprints their customer's card with an imprinter to create a customer receipt and merchant copy, then process the transaction instantaneously over the phone.

10.20.4 Payment Gateway

A payment gateway is an e-commerce service that authorizes payments for e-businesses and online retailers. It is the equivalent of a physical POS (point-of-sale) terminal located in most retail outlets. A merchant account provider is typically a separate company from the payment gateway. Some merchant account providers have their own payment gateways but the majority of companies use 3rd party payment gateways. The gateway usually has 2 components: a) the virtual terminal that can allow for a merchant to securely login and key in credit card numbers or b) have the website's shopping-cart connect to the gateway via an API to allow for real time processing from the merchant's website.

10.20.5 Level 2 or Level 3 Processing - Purchasing Cards

Visa and Mastercard have created a specialized type of credit card used primarily by government agencies and businesses. Increasingly, corporations and government agencies are relying on this form of payment to compensate their service providers and suppliers. Businesses benefit by receiving their funds quickly and by winning competitive bids and government contracts where purchasing cards are the required form of payment. The downside, however, is the increased costs associated with receiving these payments. These costs will usually be much higher than accepting a standard consumer credit card.

The solution is that some businesses may qualify for ways to process these transactions that allow them to pay lower fees if they can supply additional information, called "level 2 or level 3 data". For example, if government transactions are over $5,000, businesses can significantly reduce their transaction costs by including "level 2 or level 3 data" about the purchase along with each transaction. Examples of level 2 or level 3 data is a purchase order number associated with the transaction that the credit card will be paying. This data is passed on to the purchaser so that it may be many times easier to reconcile the transaction. If all the required data is not collected and passed on during the transaction, the merchant can have surcharges added to the basic fees or be forced into a non qualified transaction category.

10.21 MERCHANT ACCOUNT MARKETING

Merchant accounts are marketed to merchants by two basic methods: either directly by the processor or sponsoring bank, or by an authorized agent for the bank and additionally directly registered with both Visa and MasterCard as an ISO/MSP (Independent Selling Organization / Member Service Provider). Marketing details are by card issuers like Visa and MasterCard, and are enforced by various rules and fines. A few of the largest processors also partner with warehouse clubs to promote merchant accounts to their business members.

10.21.1 Marketing by Banks

A bank that has a merchant processing relationship with Visa and Mastercard, also known as a member bank, can issue merchant accounts directly to merchants. To reduce risk, some banks limit approval to merchants in its geographical area, those with a physical retail storefront, or those that have been in business for 2 years or more.

10.21.2 Marketing by Independent Sales Organization (ISO)/MSPs

To market merchant accounts, an ISO/MSP must be sponsored by a member bank. This sponsorship requires that the bank verify the financial stability and suitability of the company that will be marketing on its behalf. The ISO/MSP must also pay a fee to be registered with Visa and Mastercard and must comply with regulations in how they may market merchant accounts and the use of copyrights of Visa and Mastercard. One way to verify if an ISO/MSP is in compliance is to check a website or any other marketing material for a disclosure "company is a registered ISO/MSP of bank, town, state. FDIC insured". This disclosure is required by both Visa and Mastercard and will cause a fine of up to $25,000 if it is not clearly visible. In almost all cases, if there is no disclosure, the company is likely to be an uninformed 4th party or worse. In many cases unregistered operators have been responsible for some of the worst horror stories from merchants.

10.22 HOW TO GET APPROVED FOR A MERCHANT ACCOUNT

There are many examples of high-risk merchants, such as telemarketers (inbound or outbound), Internet/e-commerce businesses, merchants in the travel and cruise industries, Internet auctions and businesses offering membership clubs.

But owning a high-risk business doesn't mean you won't be able to open a merchant account. It does mean, though, that it may be more challenging to set one up. Merchant account providers--banks and independent sales organizations--will also consider how long you've been in business, your credit history and any previous merchant accounts you've held with other processors To increase your merchant account eligibility, follow these tips:

- Ensure a positive credit rating. Remove any past bankruptcies, late payments or liens from your credit report before you apply for a merchant account. To obtain your credit report, contact a credit reporting bureau such as TRW or a company that provides merged credit reports from major reporting agencies, such as Equifax, Experian or Trans Union. Write to them, explain that these matters have been cleared up and ask that they're removed from your credit report. Whether you own a small or large business, having a good credit rating will make a lasting and favorable impression with a transaction processor.
- Be honest about previous merchant accounts, bankruptcies, liens or judgments. By acknowledging past financial challenges, you improve your credibility and may encounter one less barrier to opening a new merchant account. You cannot hide information that's part of the public record.
- Be willing to pay higher fees or accommodate special account requirements. If you need to abide by special restrictions or pay slightly higher fees in order to open a merchant account, by all means do it! It's worth it to provide your customers with as many noncash payment options as possible. It will help you generate revenues and stimulate impulse purchases.
- Shop around for a credit card processor that best suits your needs. Talk to several different processors and don't be afraid to ask questions. Find out about:
  - **The discount rate:** The percentage of each transaction paid to the merchant account provider. If your monthly charges are less than a certain volume, the processor may charge a higher percentage.
  - **Transaction fee:** A flat rate charged for each transaction processed.
  - **Equipment:** Some examples include point-of-sale terminals, printers and peripherals. Also find out about installation costs.

- **Monthly minimum fees:** These are minimum fees that the merchant account provider collects each month from the merchant if the merchant's discount rate and transaction fees don't add up to the monthly minimum specified on the original merchant application. It is usually about $25 per month if the monthly minimum volume isn't reached.
- **Reserve fees:** If your credit history is in question, or if you own a new or high-risk business, you may be required to set up a reserve account, which protects the processor from any future losses. The reserve account is calculated as a percentage of your sales.
- **Chargeback fees:** These are the costs charged by a processor to cover disputed charges.
- **E-Commerce:** If you're an e-commerce merchant, ask your prospective processor about the costs of storefront solutions that you must have to effectively operate your Web site, such as shopping carts, Web hosting, payment gateways, virtual terminals, virtual checks, databases for fulfilling orders, customer tracking, and a way to calculate tax and shipping charges.

Operating a high-risk business does not exclude you from being able to process credit cards. When you shop around for the right transaction-processing organization, go into it knowing what to expect. Follow the strategies outlined above, and the experience of opening a merchant account will hopefully go smoothly. And in the end, getting approved will put you on your way toward generating more revenues for your business.

Getting a merchant account is a necessary step before you can take credit and debit card payments. That's essential for the vast majority of Software-as-a-Service (SaaS) start-ups, and for many other kinds of business too. Unless you'll be making all your money from advertising, you'll need to be able to take payments, and if you want to be able to do so efficiently, you need a merchant account.

Considering how many businesses there are out there, one would think this process might be smooth and painless by now. Just apply for a merchant account, sign on the dotted line, and receive your merchant id in the mail a couple of weeks later. Unfortunately, this is not the case. Obtaining a merchant account can be a long and complex process, particularly if you're a new, small business that's going through this process for the first time.

I don't claim to be an expert on this process. However, I've gone through it a few times, and I know people who are very familiar with it, so I put together this guide to obtaining a merchant account, from the cash-strapped start-up's point of view.

10.22.1 Why do We Need a Merchant Account

If you're building a typical SaaS business, you'll need a merchant account in order to process credit and debit card payments. You could use Paypal, but some customers may feel you're less credible because you don't charge like everyone else. You could use one of the gateways that don't require a merchant account, but typically they take fees of up to 10% of the transaction amount.

As of the publication of this post, the standard, most cost-effective way to take payments for SaaS products is still merchant accounts, managed by a regular bank, and going through a payment gateway.

1. When should you start this process

Getting a merchant account can take anything from a few days to more than six months (if you make many mistakes). If you're going through it for the first time, you may find yourself stuck at various points in the process. These sticking points can result in massive delays. You don't want to be sitting there with a business that has users who want to pay you, but can't because you don't have a merchant account. Unforeseen delays in this process can cost you dearly, and if you're going through this for the first time, there will probably be unforeseen delays.

On the other hand, there is little to no cost in obtaining a merchant account too early. Until your first transaction, the account just waits, unused, costing you nothing.

Therefore, you should start this process as soon as possible - today, if you can. Don't underestimate how long this might take. Banks are often ridiculously slow in processing merchant account applications, when compared to the pace of the internet.

A small addendum to this advice: you need to have some sort of website (even if it's just a placeholder) up before you start the application process. The bank will look at it. But this needs not be the same website that you actually launch with.

2. Apply to more than one bank

When you apply for a merchant account as a fresh new start-up, you're in a position of overwhelming inferiority. The bank can dictate whatever terms they want to you, ask you for money up-front, impose ridiculous charges, etc. There's a simple way around this: apply to several banks.

It takes more time and effort, but it gives you bargaining power. Banks don't talk to each other much, so you can play them against each other. If all the banks are demanding an up-front payment, you can tell each one that another bank that you've applied to didn't demand it. Banks do want your business, especially if you've conveyed the right impression, and so they'll be willing to negotiate terms if it looks like you're going to go somewhere else.

If you end up with more than one merchant account, so much the better. Sometimes banks can act irrationally and freeze your merchant account (particularly early on when you're still relatively tiny), at the first hint that maybe there could be fraud going on (whether there really is or not). Having another merchant account set up gives you the ability to minimise the damage by switching over to your backup account. And, as I said earlier, unused merchant accounts don't cost much.

3. Exaggerate your volumes

When you're preparing your internal business plan, you should be conservative with your sales forecasts. However, when you're talking to the bank, you should convince them that you will be a successful business that will bring them significant revenues. This shouldn't be too hard - after all, you are optimistic about your start-up's prospects, aren't you?

Don't lie. You need to be able to justify those numbers. However, if your internal, conservative goal is to get 500 sales a month by the end of the year, say you're looking at internal projections of 1500 to 2000 sales a month. Be realistic, but optimistic. Ideally, you want to convey a turnover that will soon rise above a million dollars, so that your account manager feels that it's worthwhile dealing with you and giving you a good deal. Don't tell them that you're hoping for those numbers. Tell them that those are the numbers you expect, based on current usage patterns. Now is the time for unwarranted confidence and optimism, not for cautious realism.

Your projected volume will also influence how big a cut the bank asks for. If your volumes are very small, they will want a comparatively large percentage of your transactions. If you're planning to process a lot of transactions, on the other hand, they may be happy with a smaller cut.

Once your rates are negotiated, the bank is extremely unlikely to increase (or decrease) them if you fail to reach the volumes you predicted. So make sure you get good rates from the start by being optimistic.

4. Know your fraud-stuff

Banks still exist in a universe where "online businesses" are a scary new idea. They often don't quite understand it, and they are scared to death of fraud. Even though you are honest, some of your customers may not be.

Your account manager will need to convince her fraud department that you're not a great fraud risk. In order to do this, you need to convince her that you know all about online fraud, and that your business has covered all the bases to prevent fraudulent activity.

You should also think ahead and figure out how someone might attempt to defraud you. This is harder because there is not all that much advice about how fraudulent individuals screw over businesses. Most of the readily available advice focuses on helping consumers avoid fraudulent businesses, but many businesses go broke dealing with fraudulent customers. It's important to think ahead to what you're going to do when (not if) someone uses a stolen card number on your service.

Do you pay commissions to affiliates? You're automatically a higher fraud risk. Do you sell intangibles (like a web service)? People might call in chargebacks to get refunds. Sell to businesses? You're a lower fraud risk, so make sure you highlight that. Adult industry? Multi-level marketing? Other "shady" businesses? Chances are the bank will not even touch you.

It is important for your own business that you think about fraud ahead of time. And it is extremely important for your merchant account process that you convey that you've thought about fraud and have it covered. Make the bank feel safe, or they'll delay your application forever.

5. Be serious

The last thing any bank wants, understandably, is someone who's going to blunder their way through figuring out how to charge credit cards, making costly mistakes along the way, getting defrauded left and right, and finally going broke and winding down the business because they couldn't handle the complexity of it all. As part of your discussions and emails with your account manager, you must convince him that you're serious, you know what you're doing and, ideally, that you have help from someone who's done it before, successfully.

If you don't have access to such a helper, find one. Again, this shouldn't be too hard - presumably you know other people who have started businesses before and they had to apply for a merchant account too. Once you've found that person, make sure your account manager is aware that you're not helpless.

Be serious about security too. There are a lot of security regulations tied to internet transaction processing, and you want to be aware of them and convey that you are aware of them. For example, it's probably a good thing to name-drop PCI-DSS in the conversation, and explain how you're compliant with it.

Finally, do convey that you're a serious business and you're going to succeed. This is not the time to declare that you're a fresh new business and you don't have formal titles within the company, and don't care much for rigid formality. This is the time to introduce yourself as the managing director and sound exactly like your stodgier competitors might.

6. *Read the fine print and negotiate the charges*

Banks will often present you with complex charges that are hard to compare with the offers from other banks. Unscrupulous ones may even use tricks like high termination fees that hit you when you least expect it. Others may ask for high up-front fees, suggest they hold your money for 3 months, etc.

All those points are negotiable.

The extent to which you can negotiate is largely driven by how much they value your business (see point 3) and by how many other offers you can choose from (see point 2). None of the merchant accounts I've been involved in have ended up having to pay an up-front fee, although the bank always asked for one.

Rates are an obvious one to compare, but don't forget to also negotiate how long the bank will hold your money before passing it to you (many banks hold your payments in a separate account and pay your corporate account at the end of the month). Anything more than 1 month should be considered unacceptable. You should consider how important that is for your cash flow.

10.22.2 Conclusion

Getting your first merchant account can be a real nightmare, but it doesn't need to be so. Following these tips will maximise your chance of looking back at this process and thinking "Heh, it wasn't so hard after all". Doing the opposite of these tips can practically guarantee you'll never get a merchant account. Here they are again:

- Start the process early because it might take much longer than you think it should
- Apply to several banks to give yourself leverage in negotiations
- Exaggerate your volumes (realistically) to obtain good terms and good attention
- Know all about fraud to make the bank feel safe about doing business with you
- Be serious to ensure the bank feels you're a trustworthy business
- Read the fine print and negotiate the terms, as you may be able to get much better terms than initially offered

10.23 MERCHANT ACCOUNT SERVICES

Selecting payment options for the customers of your internet business will directly affect your revenues and your bottom line. Considerations for selecting options must include factors such as trust, reliability and cost. Payment options for online businesses at this stage of the game must include E-Commerce credit card processing.

E-Commerce credit card processing in the internet economy is an important element in operating an online business. Online business owners that contract with a merchant account provider and E-Commerce credit card processing service to meet their customer's purchasing needs increase their potential for sales and sales revenues over those merchants who are not set up with the capacity for credit card transactions.

By incorporating E-Commerce credit card processing into your company you will speed up the process of receiving money from sales purchases. Accepting payments by providing E-Commerce credit card processing is a further shopping convenience for your customers. The result will be to put more funds from sales back into the company faster for production, expansion and inventory.

Some Factors to Consider when Shopping for an E-Commerce Merchant Account:

- Number of Transactions
- Average Transaction Amount
- Sales Volume per Month

E-Commerce credit card providers and merchant account providers are in the volume business. The higher the number of transactions and average transaction size; the lower the fixed monthly fees on your account will be. The lower the monthly fixed fees for you the less money out of your pocket each month. Where transaction fees are paid out of the proceeds of a sale you don't pay them until the sale is made. You may have to start with higher fixed fees until your volume increases and then change plans to reflect the new sales volume and number of transactions.

If your business plans on using telemarketing as a contact system to enhance online sales; setting up an E-Commerce credit card processing system has many advantages. Closing sales with customers is much easier when you can take payment immediately with a credit card. Up selling of customers is much easier as well because customers are usually much more open to up selling after they have made the initial decision to make a purchase from your company. With a very small amount of training sales staff personnel can increase your sales numbers and subsequently your revenues.

By adopting a E-Commerce credit card processing system and contracting with a merchant account provider you will be encouraging your customers to make much faster purchasing decisions and will create an environment where higher per sale revenues are possible.

As they say you don't get something for nothing and E-Commerce credit card processing services are going to require an investment on your part. Not a huge investment but an investment none the less. It can seem intimidating with all the jargon and fees involved but you can navigate through it but be careful before you sign an agreement and be certain you fully understand the terms of the agreement. Now let's talk about fees.

Factors in Choosing a Merchant Account Provider:

1. Set Up Fees
2. Monthly Service Fees
3. Chargeback Fees
4. Transaction Fees
5. Statement Fees

1. **Set Up Fees :** A merchant account provider may charge a set up fee to open an account and get your online business into their system. A merchant account provider sets up the financial relationship between your online business, a bank and an E-Commerce credit card processing service. The merchant account provider enables E-Commerce credit card processing as an option for customers who purchase from your online business.

2. **Monthly Service Fees :** In order to allow customers the option of paying for purchases with credit cards an E-Commerce credit card processing system will need to be put in place. Once you start receiving money from purchases you'll need a place to put it; the merchant account is where your money is deposited. The merchant account provider will service your merchant account and manage your E-Commerce credit card processing. A minimum monthly fee will be charged for these services.

   The merchant account provider will establish a merchant account where credits, refunds, fees and withdraws are transacted and recorded. After a sale is complete for a credit card transaction the funds from the sale will be deposited by the E-Commerce credit card processing service into you merchant account.

3. **Chargeback Fees :** If a transaction is reversed for any reason such as a credit or refund a fee is charge for the reversal of the transaction. This type of charge doesn't happen often for some online businesses except in the case of less than value exchanges where the customer returns product and exchanges it for less valued product. Many online businesses will give credit instead of refunds to avoid this chargeback fee.

4. **Transaction Fee :** Each time a customer makes a purchase with a credit card a fee is charge to your merchant account for that individual transaction and can vary for different merchant account providers. Each fee is small 10-30 cents each and is charge to the merchant for each transaction made with the E-Commerce credit card processing service.

5. **Volume Fees :** Depending on your merchant account provider and the plans available to you the total volume of credit card transactions must equal a certain amount each month and if the volume drops below the set amount a volume fee is charged. Volume amounts are generally set when you open the merchant account in anticipation of transaction activity. If the volume falls below a certain amount on a consistent basis you might want to change your plan. Monthly fees are generally lower for high volume plans and higher for lower volume plans so be realistic in choosing a volume level. You may get a break on the monthly fee with a higher volume plan but if volume drops you will pay more with a volume fee instead.

6. **Statement Fees :** E-Commerce merchant providers will compile reports that reflect the data on daily, monthly and annual activities of your online business which can be used for budgeting, accounting and planning projects. A statement fee will be charged either monthly or annually for the merchant account provider to compile the reports reflecting the activity taken place within your merchant account.

   The number of E-Commerce credit card processing companies and merchant account providers has increased substantially with the ongoing development of E-Commerce. Take you time and consult with your advisors if you are unsure about any agreement you are considering entering into with a company.

10.24 ONLINE TRANSACTIONS

To process online orders, you must offer online payment options. The most widely used form of payment currently is the credit card. Marketing studies show that you'll lose 60 percent to 80 percent of your potential orders if your Web site is not set up to accept credit cards; they also show that if you offer credit card payment, not only will you receive more orders, but those orders will be substantially larger.

Credit cards enable impulse buying, reassure customers of your legitimacy, and simplify your billing. Other methods of collecting payment are becoming available and include charging purchases to a phone bill, using electronic funds transfers (EFT), paying by electronic check and various forms of prepayment. Each of these methods requires payment processing either in the form of software added to your Web site or by linking to a payment processing service.

Understand Merchant Accounts and Their Fees

To accept credit cards, you must establish a merchant account, a special bank account for handling the revenue (and fees) from credit card transactions. Your merchant account provider (MAP)-a bank or other institution that processes online credit card transactions-will verify the credit card, process the transaction, and deposit the results into your account, usually within two to four days.

Evaluate Alternative Online Payment Methods

Credit cards still reign as the leading method of payment for online purchases, but other payment options are available. Your product and your customers' buying preferences will influence which payment methods you accept. In other countries, credit cards are not as pervasive, so you may want to consider offering alternatives for your international customers.

Offering multiple payment options on your Web site, if you can afford it and maintain your profit margin, is a means to increase sales by increasing customer convenience and confidence. Many alternative methods are better suited to micro-payments, charges under $1, because the processing costs are often lower and credit card merchant-account fees don't apply.

Determine The Fee Structure That Maximizes Your Profit Margin

Not every product sells the same way, and not every merchant account provider charges you the same way. Choose a provider that suits your business. Begin by considering the nature of the products you sell-are they large and expensive? Perhaps then you ought to seek a MAP that offers a higher flat-rate transaction fee and minimizes the discount rate, since even a hefty $1 transaction fee will be far lower than a 2.5 percent deduction from the charge. On the other hand, if you rely on small, high-volume sales, even a $0.30 transaction fee can erase your profits.

Specify Your Technical Requirements

Different MAPs require different "gateways" on your site. These gateways are the pieces of code that transmit your customers' orders to and from your bank's transaction authorizing agent. If you plan to manually process your orders, a secure Web form might be good enough to capture credit card information that you can process offline.

Evaluate Your Business's Credit-Worthiness

MAPs, like most banks, pay close attention to the companies with which they do business. Such factors as your company's length of time in business, outstanding debt, debt payment history, goods and services offered and even your personal history (for new businesses) will affect the fees your company pays to process credit card transactions on the Net.

Find MAPs You Can Work With

Many merchant account providers refuse accounts to start-up firms or firms and individuals with bad credit histories. Some MAPs will not accept "high-risk" accounts, a term that usually encompasses adult sites, online casinos, and sites operated by firms outside the MAP's own nation. Others refuse to process any transactions that originate on the Internet-even from their own existing brick-and-mortar clients-or may require that you create a separate merchant account to process orders that are not taken face-to-face but are received by mail, phone, or via the Internet.

Compare Fees and Technical Capabilities

Once you've developed a list of merchant account providers who might offer you an account, you need to compare the different MAP offerings. Be certain to ask detailed questions about each MAP's technical requirements, and make sure your system can work with your MAP's gateways-the software that actually submits your customers' credit card information for payment authorization.

Minimize Credit Card Chargebacks

Discussion about consumer credit card protection for Internet purchases has become intense. But the fact is that U.S. federal law limits a consumer's liability for unauthorized charges to $50, whether the purchase was made face-to-face or on the Internet. No such protective legislation exists for merchants, however, and they bear the full cost of fraudulent charges as chargebacks from their banks.

When a fraudulent credit card transaction takes place without the physical card being presented to the merchant, or funds are uncollectible for some other reason, merchants are charged the sale amount by the cardholder's bank. This is known in the industry as a chargeback. Merchants may also be asked to pay penalty fees in addition to the cost of the original charge. Though it has not been as hot a topic for e-tailers, credit card chargebacks pose a serious threat to profits. To reduce revenue losses due to credit card fraud, online businesses need to take steps to reduce the risk they take with every order received through their Web sites. Find out how credit card chargebacks occur and what you can do to protect yourself.

Secure All Your Transaction Data and Prevent Fraud

Credit card information is extremely sensitive, and plenty of villains are waiting to exploit any breach in your security. Additionally, online merchants are as susceptible to credit-card fraud as face-to-face retailers. Make sure your merchant account provider has addressed these issues.

Prepare for International Payment Processing

Many payment processing and merchant account providers do not accommodate international commerce. If you plan to market your product globally, you may need to search specifically for an international provider.

SUMMARY

Any web site that offers products and/or services for sale is a commercial web site. There are thousands of commercial web sites on the Internet. Some of them have been successful, and some weren't so lucky. What elements make up a good commercial web site? Of course, web pages should look attractive to a customer. However, even the most attractive web pages will not make a person come back to a web site where it takes too long to find the right product or where order forms don't work. In this lecture we will discuss what functionality is needed for a successful commercial web site and what technology implements various web site elements.

EXERCISE

1. Write down the E-Commerce technology.
2. What are three Most Important Elements of good Website
3. Justify this statement E-Commerce should have a good Website
4. What is the Significance of good E-Commerce website
5. Write down a five-step approach to developing an E-Commerce system
6. What is E-Commerce system life cycle
7. Describe about Merchant Account
8. How to Get Approved for a Merchant Account
9. Describe all Merchant Account Services
10. What is Online Transactions.

Questions Bank

1. What is E-Commerce? What is the Limitation of E-Commerce
2. Difference between E-Commerce and E-Business?
3. Identify the unique features of E-commerce technology and their business significance
4. What are the steps required to transform business to E-Business? How can electronic commerce help to reduce the production cycle time?
5. What are the various categories of E-Commerce based on the parties involved in a transaction?
6. Differentiate between Internet and Intranet based E-Commerce?
7. What is the impact of E-commerce on Business? Explain with the help of example?
8. What are the Models of E-Commerce?
9. What is need of E-Commerce? What are the disadvantages of E-Commerce?
10. Explain framework of E-Commerce?
11. Explain how the WAP protocol is structured and how the different WAP layers map into internet protocol layers
12. Discuss the mobile computing application in details.?
13. How can information from the internet be accessed using a WAP device? Discuss in details the functionality of a WAP gateway?
14. Discuss why new and improved security measures are not enough to stop online crime?
15. Why are some online merchants hesitate to ship to international addresses? What are some of the risks of doing so?
16. Describe the key dimensions of E-Commerce security.?
17. Differentiate between Mobile Commerce and E-Commerce?
18. What are the Network Infrastructure for E-Commerce?
19. Write a short note on Broadband Telecommunication?

20. What is Mobile Information Device? What is the use of this in Mobile Commerce?
21. Identify the major points of vulnerability in a typical online transaction?
22. How does spoofing threaten a website's operations?
23. What are the components of Firewall ? What are its limitations?
24. Write about security issues on web in details?
25. Write the steps involved in the asymmetric encryption process?
26. What are the Security Threats of E-Commerce?
27. What are the Factors that to be consider while designing a Firewall?
28. Why is E-Commerce Security important?
29. What is the difference between internal and external threats?
30. What motivates Hackers in E-Commerce?
31. Explain how symmetric encryption works.?
32. What are the dimensions of E-Commerce security not addressed by symmetric encryption?
33. Describe the working of public key cryptography?
34. How does the addition of a digital signature change the process of cryptography?
35. Discuss the features of IPSec protocol useful for setting the virtual private networks.
36. What are the advantages of setting virtual private networks?
37. What are digital signatures? Write the steps involved in computation of a digital signature?
38. How Symmetric key is different from Asymmetric key?
39. What is payment Gateway? Why it is important fro the money transaction on Internet?
40. Discuss the various issues that are involved in electronic payment system?
41. How is magnetic Strip cards is different from other plastic money?
42. Explain SET? What is the Need of SET? And explain the features of SET?
43. Differentiate between Home Banking and Online Banking?
44. What are the problems with traditional payment system ? Explain how the problems are solved in digital token based electronic payment system?
45. What are the limitations of online credit card payment systems?
46. Write about factors that need to be addressed in the design of any new E- payment system?
47. What are smart cards? How are they different from credit cards?
48. Explain EDI Application in Business?
49. What is E-Commerce Law ? What is the need of E-Commerce Law?
50. What are the Govt. Policies and Agenda for EDI?

51. What is Merchant Account?
52. What are the first things to consider when starting up an online business?
53. What is the biggest challenge in starting up a successful online business?
54. What are the most common misconceptions about owning an eBusiness?
55. How do I overcome the language barrier when trying to product-source overseas?
56. Should I buy inventory or use a drop ship supplier when first starting out?
57. Do I need a merchant account or can I just use Paypal and money orders?
58. What are the differences between online storefronts and selling on eBay?
59. Do I need to consult with an attorney before opening up my eBusiness?
60. What trademark, copyright, tax or other online retail laws should I research?
61. Can you dispel the myth on collecting tax online?
62. How has selling online changed since the Web first began?
63. How will selling online change in the future and how can I stay current?

Common Questions About eCommerce Store Design

64. Are flashy graphics more appealing or quality text and descriptions?
65. Should I hire a professional ad copy editor or writer to create content?
66. Should I build my own storefront or hire a professional web designer?
67. What should I know about web design before I hire a professional?
68. What programs are used to build eCommerce stores or web sites?
69. Do I need to buy any software if I plan to use a web store designer?
70. What should I look for when hiring a professional designer?
71. What are the costs associated with building an online store or site?
72. What's the average shopping cart abandonment rate and how is it lowered?
73. What do potential customers look for once they land on the homepage?
74. Which tools, such as user reviews and live chat, should I offer users?

Common Questions About eCommerce Marketing

75. When is the ideal time to start marketing my store brand and products?
76. How can I establish word-of-mouth marketing buzz about my products?
77. Should I consider hiring a professional marketing firm or can I do it myself?
78. When should I consider alternative advertising like pay-per-click ads?
79. Can I write articles about my products and use them on my site?
80. How much capital should I invest in marketing and advertising?
81. Should I get printed business material even though I have an eBusiness?
82. What is the purpose of free shipping and how effective is it?

83. How can I keep my prices competitive and still make money?
84. Is it a good idea to use suggested retail price if I sell discounted items?
85. How can I beat out competitors if our prices are the same?
86. What are the best ways to increase customer conversion rates?
87. How can I improve customer loyalty and repeat buyers to raise retention?
88. Should I offer an affiliate program and tracking system?
89. What are some ways I can recruit affiliate partners like my competition?
90. What ways can I increase landing page conversions for deep level pages?

General Questions

91. Give full form of B2B,B2C?
92. How E-Commerce Works?
93. What is a Difference between Credit card and Debit card?
94. What is VPN?
95. Does E-Commerce need Security?
96. What is Difference between Smart card and Credit card?
97. How digital signature is different from Conventional signatures?
98. What are the Types of E-Commerce?
99. What is the need of Payment Gateway?
100. Who is Merchant Account?
101. How E-Commerce help to Customer?

Model Papers

MODEL PAPER - 1

1. Attempt any two parts of the following :

(a) Define E-commerce and describe how it differs from E-Business

(b) Identify the unique features of E-commerce technology and their business significance.

(c) What are the steps required to transform business to E-business?

2. Attempt any two parts of the following

(a) Explain how the WAP protocol is structured and how the different WAP layers into Internet Protocol layers.

(b) Discuss the mobile computing application in details.

(c) How can information from the internet be accessed using a WAP device?

3. Attempt any two parts of the following

(a) Discuss why new and improved security measures are not enough to stop online crime

(b) Why are some online merchants hesitant to ship to internationals addresses? What are some of the risks of doing so?

(c) Describe the key dimensions of E-Commerce security?

(d) Identify the major points of Vulnerability in a typical online transaction.

4. Attempt any two parts of the following :

(a) Explain how symmetric encryption works. What are the dimensions of E-Commerce security not addressed by symmetric encryption?

(b) How does spoofing threaten a website's operations?

(c) What are the components of firewall? What are its limitations?

5. Attempt any two parts of the following:
   (a) What are the current limitations of online credit card payment systems?
   (b) Explain how SET protocol functions. What are the differences between the SSL protocol and the SET protocol?
   (c) How are client-based and server based digital wallets different? Why have server based digital wallets been more successful at being adopted?

MODEL PAPER- 2

1. Attempt any two parts of the following :
   (a) Define E-commerce ? Differentiate between Internet and Intranet?
   (b) How E-commerce help in Globalization?
   (c) How can electronic commerce help to reduce the production cycle time?
2. Attempt any two parts of the following :
   (a) Explain how the WAP protocol is structured and how the different WAP layers into Internet Protocol layers
   (b) Discuss the mobile computing application in details.
   (c) Identify the major points of Vulnerability in a typical online transaction.
3. Attempt any two parts of the following :
   (a) Discuss why new and improved security measures are not enough to stop online crime?
   (b) Why are some online merchants hesitant to ship to internationals addresses? What are some of the risks of doing so?
   (c) Discuss the features of IPSec protocol useful for setting the virtual private networks. What are the advantages of setting virtual private networks?
4. Attempt any two parts of the following :
   (a) Explain how symmetric encryption works?
   (b) How are client-based and server based digital wallets different? Why have server based digital wallets been more successful at being adopted?
   (c) What are smart cards? How are they different from credit cards?
5. Attempt any two parts of the following:
   (a) What are the current limitations of online credit card payment systems?
   (b) Write about factors that need to be addressed in the design of any new E- payment system?
   (c) Explain how SET protocol functions. What are the differences between the SSL protocol and the SET protocol?

MODEL PAPER 3

1. Define E- Commerce. Write down the needs of E- Commerce with advantage and disadvantage.
2. Describe all the Models of E- Commerce with suitable Examples.
3. Write down the technology and Prospects of E- Commerce with incentives for engaging in Electronic commerce
4. Draw a suitable diagram of E- Commerce framework and elaborate it in detail.
5. Describe the I-Way and with down the impact of E- Commerce on business.
6. Write down in detail the Network Infrastructure for E-commerce.
7. Describe internet and intranet based E-Commerce issues, problems and prospects.
8. Write down all network Access Equipments also elaborate the Broadband Telecommunication (ATM, ISDN, FRAMERELAY)
9. What is mobile Commerce. Write down all the mobile Information devices.
10. What is Wireless Application Protocol. Explain it with WAP Technology.

MODEL PAPER 4

Note: Attempt all question. All question carry equal marks.

1. Define E- Commerce. Write down the needs of E- Commerce with advantage and disadvantage.
2. Describe all the Models of E- Commerce with suitable Examples.

   Write down the technology and Prospects of E- Commerce with incentives for engaging in Electronic commerce.
3. Draw a suitable diagram of E- Commerce framework and elaborate it in detail.
4. Describe the I-Way and write down the impact of E- Commerce on business.
5. Write down in detail the Network Infrastructure for E-commerce.
6. Describe internet and intranet based E-Commerce issues, problems and prospects.
7. Write down all network Access Equipments also elaborate the Broadband Telecommunication (ATM, ISDN, FRAMERELAY)
8. What is mobile Commerce? Write down all the mobile Information devices.
9. What is Wireless Application Protocol? Explain it with WAP Technology.

MODEL PAPER - 5

1. Describe the advances in technology, which has facilitated e-commerce.
2. Discuss the advance of e-commerce in reference to the following:
   (a) Society
   (b) Customer
3. Why is network reliability very important for e-commerce? What factors cause problems for network reliability?
4. The architectural framework for e-commerce consists of six layers of services. List down each service and explain in short.
5. Discuss the impact of e-commerce on business.
6. Explain C2C e-commerce with an appropriate example.
7. Which types of organizations prefer to maintain their own private network? What are the advantages of a private network?
8. What is the communication protocol used by Internet? What is the advantages of using such a common standard protocol to interconnect computers?
9. Write down the advantages of broadband telecommunication? Why is it important for e-commerce?
10. Name the various mobile information access devices and discuss their roles in mobile computing.
11. What is WAP protocol stack/suite? Write down a brief description of all parts of WAP suit.
12. Write down the use of the following equipments:
    (a) Digital switches
    (b) Routers
    (c) Hubs
    (d) Cable TV set-top boxes.
13. What is Web? What do you mean by Web security? Discuss the goals of web attackers.
14. Explain the following security threats for e-commerce:
    (a) Secrecy threats
    (b) Integrity threats
    (c) Necessity threats
    (d) Server threats.
15. Discuss the various methods that can be implemented for network security.
16. Why are firewalls used in organizations? What are its main components?
17. How do you select firewell for an organization? Discuss.
18. What is VPN? What are its benefits for organizations?

19. What is the need of secure transaction is e-commerce? When a message is sent by A to B on the Internet, what are the types of security problems which may be encountered?
20. What do you mean by cryptography, encryption and decryption? Discuss any two encryption techniques.
21. What is digital signature? How is an e-document signed by a sender and sent to a receiver? How does the recipient of a signed e-document authenticate the signature?
22. What is smart card? What are the advantages of smart card over credit cards? Also explain about the different types of smart cards.
23. What do you mean by online banking? What are their advantages over traditional banking? What services are usually provided by online banking? "Online banking is secure." Justify the statement.
24. Write short notes on the following:
    (a) E-commerce laws
    (b) SET protocol.

MODEL PAPER -6

1. What are the benefits of E-commerce. Also write down the limitations of E-commerce.
2. What are internet, intranet and extranet? list advantages a company can derive from using each of the three.
3. Discuss the role of communication technologies in development of e-commerce? What is the last mile in communication technology term?
4. How e-commerce influences the elements of market?
5. What is B2B e-commerce? Who are the players involved in it?
6. What is the role of certification authority in E-commerce framework?.
7. Characterize the three generations of mobile telephony.
8. What are some ways of achieving frequency reuse in wireless communications?
9. Describe what a denial of service attack is and how it affects e-commerce. How it can be prevented?
10. What are major threats posed by a sniffing attack?
11. Discuss the advantages of using a proxy server.
12. What is meant by DMZ? What are its advantages and disadvantages?
13. What are major issues in e-mail security? What are various schemes that are used to ensure the privacy of e-mails.
14. What is a digital certificate? Describe the commonly used standards for digital certificate.

15. Universal access, regulation and information privacy are three issues that are shaping the I-way. Discuss the positive and negative aspects of these issues. What do you see as the future of the Internet in those areas?
16. Discuss the role of EDI in B2B e-commerce. How can Internet-EDI affect the balance of power in businesses?
17. Extranets are designed to allow companies to share data among themselves. How can a firm share data over their Extranet and the Internet and still restrict access to hackers?
18. Explain how a hybrid approach using both DES symmetric keys and RSA public-private key pairs works?
19. Digital signature
20. Transaction security in E-commerce
21. Market forces behind I-way
22. WAP technology.
23. E-Wallets
24. E-Advertising.

MODEL PAPER - 7

1. What is Electronic Commerce? Describe five potential benefits of Electronic Commerce of business.
2. Describe the architectural framework of Electronic Commerce. What are the Applications of this?
3. Describe Intra Organizational Commerce and its applications in the area of Business of Employee services.
4. What is the Global Information Distribution Network? What are the issues of Public Policy Shaping the I-way?
5. Explain the various issues involved in Electronic Payment System. Also give the various types of EPS.
6. What do you understand by protocol and brief describe the role of TCP/IP in internet?
7. What is the basic Network Infrastructure of for E-Commerce?
8. Describe the Market forces influencing the I-way.
9. What is the Global Information Distribution Network? What are the issues of Public Policy Shaping the I-way?
10. Write the short notes of any two:

    (a) Online Bnaking

    (b) Digital Signature

MODEL PAPER - 8

1. Give the layered structure of EDI and compare EDI versus e-mail. Conceptualize EDI and compare EDI versus e-mail. Discuss the Legal issues related with e-commerce.
2. What do you mean by Mobile Commerce? Which type of Protocols are necessary for wireless application.
3. What do you mean by Encryption? How Encryption is used in Vertual Private Network (VPN)?
4. Discuss the importance of client serves network model. How can Security be achieved with this model?
5. (a) What is WAP technology? Discuss the various mobile Information devices.
   (b) Discuss the benefits of Supply Chain Management.
6. List the different models of Electronic Payment. Explain in details the digital token based electronic payment system.
7. What do you understand by customer relationship management? What importance has customer relationship mgmt in your Organization?
8. Describe Intra organization Commerce and its applications in the area of Business of Employee services.
9. Describe the architectural framework of electronic commerce. What are the Aplplication of this?
10. Short notes:
    (a) Legal requirement in E-commerce
    (b) Firewall and network security
    (c) World Wide Web and Security

MODEL PAPER - 9

1. Discuss the importance of Mobile Commerce. Explain various Mobile information devices in the light of Mobile Commerce.
2. Describe the Layered architecture of EDI in E-Commerce. What are the benefits of EDI over traditional business, also describe the Application of EDI in business.
3. What do you mean by Encryption? Discuss various Encryption Techniques used for web security?
4. State the difference between Mobile Commerce and E-Commerce. Explain various applications of Mobile Commerce in the current Scenario.
5. (a) Explain, clearly, the concept of supply chain management giving Suitable example.
   (b) Explain the difference between a packet-filtering firewall and an Application-levle proxy server.

6. Discuss the various driving forces behind e-commerce. Also explain the industry frame work and the practical problem in implementing the e-commerce.
7. Critically comments on E-commerce as a new and effective way for conducting business product and providing better customer services on the Internet.
8. What is the likely Impact of electronic commerce on economic structures like Manufactures, dealers and consumers?
9. What is system reliability assurance also describe the characteristics of reliable Information system?
10. Short notes:
    (a) Legal requirement in E-commerce
    (b) Firewall and network security
    (c) World Wide Web and Security

MODEL PAPER - 10

1. (a) Discuss the client-server architecture of E-commerce, is client-server architecture a necessary of E-commerce.
   (b) Write short notes on:
      (i) Fiber optics
      (ii) Satellites
2. (a) Discuss the mechanism of Video on demand system/server
   (b) Write short notes on:
      (i) Virus
      (ii) Trojan Horse
      (iii) Worm
3. (a) What re the various components of the I-way, discuss it along with a proper diagram.
   (b) Differentiate between E-commerce and M-Commerce.
4. (a) Define and explain:
      (i) Just-in-time Manfacturing
      (ii) Quick Response Retailing
   (b) What do we mean by a firewall, where it is located, what are the various types of firewalls employed in practice, what are the various rules governing the firewalls.
5. (a) Differentiate between Set-top Boxes and a PC.
   (b) Define the various statistics of a website in points.
   (c) Discuss the HTTP mechanism to connect to the Internet, can we connect the internet without using HTTP connection.
6. (a) What do we mean by Mobile code and message overloading.

(b) Discuss the Electronic Commerce framework, what is specified by the two Poles in the framework.

7. (a) Discuss the role of E-commerce in light of business to customer and business.

   (b) Describe the E-commerce infrastructure and support services.

8. (a) What is electronic Commerce? Describe five potential benefits of electronic Commerce for business.

9. What is the Customer-Oriented value chain? Describe three forces lead to the www's emerges as the single most dynamic force in information technology.

10. Short Notes:

   (a) EDI
   (b) Client Server Network
   (c) Digital Signature
   (d) Video and Demand

MODEL PAPER - 11

1. (a) What is WAP; discuss it with reference to mobility

   (b) What do we mean by TDMA, what technology is used in TDMA. List the various benefits of TDMA over CDMA

2. (a) Write a short note on EDI, what are the various benefits of EDI. Can EDI be done without Electronic Commerce infrastructure?

   (b) Discuss the layered architecture of EDI along with a proper diagram. What are X.12 and EDIFACT IN EDI.

3. (a) What are the two broad areas of security concerns in E-Commerce?

   (b) What are the various protection mechanisms employed for security.

   (c) Discuss Firewalls and Network Security.

   (d) What is health care EDI?

4. (a) Discuss the Electronic Commerce framework (various building blocks in the infrastructure), show it using a proper diagram.

   (b) What are the various components of the I-way, discuss in short.

   (c) What do we mean by e-cash, what are the various properties of e-cash, what are the various problems associated with e-cash.

5. (a) What do we mean by CDMA, CDMA is based on wireless or wire based technology illustrate it, why CDMA is called wide band and spread spectrum technology, discuss it.

   (b) Discuss cellular communication; what is the "Hand Off" situation in cellular.

6. Write a short note on any, one of the following:

   (a) Digital token based Electronic payment systems.

(b) Smart cards based Electronic payment systems.

(c) Differentiate between EDI and E-mail.

7. (a) What is the difference between public key encryption and private key encrption?

(b) Discuss the importance of E-commerce.

(c) State the advantages and disadvantages of home banking.

(d) What are the legal requirements in E-commerce?

8. (a) What is online banking? State the merits and demerits of online banking.

(b) State the differnce between inter and intra organizational E-commerce.

(c) What are the two pillars of e-commerce business? Describe in detail.

9. (a) Discuss the WAP application architecture, i.e. how the WAP device accesses the application server.

(b) Explain smart cards, as Internet payment method. What are the components of smart card chip?

10. (a) Define E-Governance, what do we mean by G-to-C and G-to-G E-commerce methods.

(b) What is the difference between online and offline transaction? How does e-commerce support then online transaction?

Previous Year Questions Papers

B.Tech.

(SEM. V) EXAMINATION 2010-11

E-Commerce

Time: Three Hours **Total marks: 100**

Notes: Attempt All questions.

Q.1 Attempt any four parts of the following: **5 × 4 = 20**

(a) Describe the advances in technology, which has facilitated E-Commerce.

(b) Discuss the advantages of E-Commerce in reference to the followings:

(i) Society (ii) Customer

(c) Why is network reliability very important for E-Commerce? What factors cause problems for network reliability?

(d) The architectural framework for E-Commerce consists of six layers of services. List down each service and explain in short.

(e) Discuss the impact of E-Commerce on business.

(f) Explain C2C E-Commerce with an appropriate example.

Q.2 Attempt any four parts of the following: **5 × 4 = 20**

(a) Which types of organizations prefer to maintain their own private network? What are the advantages of a private network?

(b) What is the communication protocol used by Internet? What is the advantage of using such a common standard protocol to interconnect computers?

(c) Write down the advantages of broadband telecommunication? Why is it important for E-Commerce?

(d) Name the various mobile information access devices and discuss their roles in mobile computing.

(e) What is WAP protocol stack/suite? Write down a brief description of all parts of WAP suit.

(f) Write down the use of following equipments:

(i) Digital switches (ii) Routers

(iii) Hubs (iv) Cable TV set-top boxes.

Q.3 Attempt any four parts of the following: **5 × 4 = 20**

(a) What is Web? What do you mean by Web security? Discuss the goals of web attackers.

(b) Explain the following security threats for E-Commerce:

(i) Secrecy threats

(ii) Integrity threats

(iii) Necessity threats

(iv) Server threats.

(c) Discuss the various methods that can be implemented for network security.

(d) Why are firewalls used in organizations? What are its main components?

(e) How do you select firewall for an organization? Discuss.

(f) What is VPN? What are its benefits for organizations?

Q.4 Attempt any two parts of the following: **10 × 2 = 20**

(a) What is the need of secure transaction in E-Commerce? When a message is sent by A to B on the Internet, what are the types of security problems which may be encountered?

(b) What do you mean by cryptography, encryption and decryption? Discuss any two encryption techniques.

(c) What is digital signature? How is an e-document signed by a sender and sent to a receiver? How does the recipient of a signed e-document authenticate the signature?

Q.5 Attempt any four parts of the following: **5 × 4 = 20**

(a) What is smart card? What are the advantages of smart card over credit cards? Also explain about the different types of smart cards.

(b) What do you mean by online banking? What are their advantages over traditional banking? What services are usually provided by online banking? "Online banking is secure." Justify the statement.

(c) Write short notes on the followings:

(i) E-Commerce laws

(ii) SET protocol.

B.Tech.
(SEM. V) EXAMINATION 2009-10
E-Commerce

Time: Three Hours **Total marks: 100**

Notes: Attempt All questions.

Q.1 Attempt any two parts of the following: **10 × 2 = 20**

(a) Give the timeline history of E-Commerce development. What are inter-organizational E-Commerce? Describe the client-server architecture of E-Commerce.

(b) Write notes on the following:

(i) Electronic Commerce and Retail industry

(ii) Marketing and Electronic commerce.

(c) Describe global information distribution network with reference to:

(i) Long distance networks

(ii) Satellite networks

(iii) Broadband telecommunication

Q.2 Attempt any two parts of the following: **10 × 2 = 20**

(a) What do you understand by mobile commerce? Describe the mobile computing application with reference to:

(i) Remote communication

(ii) Remote data access

(iii) On line transaction processing

(b) Describe in brief, the concept of WAP technology. Describe the model of internet based mobile computing. What is mobile ICP/IP based networking.

(c) Write a note on firewalls and network security.

Q.3 Attempt any two parts of the following: **10 × 2 = 20**

(a) What do you understand by Virtual Private Network (VPN)? How it maintains the confidentiality of resources from the existing physical network to a selected group of nodes within the same network?

(b) What is the public key encryption system? How can it be used for providing authentication in E-Commerce? Use suitable examples to explain it.

(c) What does the web encompass? Describe the technology behind the web with reference to:

(i) FTP

(ii) TELNET

(iii) URL

(iv) HTTP

(v) Gopher

Q.4 Attempt any two parts of the following: **10 × 2 = 20**

(a) What do you understand by digital token based electronic payment system? What are smart cards? Describe the working of smart card readers and smart phones.

(b) Discuss the credit card based electronic payment system. What are third party processors and online credit card processors? Describe the risks involved in electronic payment systems?

(c) Write notes on:

(i) Home banking

(ii) Internet banking

Q.5 Attempt any two parts of the following: **10 × 2 = 20**

(a) Describe EDI applications in business with the reference to:

(i) International trade

(ii) Customs

(iii) Logistics of transport

(iv) Trade point global network

(b) Describe impact of the network based E-Commerce transaction on the traditional supply chain management.

(c) What is the role of certification authorities in E-Commerce environment? How can two parties either a non-repudiable legal contract in electronic commerce environment?

B.Tech.
(SEM. V) EXAMINATION 2008-09
E-Commerce

Time: Three Hours **Total marks: 100**

Notes: Attempt All questions.

Q.1 Attempt any two parts of the following: **10 × 2 = 20**

(a) Describe the need of E-Commerce in the changing business environment. What are the market forces influencing the I-WAY? What is mobile data networks?

(b) Define B2B E-Commerce and illustrate the advantages offered by B2B E-Commerce of existing business.

(c) Describe the working of broadband telecommunication system.

Q.2 Attempt any two parts of the following: **10 × 2 = 20**

(a) Compare Client-Server Security and Data and Transaction Security systems. What are the client-server security threats? Describe the security policies and firewall management.

(b) What do you understand by Wireless Application Protocol (WAP)? What are Personal Digital Assistants (PDAs)?

(c) Show that the Domain Name System (DNS) is an example of global distributed information management system. Use suitable examples to explain it.

Q.3 Attempt any two parts of the following: **10 × 2 = 20**

(a) What are secret key encryption techniques? What is the concept of public key encryption system and private key encryption system. Use suitable examples to explain it.

(b) Why are the machines on internet vulnerable to hackers? Describe various sources of vulnerabilities.

(c) Write a note a web security with reference to

(i) Secure HTTP

(ii) Secure Socket Layer-SSL

Q.4 Attempt any two parts of the following: **10 × 2 = 20**

(a) Describe the basic requirements of an online payment system.

(b) What are the emerging financial instruments used in electronic payment system? Describe the concept of electronic purse.

(c) Describe the pros and cons of credit card based electronic payment system. Use examples to explain it.

Q.5 Attempt any two parts of the following: **10 × 2 = 20**

(a) Describe the impact of network based E-Commerce transactions on the traditional supply chain management. What is Net-commerce?

(b) Discuss the issues of Customer Relationship Management?

(c) What is the likely impact of E-Commerce on economic structures like manufactures dealers, channel partners and consumers?

B.Tech.
(SEM. V) EXAMINATION 2007-08
E-Commerce

Time: Three Hours **Total marks: 100**

Notes: (i) Attempt All questions.

(ii) All parts of a question should be written at single contiguous place.

Q.1 Attempt any four parts of the following: **5 × 4 = 20**

(a) What are the benefits of E-Commerce? Also write down the limitations of E-Commerce.

(b) What are internet, intranet and extranet? List advantages a company can derive from using each of the three.

(c) Discuss the role of communication technologies in development of E-Commerce? What is 'the last mile' in communication technology term?

(d) How E-Commerce influences the elements of a market?

(e) What is B2B E-Commerce? What are the players involved in it?

(f) What is the role of certification authority in E-Commerce framework?

Q.2 Attempt any four of the following: **5 × 4 = 20**

(a) Characterize the three generations of mobile telephony.

(b) What are some ways of achieving frequency reuse in wireless communication?

(c) Describe what a denial of service attack is and how it affects E-Commerce. How it can be prevented?

(d) What are major threats posed by a sniffing attack?

(e) Discuss the advantages of using a proxy server.

(f) What is meant by DMZ? What are its advantages and disadvantages?

Q.3 Attempt any two of the following: **10 × 2 = 20**

(a) What are major issues in e-mail security? What are various schemes that are used to ensure the privacy of e-mails?

(b) What is digital certificate? Describe the commonly used standards for digital certificate.

(c) Universal access, regulation and information privacy are three major issues that are shaping the I-way. Discuss the positive and negative aspects of these issues. What do you see as the future of the Internet in these areas?

Q.4 Attempt any two of the following: **10 × 2 = 20**

(a) Discuss the role of EDI in B2B E-Commerce. How can Internet-EDI affect the balance of power in businesses?

(b) Extranets are designed to allow companies to share data among themselves. How can a firm share data over their Extranet and the Internet and still restrict access to hackers?

(c) Explain how a hybrid approach using both DES symmetric keys and RSA public private key pairs works?

Q.5 Write short notes on any four: **5 × 4 = 20**

(a) Digital signature.

(b) Transaction security in E-Commerce

(c) Market foces behind I-way

(d) WAp technology

(e) E-Wallets

(f) E-Advertising.

B.Tech.
(SEM. V) EXAMINATION 2006-07
E-Commerce

Time: Three Hours **Total marks: 100**

Notes: (i) Answer All questions.

(ii) All questions carry equal marks.

(iii) In case of numerical problems assume data wherever not provided.

(iv) Be precise in your answer.

Q.1 Attempt any four parts of the following: **5 × 4 = 20**

(a) What is the intra organizational E-Commerce and what are is potential benefits?

(b) Which type of transactions come under the category of C2B E-Commerce?

(c) E-Commerce is the buying and selling of information, products and services via computer networks. Does this definition include all aspects that you would consider as part of E-Commerce? Why do why not?

(d) What is supplier-centric B2B E-Commerce.

(e) Discuss the role of I-way in development of E-Commerce.

(f) What are Internet and Externet? What are their potential advantages?

Q.2 Attempt any four parts of the following: **5 × 4 = 20**

(a) Why is the internet vulnerable to hackers? Describe various attack types web-server is prone to?

(b) What are threats posed by a DNS spoofing attack?

(c) Compare the stateful inspection firewell with the application level proxy firewall.

(d) Discuss the main features of WAP technology.

(e) How does AMPS differs from GSM?

(f) Compare and contrast the concepts of universal personal telecommunications and universal communications access.

Q.3 Attempt any two parts of the following: **10 × 2 = 20**

(a) Compare Secure Socket Layer (SSL) and Secure Electronic Transaction (SET) protocols. Why Payment Cards (debit, credit and charge cards) are much more popular for online payments that e-cash and e-wallets.

(b) Propose a Security Model for an E-Banking Application.

(c) What is Public key Infrastructure? Describe the role of the certification authority and reigstration authority.

Q.4 Attempt any two parts of the following: **10 × 2 = 20**

(a) Describe the functioning of a fully integrated EDI system. What ate its benefits over a Non-EDI based system?

(b) What are the major components of supply-chain management? How E-Commerce can be helpful in each of them?

(c) Discuss various types of E-payment systems and their comparative advantages and disadvantages.

Q.5 Write short notes on any four: **5 × 4 = 20**

(a) Emerging Financial Instruments.

(b) Virtual Private Networks (VPN).

(c) CDMA technology.

(d) Broad Band telecommunications.

(e) Role of multimedia in development of E-Commerce.

Index

A

B

F

G

H

I

N

O

P

Q

R

S

T

U

V

W